Defining Democracy

Defining Democracy

Democratic Commitment in the Arab World

Hannah M. Ridge

LYNNE
RIENNER
PUBLISHERS

BOULDER
LONDON

Published in the United States of America in 2023 by
Lynne Rienner Publishers, Inc.
1800 30th Street, Suite 314, Boulder, Colorado 80301
www.rienner.com

and in the United Kingdom by
Lynne Rienner Publishers, Inc.
Gray's Inn House, 127 Clerkenwell Road, London EC1 5DB
www.eurospanbookstore.com/rienner

© 2023 by Lynne Rienner Publishers, Inc. All rights reserved

Library of Congress Cataloging-in-Publication Data
Names: Ridge, Hannah M., 1991– author.
Title: Defining democracy : democratic commitment in the Arab world /
   Hannah M. Ridge.
Description: Boulder, Colorado : Lynne Rienner Publishers, Inc., 2023. |
   Includes bibliographical references and index. | Summary: "Explores the
   'democracy paradox' in the MENA region, showing that democracy and the
   Arab word *dimuqratiyya* often do not mean the same thing—and how
   conflating the two has led to misconceptions about public support for
   democratic governance"— Provided by publisher.
Identifiers: LCCN 2023013497 (print) | LCCN 2023013498 (ebook) | ISBN
   9781685859558 (hardcover) | ISBN 9781685856533 (ebook)
Subjects: LCSH: Democracy—Middle East—Public opinion. |
   Democracy—Africa, North—Public opinion. | Public opinion—Middle East.
   | Public opinion—Africa, North. | Democracy—Middle East. |
   Democracy—Africa, North. | Middle East—Politics and government—21st
   century. | Africa, North—Politics and government—21st century.
Classification: LCC JQ1758.A91 R54 2023 (print) | LCC JQ1758.A91 (ebook)
   | DDC 320.417/4927—dc23/eng/20230422
LC record available at https://lccn.loc.gov/2023013497
LC ebook record available at https://lccn.loc.gov/2023013498

British Cataloguing in Publication Data
A Cataloguing in Publication record for this book
is available from the British Library.

Printed and bound in the United States of America

∞ The paper used in this publication meets the requirements
of the American National Standard for Permanence of
Paper for Printed Library Materials Z39.48-1992.

5 4 3 2 1

To Mathew McCubbins (1956–2021)

Contents

List of Tables and Figures	ix
Acknowledgments	xi
1 A Democracy Paradox?	1
2 Defining Democracy	27
3 Defining *Dimuqratiyya*	51
4 *Dimuqratiyya* and Political Behavior	83
5 Democratic Commitment in Egypt	107
6 Democratic Commitment in Morocco	133
7 Making Choices	157
8 For the People	177
Appendixes	
A. *Conducting Surveys in the Middle East*	193
B. *Survey Questions for Egypt and Morocco*	199
C. *Variable Operationalization*	207
D. *Partial-Credit IRT Models*	227
E. *Conjoint Experiment Results*	231
F. *Conception of* Dimuqratiyya *(Arab Barometer V)*	237
by Country	
G. *(Non)democratic Regime Country Suitability*	239
Works Cited	245
Index	257
About the Book	267

Tables and Figures

Tables

2.1	Extent of *Dimuqratiyya* in the Country Rating	37
2.2	Correlation of *Dimuqratiyya* and Democracy Ratings	40
2.3	How *Dimuqratiyya* Is the Country?	42
3.1	Crosstabulation of *Dimuqratiyya* Characteristics in Egypt	62
3.2	Crosstabulation of *Dimuqratiyya* Characteristics in Morocco	64
3.3	Relationship Between Most Important Characteristic and Characteristic Importance in Egypt	68
3.4	Relationship Between Most Important Characteristic and Characteristic Importance in Morocco	69
3.5	Relationship Between Most Important Characteristic and Very Important Characteristics in Egypt	70
3.6	Relationship Between Most Important Characteristic and Very Important Characteristics in Morocco	71
3.7	Conception of *Dimuqratiyya* (Arab Barometer V)	74
3.8	Conception of *Dimuqratiyya*	75
4.1	Political Behavior Correlations	89
4.2	*Dimuqratiyya* and Political Behavior	90
4.3	Correlation of Meanings	96
4.4	Conception of *Dimuqratiyya* per Wave	98
4.5	*Dimuqratiyya* Is Good	100
4.6	*Dimuqratiyya* and DAP	102
5.1	Conception of *Dimuqratiyya* and Democratic Attitudes in Egypt	120
5.2	Democratic Commitment in Egypt	122

x　　*Tables and Figures*

5.3	Regime-Type Preferences in Egypt	124
6.1	Conception of *Dimuqratiyya* and Democratic Attitudes in Morocco	145
6.2	Democratic Commitment in Morocco	147
6.3	Regime-Type Preferences in Morocco	149

Figures

| 3.1 | Importance of Elements of *Dimuqratiyya* in Egypt | 53 |
| 3.2 | Importance of Elements of *Dimuqratiyya* in Morocco | 55 |

Acknowledgments

More people have contributed to this book than can be individually thanked. It has come a long way from its inception, which saw me sitting on the floor of the cubicle farm in Duke University's Political Science Department with stacks of journal articles and Arab Barometer questionnaires. I saw surveys asking people what *dimuqratiyya* meant to them—from elected governments to redistributive economies—and I pondered the empirical ramifications of these different meanings. How did this word, which I had learned as a student of Arabic meant *democracy*, have these varied meanings? How could we use these surveys if the people surveyed were hearing such varied questions? What did it mean, then, to want *dimuqratiyya*, which the surveys said people did?

The multiple meanings made me recall a discussion after the military coup in Egypt, during which an Egyptian speaker characterized the coup as a *dimuqratiyya* act. *Dimuqratiyya* possibly included antidemocratic acts. *Dimuqratiyya* could be a government (possibly) for the people that is not (entirely) of or by the people. This book explores this (dis)continuity between democracy and *dimuqratiyya*.

I am deeply indebted to the scholars who oversaw the earliest phases of this project. Timur Kuran and Abdeslam Maghraoui gave invaluable guidance on MENA research. Alexander Kirshner contributed heavily to the treatment of democratic theory and the distinction between intrinsic and instrumental support. Most important, I am grateful to Mathew McCubbins. He believed in careful measurement and construct validity, and he advised assiduously on the empirical models. Without his support, this project would not have been possible. John Aldrich has also been a great mentor in academia, modeling so much of what I want to be as a scholar and a professor. He encouraged

xii *Acknowledgments*

me to study public opinion on democracy and advocated for my writing the book. I am continually indebted to his advice.

My scholarly community has also provided feedback and guidance along the way. Sunshine Hillygus and Kyle Endres commented on my survey instrument. Joshua Lerner and Kiran Auerbach read chapter drafts and shared my interest in questions of measurement. Much of the manuscript was written during a fellowship at the University of Chicago Pozen Center for Human Rights, for which I am grateful. Rochelle Terman, Paul Kohlbry, and Lindsay Gifford gave crucial advice.

Kelsey Ridge provided tremendous assistance and patience during the research and writing process, including reading every page of the manuscript. She also frequently reminded me that a survey respondent thought that this research could topple the Egyptian government. I still believe that if asking whether elections are a good idea is enough to foment a rebellion, the democratic spirit is already at work. I thank, as well, my parents for tolerating my "desert-loving" ways.

Survey research is resource intensive. My work benefited from financial support from the Duke University Political Science Department, Mathew McCubbins, and the Association for the Study of the Middle East and Africa. The Institute for Humane Studies provided financial support for the index. I also thank Jasvinder Notra, my contact at YouGov MENA, for withstanding dozens of emails on the translation, formatting, and fielding of my surveys. I am grateful to the Arab Barometer team for creating and continuing that tremendous dataset.

This book is not meant to be the final word on any of the questions addressed. I hope, though, that more scholars will consider how key institutions and constructs are popularly understood, how our interlocutors understand us, and whether we are comprehending their statements and actions. I extend my sincere gratitude to those who have helped that project come this far.

1

A Democracy Paradox?

But why does no one explain this dimuqratiyya *to us? Is it a country or an 'afrita or an animal or an island?*
—Fatima Mernissi, *Islam and Democracy*[1]

In 2010, a Tunisian fruit seller was interrogated by the police for operating without a license. When he could not pay the fine—or bribe —that they required for his unpermitted cart, they confiscated his wares. After unsuccessfully seeking redress from Sidi Bouzid officials, Mohamed Bouazizi publicly set himself on fire. His death kick-started protests by his family and other informal workers. Social media spread word of the protests, and more suicides bolstered the public's commitment and expanded the demonstrations.

Following a familiar pattern in Tunisia, antiregime protests started in southern and central regions of the country, which were poorer and had engaged in previous demonstrations. However, unlike during those protests, the security services could not shut down the demonstrations before they reached the wealthier capital and coastal areas (King 2019). The Zine El Abidine Ben Ali regime faced mass movements against corruption, economic stagnation, and human rights abuses. Most crucially, these demonstrations spread beyond Tunisia.

Millions of people across the Middle East poured into the streets to call for social change. International media coverage highlighted chants for the downfall of authoritarian regimes. The situation, from the popular outpouring to the observers' awe, recalled the suddenness of the collapse of the Soviet Union. Like in the USSR, "the leadership was generally despised, lofty economic promises remained unfulfilled, and freedoms

2 Defining Democracy

taken for granted elsewhere existed only on paper" (Kuran 1991, 12). The surprise was not the rebellion but the timing.

Western leaders, though reticent initially to support the ouster of their political allies, publicly lauded calls for democracy. President Barack Obama, speaking at the State Department in May 2011, called Tunisia the "vanguard of this democratic wave." He also committed US support: "There must be no doubt that the United States of America welcomes change that advances self-determination and opportunity. Yes, there will be perils that accompany this moment of promise. But after decades of accepting the world as it is in the region, we have a chance to pursue the world as it should be." On behalf of the United States, he endorsed liberal democracy as the framework for foreign policy:

> The United States opposes the use of violence and repression against the people of the region. The United States supports a set of universal rights. And these rights include free speech, the freedom of peaceful assembly, the freedom of religion, equality for men and women under the rule of law, and the right to choose your own leaders—whether you live in Baghdad or Damascus, Sanaa or Tehran. And we support political and economic reform in the Middle East and North Africa that can meet the legitimate aspirations of ordinary people throughout the region. (Obama 2011)

Baghdad and Damascus residents might argue that the administration failed to live up to its commitments. Overall, however, Western media and Western leaders were quick to identify the Arab Spring as a democratic revolution.

It was, in the short term, for some countries. Egypt and Tunisia successfully removed their long-standing leaders, wrote new constitutions, and held elections. For many, though, the Arab Spring has fallen into what some call the Arab Winter (Magharoui 2019; Feldman 2020). Wars are raging in Syria and Yemen. Libya spent most of a decade in war. Non-democratic regimes persisted in states like Morocco and Algeria. A military coup upended the elected government in Egypt. After nearly a decade of democracy, Tunisia—the success story of the uprisings—seems to have lost its democracy to a self-coup. After decades of struggle—the democratization efforts did not start with the Arab Spring—the Middle East/North Africa (MENA) is the least democratic region of the world.

This lack of democratization flies in the face of high expressed public support for democracy in the Middle East. The extensive support predated the Arab Spring, and it continues in the most recent surveys. Researchers have termed this discrepancy the *democracy paradox*. Why has the region not democratized? Why, in particular, do we see such strong and recurrent expressions of support for democracy in such an undemocratic region? This book contributes to answering these questions about the Arab world. To do so, it looks at what people mean when they protest for democracy, evaluate political reforms, and express this supposed democratic support. Understanding how Arabic speakers are using the language of democracy grants insight into the political behavior, social movements, and popular will of the Middle East. This information is vital to promoting or supporting self-determination and regional democratization.

Fundamentally, *dimuqratiyya*, the Arabic word that typically stands in for *democracy* in this discourse and in these public opinion polls, does not always signify what political scientists and foreign observers mean when they say *democracy*. *Democracy* refers to a system of government based on binding elections—though some advocates append liberal values and economic success to the agenda. *Dimuqratiyya*, in fact, has two meanings. For about half of listeners, it refers to political institutions, like elections and freedom of speech. For the other half, *dimuqratiyya* describes a set of socioeconomic outcomes, independent of the political structures that generate those outcomes. Thus, to look at any invocation of *dimuqratiyya*—by protestors or pollsters—and assume that it is an invocation of *democracy* is potentially to misconstrue what is being said. To properly understand Middle East/North African citizens' politics and preferences, we must ask the right questions and listen for the answers.

A Democracy Deficit

The democracy deficit in the Middle East/North Africa is overdetermined. Myriad explanations are given for why democracy has not taken root. Some resign these states to authoritarianism because the fault is historical. If the cause is in the unchangeable past, then the future is a foregone conclusion. Others would allow for regional development. Decades of democratic struggles demonstrate that Middle East/North Africa residents do not think democratization is impossible. I consider these impediments briefly before turning to how people inside and outside the Middle East/North Africa view democracy.

The most famous "cause" of the regions' failure to democratize is Islam. Researchers point out that a country's likelihood of being a democracy is lower when its Muslim population share is higher (Potrafke 2013).

4 *Defining Democracy*

They argue that this results from the tenets of the faith itself, which they argue oppose freedom, pluralism, or voting (Fukuyama 2006; Minkenberg 2007). Others argue that it stems from Islam's failure to separate religion from the state (Lewis 2002). Huntington (2000) posited that Islam suffused the region's culture and traditions, as opposed to supposedly Western values like human rights and democracy. For an expert unpacking of the arguments for and against Islam's philosophical support for and opposition to these values, see Ciftci (2022).

Islam's influence could also be instrumental and indirect. Islamic systems pervading society, such as Islamic endowments (*waqf*), inhibited the development of civil society organizations and political participation that might have pressed for democratization (Lewis 2002; Kuran 2012). Islamic law caused the region's retrenchment in global status and restrictions on human development. From the other side, the insufficiency of Protestant missionaries to the region and the attendant educational and organizational development their involvement created elsewhere relatively stunted democratic development (Woodberry 2012). Lewis (2002, 156) counters that "to blame Islam as such is usually hazardous, and rarely attempted. Nor is it very plausible," since the predominance of Islam has not varied substantially with the centuries. A constant cannot explain variation. The influence of Islam on personal preferences, cultural norms, and legal precepts is an ongoing question.

Another factor is colonialism. The reshaping of regional boundaries and interference in constitutional processes by European and, eventually, American forces have received substantial blame for MENA politics. Europeans replaced the Ottoman political institutions, promoted secularism, and failed to develop domestic civil society. Europe also endorsed the state of Israel, itself blamed for the Middle East's ills (Alkadry 2002). The empirical evidence for a colonial effect, however, is weak (El Badawi and Makdisi 2007; Fish 2002). Lewis (2002, 153), while acknowledging nationalism as a European "import," criticizes this argument: "In the Middle East, there have been good reasons for such blame. . . . But the Anglo-French interlude was comparatively brief and ended half a century ago; the change for the worse began long before their arrival and continued unabated after their departure."

Much of the region was controlled by the Ottoman Empire. The empire's policies did not set the region on the path to democratization (Kuran 2012). Why would they, when the sultan sought to retain power? Even prior to that, the Middle East had been subject to the Arab conquests. These domains saw widespread use of slave armies and treated "religious leaders as the primary check on the power of the sovereign"

(Chaney, Akerlof, and Blaydes 2012, 382). The areas of the Muslim world that were conquered by Arab armies in the early decades of Islam, to this day, have lower rates of democratization. This is consistent with the gap between Arab and non-Arab Muslim-majority states in democratization (Stepan and Robertson 2003). The historical persistence of Arab-conquest and Ottoman institutions and resultant weakness in democratic and civil society organizations keeps them down.

The Middle East's history of armed conflict also has been indicted. Muslim-majority states are not significantly more likely than others to have experienced armed conflict, but the Middle East has seen substantial conflict in the last century. The Arab world is the exception to the assertion that conflict encourages democratization (El Badawi and Makdisi 2007). The Gulf wars and US-led incursions in Iraq are pertinent. The conflict over Israel is particularly central to this discourse. Stepan and Robertson (2003, 42) posit that neutralizing the Israel conflict by establishing a recognized two-state solution would obviate a foreign policy question that MENA governments use to sustain "high military spending, authoritarianism, the world's greatest concentration of traditional autocratic monarchies, and the willingness to sacrifice, or interfere with, national goals in the name of pan-Arabism and pan-Islamism."

Another supposed source of nondemocracy is a resource curse. Oil deposits and mineral wealth allow rentier regimes to keep their publics demobilized, to provide services without taxation, to finance systems of repression, and to avoid investing in human capital (Ross 2001; El Badawi and Makdisi 2007). Oil resources stabilize the authoritarian power structure. The negative effects of oil are not unique to the Middle East (Ross 2001; Fish 2002). The threat, however, is greater in poor countries, for which the resource wealth will represent a larger share of the economy. Furthermore, oil-based economies are more likely to exclude women from the labor force (Ross 2008), especially in countries with "strong patriarchal structures" (Groh and Rothschild 2012, 84). The exacerbation of gender-based inequalities undermines representation in government of the full populace, undercutting democracy and democratization (Abdo-Katsipis 2017; Fish 2002; Inglehart and Norris 2003).

Democratic culture theory posits that for regions to democratize durably, there must be a coterie of supportive institutions and pro-democracy values. Durable democracies require sufficient economic deliverables, self-expressive values, tolerance, interpersonal trust, and a propensity toward social and political participation (Inglehart 2003). The Middle East faces challenges in these domains—the democratic culture is uneven and decoupled from democratic attitudes (Welzel

6 Defining Democracy

2021b; Ridge 2022a, 2022b). In this theory, any democracy that is instituted will be on shaky foundations.

Subjective well-being in the region is low. There are high rates of unemployment and poverty. The regimes sometimes target these needs instead of ameliorating the political deficits, creating a tacit nondemocratic social contract. The regimes also perform poorly on human rights indicators. Scholars have singled out two particular values as holding the region back. Low support for women's rights constrains human development (Inglehart and Norris 2003; Fish 2002). Although expressed support for democracy is high, opposition to women's rights discourages support for a democratic regime that might liberalize that dimension. Conversely, women in the region may fear democratization if they believe the elected government would roll back extant rights (García-Peñalosa and Konte 2014). For instance, if elected, an Islamist party could promote a conservative interpretation of personal status law or undermine women's education. That is why Rizzo, Abdel-Latif, and Meyer (2004) argue that women in Arab countries are less likely to support democracy than women in other Muslim-majority countries. Ridge (2022a) finds that Egyptian women are not more or less likely to be democrats if they are assured of a liberal regime; however, they are less supportive of illiberal democracies than men are.

The other value highlighted is religious freedom. Muslim-majority states have less religious freedom than other states. Rowley and Smith (2009) posit that constraints on religious freedom result in restraints on religious and political discourse. They suppose that the constraints come from Islam. Fear of being viewed as an apostate causes self-censorship, which undermines political development. The states' control of religious groups and religious people has both organizational and individual-level effects. Limitations on religious freedom in Muslim-majority countries impact citizens' compliance with religious law and popular displays of religiosity (Ridge 2019, 2020). To the degree that religious beliefs and religious participation drive political behavior, these policies have knock-on effects (Hoffman and Jamal 2014; Arikan and Bloom 2019). The regulations states use to repress religious freedom in Muslim-majority countries restrict political competition by suppressing civil society groups that the regimes see as threats to their power (Sarkissian 2012). This perceived challenge is part of why some regimes place greater restrictions on Islam-affiliated organizations than on minority-serving organizations. The states' regulatory capacity in turn discourages democratic transition. Once the role of regulation is taken into account, the empirical predictive power of Islam for a country's level of democracy "disappears" (502).

Each or all of these factors could contribute to the democracy deficit in the Middle East/North Africa. Some of the theories produce a bleak outlook. After all, a history of colonization or regional conflict cannot be rewritten. Theoretically changeable characteristics are also not necessarily actionable. "Stop being Muslim" is not earnest political advice. In other cases, the future may be more optimistic. Economic development can transpire, and gender egalitarianism can spread. Oil deposits will eventually run out. Whether those changes truly would facilitate democratization, though, is hypothetical at this point.

What these theories cannot do is explain the democracy paradox. They do not convey why democracy would poll so highly in the Arab world, even while democracy is rare. Some of these theories themselves even suggest that the support should be low. For instance, the supposed antidemocratic nature of Islam or Islamic culture should lower support. This is not what is found. That could mean the theory is wrong or that the support for democracy is disingenuous.

If the high support is genuine, maybe the paradox results from the overwhelmingness of these forces. The public may wish to democratize but is doomed by the past. Since the past is unchangeable, pro-democracy efforts are in vain. Again, this is bleak. It is also a diagnosis by default. It takes the lack of democracy as given and functionally unrelated to the popular will. Such a fatalistic view that obviates popular will is by its own nature antidemocratic.

Another set of analyses calls the support itself into question. Maseland and van Hoorn (2011, 481) explicitly state that "there is no puzzle." It is a question of diminishing marginal utility to democracy or thermostatic preferences (Claassen 2020). That is to say, because Muslims live in places that are less democratic, they will "have a craving for more democracy," not as paradox but as "basic microeconomics" (Maseland and van Hoorn 2011, 482). The marginal value is not a phenomenon unique to the Muslim-majority states, but it impacts the Middle East because of the lack of democracy on the ground. The paradox is thus resolved because the support is not itself real.

The marginal value hypothesis would then predict that Tunisians would place less value on democracy than other MENA-country nationals, since Tunisia was the only regional democracy for a time. That is not what the 2018 Arab Barometer results show. Tunisia had some of the highest rates of belief that *dimuqratiyya* may have problems but is still the best form of government. Other high-support countries had diverse regime structures.

There is, of course, always the threat that people are just lying. Strategic and intentional misrepresentation of attitudes, opinions, and

8   *Defining Democracy*

preferences is known as *preference falsification* (Kuran 1997). Preference falsification is, by necessity, a concern in any survey. In this case, the argument would run that citizens in nondemocracies feel compelled to lie and say they like democracy or hate it because of fear of the regime. However, "the positive relation between democratic attitudes and Islam exists not only at the country level but also at the level of individual Muslims. For these reasons, biases due to repressive environments likely do not cause the positive relation between Muslim identity and democratic attitudes" (Maseland and van Hoorn 2011, 485).

In general, researchers have found that Middle East/North African citizens are eager to participate in survey studies (Gengler et al. 2019; Corstange 2014). In original surveys conducted for this book, some individuals noted that they welcomed the opportunity for the public to express its opinions and interests. For instance, an eighteen-to-twenty-four-year-old Muslim Moroccan woman said, "This questionnaire pleased me a lot, because it is good to know the people's opinions about politics and the government system in their country."[2] Another Muslim Moroccan woman, forty plus years old, wrote, "This type of survey is very useful to know the citizens' opinions and also to advance the country to the highest of positions."[3] This is not to say that every respondent was positively disposed to discussing politics. One respondent in Egypt even thought that the survey was a prelude to an attempt to overthrow the government or that the responses, if made public, could be destabilizing for the regime. The forty-plus-year-old Cairene Muslim man with an advanced degree wrote, "[This is] a political poll that is intended to shake citizens' confidence in the political leadership and to spread the spirit of rebellion against the current regime in order to destroy the country."[4] He still filled out the survey. Furthermore, arguably, if a survey could trigger a revolution, the antigovernment sentiment was already boiling under the surface.

Concern about being spied on seemed limited. One Moroccan respondent, a forty-plus-year-old suburban Muslim woman with an advanced degree, wrote, "The worst governments in the world are Arab governments and Islamic governments."[5] This response does not betray a great fear of observation or identification, though it might indicate openness to regime change. Heightened levels of concern among researchers that ideology and regime type lead to systematic misrepresentation may reflect researchers' own biases rather than the realities of regional survey studies. Benstead (2018, 536) argues "that worries that the Arab world is a more challenging survey context—or that citizens answer dishonestly—reflect biases of 'Arab exceptionalism,' more than

A Democracy Paradox? 9

fair assessments of data quality." It is necessary to consider the choices in survey construction that can influence respondents' behavior, but the Middle East can be treated as functionally similar to other regions of the world in survey studies.

MENA residents are also reasonable but not perfectly rational actors with imperfect political knowledge (Lupia and McCubbins 1998), who can update their preferences based on "core cultural values and enduring social needs" just like other people, through "the natural combination" of intuition and deliberate reasoning (Fatas-Villafranca, Dulce Saura, and Vázquez 2011, 419). Political preferences reflect citizens' "personality traits, values, principles, group affiliations, and material interests" (Leeper and Slothuus 2014, 131). Politics is discussed at sites ranging from civil society organizations in Palestine (Jamal 2007) to khat chews in Yemen (Wedeen 2007). Citizens have also turned to bodies like political parties, religious organizations, slogans and cartoons, and unions to be informed and to express themselves (Beinin 2015; El-Ghobashy 2021).

Evaluating public opinion in the Middle East is hardly new. Public opinion (*efkâr-i umûmîye* or *efkâr-i âmme*) played a recognized role in Ottoman politics, especially after the 1860s. Şiviloğlu's (2018) *The Emergence of Public Opinion* documents the process by which the introduction of public debts and the expansion of civil society spaces gave public opinion the opportunity to flourish and drive policy, including deposing political figures. At times the sultanate was constrained by the public will, while at other points it relied on the "illusion of public consent" (56). Previously the Janissary corps had served as the embodiment and constraining force of the public voice. That the military can be the people's voice will be discussed more in Chapter 5 on Egypt. Şiviloğlu (2018) argues that the Ottoman regime was not merely mimicking the West in expressing concern for public opinion but was actively incorporating a sense of public agency into its strategic framework.

Explicitly empirical analyses of public opinion in the Middle East are, of course, more recent. Turkey has been incorporated into the World Values Survey since the second wave (1990–1994), and a variety of Arab states have been included since Wave 4 (2000–2004). The first wave of the Arab Barometer was completed in 2007. North African countries appeared on the Afrobarometer starting in the fifth wave (2011–2013). The Arab world has decades of experience with public opinion invocations and examinations. This book draws on data from the World Values Survey, several waves of the Arab Barometer, and original survey studies in Egypt and Morocco to develop its claims.

10 *Defining Democracy*

This combination of datasets means two decades' worth of public opinion studies—thousands of citizens' responses—can be brought to bear in these analyses. These original surveys included free response space for the citizens to voice any additional thoughts they had on these topics. The quotes above were some of these discursive comments; other statements will be introduced in the following chapters. For more information about the surveys conducted for this book—including additional comments from survey respondents and demographic information—see Appendix A. Although surveys should be conducted mindfully with respect to citizens' comfort and safety, there is not substantive reason to believe there have been decades of mass deception about the democratic interest.

An Alternative

I posit, in this book, a middle road. The support that the respondents are expressing is genuine. However, it is being misinterpreted and therefore misunderstood. To preview the most important finding: the support for democracy is lower than we have thought. Thus, the absence of democratization is not as paradoxical as it seems.

Why have we thought the support was higher than it is? It is because of how we have been measuring it. A concept or structure that a researcher seeks to measure is a *construct*. Trust, for instance, is an idea or interpersonal condition one might measure. Converting that idea into a numerical metric is termed *operationalizing the construct*. The accuracy of that empirical representation of the thing—the construct—is called *construct validity* (Cronbach and Meehl 1955; Adcock and Collier 2001). The typical measurement tools for assessing democratic commitment globally lack construct validity. This is because the difference between the constructs—the underlying ideas—*democracy* and *dimuqratiyya*[6] is not taken into account when formulating these questions. While the former highlights (liberal) political institutions, the latter is regularly tied to socioeconomic outcomes.

To identify this high level of support, researchers have turned to a variety of multicountry surveys, including the World Values Survey, the Arab Barometer, and the Afrobarometer. When these surveys are performed in the Middle East, questions that were developed in English are rendered in Arabic. This act of translation introduces a challenge: "Poor translation can rob researchers of the chance to ask the questions they want to ask across languages and cultures. However, we cannot always expect to notice from the data that translation problems have arisen"

(Harkness, Pennell, and Schoua-Glusberg 2004, 454).[7] If results are changed due to the act of translation, such as by inadvertently calling on a different construct or by changing the meaning of response options, then there will be mismeasurement. This measurement error introduced by translation is the *translation bias* in the estimate.[8] In this case, in place of the word *democracy*, the surveys ask respondents about their attitudes toward *dimuqratiyya*. Although democracy and *dimuqratiyya* sound alike—both derive from the same Greek root—they are not calling up the same idea for the survey takers. In fact, *dimuqratiyya* calls up different ideas even within the Middle East. As such, the surveys will misestimate the attitudes toward democracy by asking about *dimuqratiyya*.[9] The researchers are introducing *translation bias* into the survey results by conflating these different constructs.

A Global Consensus?

The widespread use of surveys to identify support for democracy has previously engendered concern that survey takers in different regions do not share similar understandings of democracy, which in turn corrupts the interpretation of survey results. Scholars have concluded, based on open- and closed-ended survey questions about meaning, that not only do mass publics understand the word *democracy* when it is put to them in a question but also that publics globally share a very similar understanding to each other and to researchers. They propose that most citizens identify democracy with freedom and the procedural and institutional elements of democracy (Dalton, Shin, and Jou 2007). Thus they conclude that global publics are construing democracy as political scientists do.

This pattern would be fortuitous. The focus on electoral or participatory institutions is consistent with researchers' expectations when asking these questions. Democracies are systems of competitive elections that rule by consent of the governed as determined by majority rule (Dahl 2008 [1971]; Schumpeter 2008 [1942]; Przeworksi et al. 2000). Democracy is an expression of the "freedoms that entitle people to self-determine their private lives and to have a voice and vote in the public sphere of which they are a part" (Welzel 2021a, 21). States can construct myriad institutions and norms befitting local preferences and traditions around the elections. These range from the particular form elected government takes, from direct election to the separation of powers, to the kinds of policies the governments create, such as welfare systems and acculturation structures. In crafting the questions used to analyze citizens'

12   *Defining Democracy*

democratic attitudes and commitments, this study has focused on *choosing the government by election.*[10] This focus on elections does not devalue other things states do or goals citizens might have for them. It recognizes that political scientists have a meaning in mind when using the word *democracy*. More will be said on how political scientists define and measure democracy as a construct in Chapter 2.

These conceptions drive survey researchers' expectations about democracy and its meaning. Fuchs and Roller (2006, 77–78) explicitly state, "We assume that citizens of Central and Eastern Europe possess enough information about democracy that cognitively it is not a difficult object," and respondents can thus be asked "directly for democracy" in survey questions; when they ask subjects about democracy, they report that subjects identify "theoretically relevant criteria of liberal democracy." Ferrín and Kriesi (2016) affirm a pan-European understanding of democracy as liberal democracy. Bratton (2009) addresses this question as well in his near-global study of democratic attitudes and political participation. He finds a "common pattern of shared meanings across all world regions" and reports that "a regime of civil liberties" is the most common meaning given for democracy (Bratton 2009, 7). Bratton includes, however, an important caveat. His results omit the Middle East and Latin America, where the open-ended question had not been posed; the Arab Barometer asked for "characteristics of democracy" by his reckoning (7). Nevertheless, he favors this globalized interpretation of questions and answers related to democracy.

However, omitting later-wave democratizing countries from the sample artificially increases the apparent cross-cultural agreement about the meaning of democracy. Ariely (2015, 632)—who avers that there is "a common understanding of the core procedures of democracy across most countries"—uses the World Values Survey to conclude that more "democratic" countries are more likely to have citizens who view procedural elements as "essential" to a country's being a democracy. Similarly, European Social Survey and Comparative Congressional Election Survey data show that "public opinion on both sides of the Atlantic, therefore, seems to converge quite strongly on what are the most important characteristics of democracy, and traditional liberal elements such as the rule of law, free and fair elections, and free media clearly are of paramount importance for most citizens" (Oser and Hooghe 2018b, 18–19). The United States and Europe are not uniform in the level of importance they place on social rights for identifying a democracy; however, the essential features are held in agreement, and they are political institutions. This pattern would bias the results toward the aforementioned impression of agreement about a proceduralist understanding of democracy. Omitting democratizing areas, intentionally or otherwise, is biasing in favor of a globally shared political-institutions-based understanding of democracy. Canache (2012) addresses this question for Latin America. Using LAPOP data, she affirms the predominance of the liberal political understanding of democracy in Latin America.

The corollary of a high rate of political conceptions of democracy is a low rate of economic conceptions. Dalton, Shin, and Jou (2007, 147) find that "few people define democracy in terms of social benefits," a category in which they include "social equality, justice, and equality of opportunities, rather than blatant economic benefits such as employment, social welfare, or economic opportunities." They interpret this pattern as a refutation of the notion that support for democratic systems derives from a desire for improved living standards. Bratton (2009, 7) finds that "fewer than 5 percent" reference "a regime of social rights or economic development" in an open-ended question, although he acknowledges the rate increases when respondents choose from a list. The purported global uniformity contributes to researchers' belief that a political conception of democracy can be assumed when analyzing survey data on democratic support.

This optimism about a uniform popular understanding of democracy is not without its detractors. Schaffer (2014) uses a case study of the Philippines to argue that the apparent conformity around liberal (political) democracy as an understanding is based on methodological errors on the part of survey compilers for the open-ended questions that create this apparent agreement in answers. He identifies three faults: compression, compartmentalization, and homogenization of open-ended answers. *Compression* is the shortening of long answers into single words and simple phrases. *Compartmentalization* is the division of the open-ended response into a number of categories by a coder that can subtract meaning in disintegrating the thoughts rather than treating them as fitting together. *Homogenization* is interviewers' glossing respondents' statements to retrospectively construct apparently unified response blocs that may not reflect nuances.[11] This problem is magnified when the responses are only recorded in a different language than the respondent is using and the interviewer has sole discretion over how the responses are rendered in the new language. Qualitative work and more rigorous questions are Schaffer's preferred solution, though these suggestions pose their own logistical and interpretative challenges. His skepticism of compressed open-ended responses and the equation of results across cultures is understandable.

14   Defining Democracy

Papacharissi (2021, 38) finds qualitatively that people think of "democracy" in terms of equality, especially with respect to freedom of expression, under a system of "consensus or majority rule." However, since her focus was not explicitly on "democracy" but on an "ideal democracy, or if it's not a democracy, what might lie after it," she is tapping more directly into what people want from their government. She follows "desire lines" to identify what should replace democracy and proposes that there is no global "disconnect" with respect to what individuals think is "wrong with democracy" (x, xii). She does this without establishing that the many words her multilinguistic study used for democracy tapped into the same construct. In fact, she argues that "coming up with a definition of democracy that lasts forever is an impossible problem. Democracy is a fixed ideal with flexible morphology, one that must be adjusted with the least measure of compromise" (49). She is not seeking to assess a construct, then. She targets an ideal government, then casts the word *democracy* onto that system. The use of the word to describe something that may not be a democracy at all—as political scientists typically measure and understand it—demonstrates the linguistic drift that complicates the use of this word. Chapters 3 and 7 demonstrate that such casting of meanings is driving the application of the label *dimuqratiyya* to different types of government.

Despite the supposed consensus, disparate understandings of democracy are on view in some closed-ended cross-national survey questions. The widely used World Values Survey is an instructive case. The World Values Survey has respondents rate how important a series of characteristics are to democracy—or, rather, whatever word is used for democracy in that survey. The scale ranges from "Not an essential characteristic of democracy" (1) to "An essential characteristic of democracy" (10).

On one hand, the World Values Survey responses seem to back up the optimistic results: people all over say political institutions are essential to the word-idea named. In Wave 7 (2017–2020), 80.5 percent of respondents indicated that the public's choosing leaders in free elections was an essential feature of democracy;[12] 73 percent stated that civil rights protections guarding people's liberties from oppression were essential. Equal rights for men and women were essential to democracy for 81.5 percent of respondents. Institutional features fit for most people. On the other hand, one might construe these frequencies as unfortunately low for features political scientists consider definitive of democratic governance.

At the same time, these surveys justify Schaffer's (2014) skepticism. According to the same World Values Survey data, 59.5 percent said that government taxation of the rich to subsidize the poor is essential for a country to be a democracy; 69.1 percent rated state unemployment aid as essential. For 54 percent of respondents, a state's making people's incomes equal was essential to democracy. Half to two-thirds of respondents label economic characteristics essential features of democracy, though they are not necessarily something democracies can, or could exclusively, provide.

Even more indicative of confusion of constructs is that many respondents rated potentially antidemocratic elements as essential to democracy. For instance, 47 percent stated that people's obeying the rules is essential; if these respondents are thinking of the rule of law, then that would make sense, but if they mean forced or unthinking obedience to a ruler, then it is undemocratic. Allowing religious authorities to interpret the laws was marked essential to democracy by 24.1 percent of respondents; 33 percent identified permitting a military takeover of an incompetent government as essential to democracy. Viewing these features as essential suggests that respondents are thinking of a different system entirely when they hear that word.

These patterns are not globally uniform. A few scholars have noted this point; however, they have not reached the same conclusions about its meaning. Cho (2015) studies global heterogeneity in the fifth-wave World Values Survey data. He reads the essentialness ratings for elections, civil liberties, military-takeover opportunities, and a role for religious leaders in interpreting the law as reflecting the degree to which respondents are "informed" or not about the meaning of democracy (241). He makes it a question of whether or not the respondents are correct about democracy rather than an indication that the multiple terms employed are not equivalent.[13]

Taking nearly a reverse position on the data, Davis, Goidel, and Zhao (2021) affirm some of the existing expectations about a shared meaning for democracy by looking at these questions in a subset of the World Values Survey countries: the democratic world. They find "general consensus *and* differences on some characteristic of democracy both within and across countries" in these democracies (854). However, "all concur generally about the importance of free elections, referendums, civil rights, and gender equality and seem to reject army rule" (857). While concluding that the multidimensional nature of democracy should be treated with "greater sensitivity" in cross-national studies, they also conclude that "despite measurable differences in public understandings of democracy, the vast majority of respondents across countries are 'pro-democracy'" (861). In fact, they take the rating of essentialness as an indicator of support rather than a recognition of an objective fact.

16 *Defining Democracy*

The "apathetic" class—which gave a low score to every feature—is considered apathetic to democracy if not "antidemocracy" (861). This elision implies that recognizing that elections are democratic is tantamount to supporting elections, which is not true. Davis, Goidel, and Zhao do not test the implications of these different understandings for democratic commitment. This book does.

Ulbricht (2018) approaches this point. He weights World Values Survey respondents' answers to the "what [do] you think about each [political system] as a way of governing this country" and "how important is it for you to live in a country that is governed democratically?" questions by how important certain features are to "democracy." The respondents were classed as authoritarian democrats, representative democrats, direct democrats, social democrats, radical direct democrats, socialist democrats, and inconsistent democrats. He uses the word *democrat* not to convey support for democracy but rather as a placeholder for the idea of viewing essential elements of democracy in that fashion.

Ulbricht (2018, 1414) concludes, "When people's stated desire for democracy is adjusted in accordance with procedural, participatory, and social variants of political liberalism, support for any kind of liberal democracy declines considerably, with striking differences across political regimes." He also argues that desire for liberal democracy is primarily a function of the regime in which the respondent lives. He reports, "Authoritarian and illiberal attitudes, which are rejected by academic definitions of democracy, are extremely common in autocracies, hybrid autocracies, and even hybrid democracies" (1414). The Middle East would certainly fall into this category. Thus, he concludes that the scholarly consensus that democracy is popular is wrong and that, globally, the support for democracy under autocracies is truly low. Ulbricht's work is a tremendous foray into the implications of different understandings of democracy. This book answers the question more explicitly by evaluating support for democratic institutions.

Meaning in the Middle East

The Middle East does not demonstrate this seeming consensus on the meaning of democracy. This can be seen in the World Values Survey results. Having people choose the government by election is well recognized as important to "democracy" in the Middle East, as in other places. Civil liberties to protect citizens are also broadly identified with democracy. The consensus, however, breaks down when other considerations are introduced. Equal rights for women are not viewed as essential in the same way that other rights protections are; survey respondents in Muslim-majority countries, including the Middle East, and in South America view this element as less essential to democracy. State interventions to control incomes is viewed as essential in the Middle East and Asia, while North America and Europe view it as far less crucial. State unemployment aid gets a higher rating on essentialness in MENA countries. The rating far exceeds the rating in North America or Oceania, while it is on par with considerations in Europe and Asian countries. In the Middle East, ratings of the essentialness of taxing the rich to subsidize the poor outstrips those in other regions, even much of Europe. Economic interests thus seem to play a larger role in MENA responses to what makes something "democratic."

Muslim-majority countries, including in the Middle East, are disproportionately represented among those with the highest ratings for religious authorities evaluating laws. This is a far cry from the position that democracy necessarily requires that religious authorities hold no sway in this domain. For instance, Davis, Goidel, and Zhao (2020, 853) assert that "secular pluralism and elected-self-determination [are] both core features of functional democracy." Identifying a military takeover of an inefficient regime as democratic is also much more likely in Muslim-majority countries, including in the Middle East.

AlAzzawi and Gouda (2017) approach it as a religious question. They compare Muslim and non-Muslim respondents in the sixth wave of the World Values Survey. Muslims, they conclude, place less value than non-Muslims on the procedural elements, such as elections and civil rights. Muslims also are more prone to what AlAzzawi and Gouda call "authoritarian democracy"—identifying military and religious leaders' control of the government as essential to "democracy"—than non-Muslims. They construe these beliefs about the essential nature of these possible elements of government as "higher preference" or "lower preference" for these institutions or as "qualms" about or "faith" in them, which is not what the question actually asks (11). They ultimately compare Muslims and non-Muslims' support for "democracy," despite the fact that they have just established that the respondents conceive of "democracy" differently. While research on global Muslim populations by necessity will invoke Middle Eastern communities, it also extends into multiple linguistic and cultural milieus, which are conflated here. These challenges are overlooked in an effort to establish a seeming religion-affiliated pseudo-consensus *opposed* to democracy.

These differences could all be attributed to the idea that the people in this part of the world are just not very democratic or do not understand what democracy is and what it is not. That is the implication of

18 Defining Democracy

scholars like Welzel (2021a, 14–15), who refer to these as "strongly twisted" understandings or "misunderstandings of democracy." Other researchers suggest that the differences come from having an instrumental view of democracy—democracy still involves elections, but these people are thinking about what those elections will get them and how much they might like those outcomes. They are then assumed to project those desires onto democracy as an idea.

Rather than suggest that these people are ignorant of democracy, I propose that researchers are ineffectually responding to the different meanings of the words introduced by the translated survey questionnaires. As such, this discussion of the so-called paradox has transpired without evidence that citizens have a solid or shared understanding of what the term even means. Consider the quote from Moroccan sociologist Fatima Mernissi (1992) at the beginning of this text. Mernissi is recounting growing up in her grandfather's harem; the women were watching the nightly news. Her aunt noted that speakers did not define *dimuqratiyya*; she wondered if *dimuqratiyya* was a country, an animal, or an *'afrita*, meaning a dirty trick. Given the way waves of democratization have played out across the world, there could be some truth in the latter interpretation. The fundamental point, though, is that *dimuqratiyya* is not one known thing.

Dimuqratiyya, this book will show, has the tenor of "the state as it should be." That means its meaning depends on the hearer. For some, the term conjures a set of political institutions. Others indicate that it describes a set of socioeconomic outcomes. It does not mean *democracy* specifically.

Arab Barometer data indicate that approximately half of the respondents view *dimuqratiyya* primarily as economic conditions rather than a political structure. In 2018, the Arab Barometer asked respondents in twelve Middle East/North African countries to identify, from a closed list, the most important characteristic of a *dimuqratiyya* (Arab Barometer V). Only 28.6 percent of the respondents, across the countries, identified one of the procedural elements—choosing a government by election and the freedom to criticize the government—as the most important; 66.8 percent identified a socioeconomic outcome—the government maintains law and order or the government ensures job opportunities for all—as the most important. In fact, jobs provision was the most commonly selected category (35.7 percent).[14] Rather than there being a consensus understanding of what is essential to *dimuqratiyya* around political *or* economic elements, this split indicates that there is the opposite of consensus. Furthermore, as Chapter 3 shows, which citizens hold which view of this construct is highly idiosyncratic. For simplicity, in this

A Democracy Paradox? 19

book, a focus on political-institutional elements is called a political conception of *dimuqratiyya* (PCD); a focus on the socioeconomic outcomes is called a socioeconomic conception of *dimuqratiyya* (SECD).

Interestingly, there is also a schism in the Middle East between liberalism and democracy. For many Westerners, the term *democracy* is "shorthand for liberal democracy," assuming into it features like "the rule of law and the freedoms of speech, assembly, religion, and the press" (Plattner 2019, 6). Recent studies in Egypt and Tunisia find that citizens' attitudes toward elected government are effectively decoupled from their support for liberal values (Ridge 2022a, 2022b).[15] The region features both illiberal democrats and liberal nondemocrats in conjunction with the liberal democrats and less-than-liberal nondemocrats. Still less than *dimuqratiyya* can be assumed to mean democracy should it be assumed to mean liberal democracy.

This lack of consensus introduces questions of what citizens are endorsing when they endorse *dimuqratiyya*. Two diverging meanings are identified in the Arab Barometer. This book examines which citizens are more likely to hold which view of *dimuqratiyya*, whether these groups of citizens perform politics differently, and whether they hold different regime-type preferences. How citizens conceive of *dimuqratiyya*, after all, is not the same as whether or not they support democracy or *dimuqratiyya* as a system of government.

One point must be openly acknowledged in this discussion. This book is not intended to argue that Arabic-speaking respondents are "wrong," "uninformed," or "misguided" about what words mean. The questions posed to them by researchers have asked about a functionally different construct. As such, their answers reflect that construct and its differences from democracy. This is thus fundamentally opposed to Cho's (2015) conclusion. The intragroup discrepancies with regard to the meaning of *dimuqratiyya*—the topic of Chapter 3—may create the sense that some respondents are more correct than others with respect to how that construct should be understood. However, insofar as there is a discrepancy between democracy and *dimuqratiyya*, error should be assigned to researchers who failed to make their questions clear rather than respondents who answered the question as they understood it.

Plan for the Book

This book addresses—to say it bluntly—the causes and consequences of this diversity of understandings of *dimuqratiyya*. It draws on multiple data sources from the Arab world over two decades. Establishing how

20 *Defining Democracy*

citizens understand *dimuqratiyya*, for instance, will draw on several waves of data from the Arab Barometer. This will be the focus of the first half of the book.

Chapter 2 presents an overview of how democracy as a construct is understood in political science. It considers both how researchers talk about the construct and how they measure it. These measurement tools identify what the discipline considers fundamental to democracy. Namely, political science focuses on elements of institutional design—such as competitive elections and universal suffrage—to measure democracy. Some researchers have proposed more maximal definitions of democracy; they may invoke liberal values or welfare economic policies. However, the most commonly used measurements take the minimal, institutional approach. These definitions are the hidden foundation of the literature on democratization, democratic erosion, and democracy deficit that utilize these measurement systems. These conceptions of democracy are thus the touchstone against which Arabs' conceptions of *dimuqratiyya* are compared in the development of that work.

The chapter then compares the factors that make political scientists call a country democratic with those that make Arabs call their countries *dimuqratiyya*. The Arab Barometer allows citizens to rate a country's level of *dimuqratiyya*. The ratings do not map well to expert ratings of countries' democracy levels. Which individual- and state-level factors lead to a state's being given a high or low rating for *dimuqratiyya*? These patterns provide a subliminal insight into how citizens understand the construct onto which researchers have cast the meaning *democracy*. It shows that citizens' evaluations of their country's elections have some influence on their *dimuqratiyya* perceptions but that economic forces and opinions about the current government's performance play a much larger and more consistent role in their assessments. These findings provide a clear demonstration that *dimuqratiyya* and democracy are not one and the same.

The next chapter distinguishes citizens by their conceptions of *dimuqratiyya*. Using the Arab Barometer data, it finds that approximately half of the citizens in the Middle East/North Africa have a primarily political construal of *dimuqratiyya*, and approximately half conceive of *dimuqratiyya* primarily in socioeconomic terms. Who is more likely to identify *dimuqratiyya* with a socioeconomic outcome or with a political process? The study finds limited patterns of cross-cultural predictability of citizens' understanding of *dimuqratiyya*. Citizens' beliefs in this regard are highly idiosyncratic. As one Moroccan woman indicated, "The concept of *dimuqrāṭiyya* is broad and comprehensive, and everyone uses it from their own perspective" (Khanani 2021, 97). Given

A Democracy Paradox? **21**

this individuation, it is challenging to predict who will use it in a given way. Furthermore, it is doubtful that conception of *dimuqratiyya* would respond to intentional manipulation by governments or policy activists. This fact, though, does not make these social blocs immaterial. As the second half of the book demonstrates, there are multiple knock-on effects of these diverging conceptions of *dimuqratiyya*.

The discussion transitions from concept to practice in the second half. That is to say, the focus shifts from how citizens understand *dimuqratiyya* to how these different conceptions of *dimuqratiyya* engender different politics. Chapter 4 assesses the impact on regime-type preferences and political behavior. Recent Arab Barometer surveys demonstrate that individuals who conceive of *dimuqratiyya* in political terms are more likely to participate in politics. This includes institutionalized participation, like joining a party, and noninstitutionalized participation, like joining a protest or perpetrating political violence.[16] Furthermore, data from early waves of the Arab Barometer hint that different conceptions of *dimuqratiyya* are associated with different attitudes toward elected and unelected systems of government.

However, because existing surveys—even those that acknowledge that survey respondents do not all understand the word *democracy* or the word *dimuqratiyya* in the same way—continue to use that word in their questions, it is impossible to use these surveys to understand the implications of this varied understanding for citizens' attitudes toward democracy. Comparing the answers across clusters of understanding is like comparing apples to oranges. Properly answering this question requires original survey items that address democracy specifically rather than *dimuqratiyya*. To do that, this book draws on original surveys conducted in Egypt and Morocco.

Egypt is the largest Arab country. It has over one hundred million inhabitants and is a driving force in Arab culture. Chants from Tahrir Square—"Al-sha'ab yurīd isqāṭ al-niẓām" (the people want the overthrow of the regime)—created defining images of the Arab Spring. Egypt's prominence during the uprisings also gives it a prime position in the global understanding of the Middle East and its efforts to democratize. The country swept out a decades-long dictatorship and held elections. For electoral democratization, Egypt had to navigate what Hassan, Kendall, and Whitefields (2018) call the Scylla and Charybdis of Egyptian politics: Islamist and military rule. Eventually, the elected Islamist president was himself replaced in a military coup. The supposedly democratic nature of this coup—because the military is populist and Islamists cannot be democrats—demonstrates the ongoing

22 Defining Democracy

negotiations between democratic means, democratic processes, and democratic commitment.

Morocco, a constitutional monarchy at the other end of North Africa, has a different state structure than Egypt. The Moroccan monarchy has engaged iteratively with political reform, including transferring more power to parliament and approving alternations in government that involve nonmonarchist parties. These reforms were not true democratization but rather a "pluralization" of power, because the monarchy retains the true power, including the loyalty of the Ministries of Sovereignty: Justice, Defense, Foreign Affairs, Religious Affairs, and Interior (King 2019; Hibou 2011). After the February 20 Movement protests, new reforms and a new constitution were instituted. The movement's underlying concerns about economic problems and corruption were not resolved, but the reforms averted greater change. Morocco's history of the "depoliticization" of politics and the prominence of the king create a strong counterpoint to Egypt's political dynamism (Maghraoui 2002, 2015). The influence of these counter-democratic structures on the relationship between *dimuqratiyya* and democratic commitment will be discussed.

Respondents were asked how they feel about *choosing the government by election*. Namely, do they think that electing the government is best, or is it sometimes better to use a nonelected government? Do they think that choosing the government by election is appropriate for their countries? Both of these questions are informative in their own light. The combination of the two identifies *committed democrats*. People who think that elected government is both right and good are the people we would expect to promote democratization and to defend a democratic regime under threat. They were also given the opportunity to reject undemocratic systems of government. Crucially, these surveys demonstrate that for many citizens who endorse democracy, it is not the only acceptable government. It is one choice among many acceptable alternatives. Thus, the obstacle to democratization is not public opposition but rather the potential to settle on a nondemocratic alternative.

Chapters 5 and 6 discuss the relationship between Egyptians' and Moroccans' individual understandings of *dimuqratiyya* and their support for electoral democracy. These studies find that expressed support for choosing the government by election is lower than reported support rates for *dimuqratiyya*. In both cases, a sizeable democracy-*dimuqratiyya* gap is identified. The standard questions have overestimated support for democracy, indicating positive translation bias. Furthermore, in the surveys from Egypt, the research finds that citizens who identify *dimuqratiyya* with a socioeconomic outcome are less likely to be invested in maintaining a democratic government and more open to several nondemocratic alternatives. The military's involvement in Egyptian political practice is particularly discussed. Parallel surveys in Morocco, however, find that while Moroccans who conceive of *dimuqratiyya* as a set of political institutions are more likely to favor electoral democracy, they are not necessarily proof against nondemocratic alternatives. The import of *dimuqratiyya* is particularly discussed in relation to Morocco's monarchy, which seems to have infiltrated *dimuqratiyya*.

The final empirical chapter considers what kinds of state structures citizens prefer. Namely, it considers whether individuals who think of *dimuqratiyya* primarily in political terms and those who think of it in socioeconomic terms would make different choices for their countries' political futures if they could through a conjoint experiment embedded in the Egypt and Morocco surveys. Respondents were shown several descriptions of potential state structures and asked to choose, of those options, in which state they would prefer to live.

Democratization and democracy are processes of perpetual political choices. What do the people want? When presented with the choice of regimes described in terms of their opportunities for political participation, the role religion and religious leaders would play in the state, and the economic outcomes that the regime would generate, the overall results from Egypt and Morocco are markedly similar. In both countries, citizens prefer a state that features elections and opportunities for political participation while generating widespread employment. Although they want the state to recognize a state religion, they seek no role for religious leaders in that government.

PCD respondents and SECD respondents, however, do reveal different preferences. Again, citizens who view *dimuqratiyya* as a political structure are more committed to choosing an elections-based state and less focused on economic outcomes. They are also more invested in keeping religious leaders out of the government. Not only, then, do these citizens conceive differently of *dimuqratiyya* as a theoretical construct, a term to be defined; they also want different things in and from their government. These differences in their state-structural preferences suggest that some respondents are casting the term *dimuqratiyya* onto the government they prefer rather than simply viewing it as an idea that exists separately from their preferences. It is, as Chapter 2 suggests, a government that works. What working means can be particularized to the respondent. It may be a government for the people, even if it is not, in both conceptions, of the people or by the people.

The conclusion considers the implications of these patterns for political science and Middle Eastern studies research. With respect to the respondents' understanding of *dimuqratiyya* and its relationship to democratic

24 Defining Democracy

commitment, that the sizeable population with an economic understanding of *dimuqratiyya* has less interest in elected governance contributes to our understanding of the democracy paradox in the Middle East. The social support for democratic governance has been systematically overestimated through translation bias. As such, this book concludes that the reported levels of support for democracy in the Middle East are likely presenting an overly rosy impression of support for electoral democracy and the interest in democratization.

This disparity in conceptions of *dimuqratiyya* also can inform researchers' understanding of protest movements—namely, the potential to misunderstand the objectives of these movements. This could apply to those from decades ago when Mernissi's aunt posed her question or to the most recent movements. Are these pro-democracy protests? Just because they endorse *dimuqratiyya* does not mean that they call for *democracy* as political scientists have used the term or that democratization is a singular or overriding objective. These findings suggest that, to a certain extent, the efficacy of some previous social movements, such as the Arab uprisings, has been inaccurately characterized, and arguably underrated, by researchers and outside observers. Afterall, if they were pro-*dimuqratiyya* movements, then their failure to install a durable democracy does not mean that they have missed the mark. Success would depend on how influential the movement was in instituting elements of *dimuqratiyya*, like equitable economic policies.

Additionally, these results highlight the options that authoritarian regimes have to co-opt or forestall opposition efforts, even potentially while portraying themselves as supporters of *dimuqratiyya*. Caution is urged in construing political agents as supporters of democracy based on appeals to *dimuqratiyya*. This conceptual mismatch introduces an avenue for supporting authoritarian persistence. Outside observers, including foreign powers, should bear these competing forces in mind when considering "pro-democracy" interventions. Durable democracy will require satisfying popular will and averting authoritarians' efforts to use *dimuqratiyya* against democracy. Securing democratization in the region will ultimately also require *dimuqratization*.

Finally, the book also notes that other central political constructs can face this challenge of diverging meanings. Ciftci (2022), for instance, unpacks the multiple meanings given to *'adl/adalet* (justice) in Turkey. Other constructs that merit such study could include secularism, nationalism, and human rights. The list is extensive. The study of democracy should also be extended to other regions. It is possible that this instance of translation bias for "democracy" is an Arabic-language-specific phenomenon. That cannot be evaluated with these surveys. However, it is also possible that the seeming global consensus about how *democracy* is understood around the world—in the many other languages that are used—has been overstated. Schaffer (2014) argues that it is. Other researchers will have to take up the mantel of examining this point in different language milieus. Countries like China have made ready use of the defense that their governments are "for the people" to claim democratic credentials for their authoritarian regimes. How has language shaped their ability to make such bold assertions? Survey methodologists and researchers will have to grapple with the potential need to alter long-standing survey questions to address these disparities or to account for the biased results the word choice is inducing. To do otherwise risks researchers and respondents talking past each other by consequence of language. First, though, we look inward at political science and how political scientists and Arab publics understand *democracy* and *dimuqratiyya*.

Notes

1. "Pourquoi on ne nous explique pas cette *dimoqratiya*? Est-ce que c'est un pays ou une effrita ou un animal ou une île?" (Mernissi 1992, 115).

2. A'jabnī al-istibyān kathīran li'annhu min al-jayyid ma'ifa arā' al-nās ḥawla al-siyāsa wa niẓām al-ḥukm fī baladihim.

3. Hādhā al-naw' min al-istiṭlā'āt mufīd jiddan li-ma'rifa arā' al-muwaṭinīn wa kadhālk li-l-nuhūḍ bil-dawla ilā a'lā al-markākiz.

4. Istiṭlā' siyāsa al-gharaḍ minhu za'za'a thiqa al-muwaṭinīn fī al-qiyāda al siyāsiyya wabathth rūḥ al-tamarrud 'alā al-niẓām al-ḥālī li-tadmīr al-dawla.

5. Aswa' al-ḥukūmāt fī al-'ālim hiyya al-ḥukūmāt al-'arabiyya wa al-ḥukūmāt al-islāmiyya.

6. Note: Arabic is a gendered language, and many modes have been designed for transliterating Arabic script into Latin characters. For consistency, the word will be rendered as *dimuqratiyya*. *Dimuqratiyya* will also be used where the adjectival form is meant, regardless of the Arabic-language gender of the referent (i.e., the difference between *balad* [masculine] and *dawla* [feminine] for country).

7. Best practices in questionnaire design for multinational, multicultural surveys involve "subject-area experts, area and cultural specialists, linguistic experts, and survey methodologists" (Lyberg et al. 2021, 52). This is a logistically challenging process. Most multicultural surveys now use TRAPD protocols based on those developed for Bible translations (Lyberg et al. 2021). The instrument is translated, then reviewed by a survey and/or topic expert and the translator(s); adjudication is made about issues in the translations, which are then modified; the instrument is pretested on the target population; and documentation is made regarding the process and decisions that were taken.

8. Pérez (2011) dubs the differences in survey questions' performance based on translation bias "differential item functioning."

26 Defining Democracy

9. Consider an analogy: if a survey asks respondents whether they would allow a cat in their homes, and some respondents picture a tabby kitten and some respondents picture a lion, the researcher—who probably meant the former—is likely to misreport and misconstrue the pet policies preferred by the latter group.

10. Democratic commitment refers to citizens' willingness to stand by democracy as a system of government. As will be discussed at greater length in the second half of the book, democratic commitment is typically measured based on the belief that democracy is the best form of government and that it is appropriate for one's country.

11. Arguably, Fuchs and Roller (2006) engage in such a targeted classification. In their open-ended answers, 12 percent of their sample reportedly identify "social justice and economic welfare" as "the meaning of democracy," but they include this population with those answering "liberty and basic rights," "political participation," and "rule of law and equality before the law" to identify "a striking homogenous and focused meaning of democracy," despite its not being a clearly political-institutional representation of democracy (78–79). Their conclusion of uniform understanding is, then, a generous estimate.

12. For this discussion, ratings from six to ten on the one-to-ten essentialness scale are considered as rating the feature essential.

13. Cho (2015, 247) concludes that "only 36 percent of respondents correctly evaluated all four regime characteristics." By default, a global majority are wrong. He attributes this supposed misunderstanding to over acceptance of the nondemocratic features, while, by and large, "the last three decades have been far more successful in enlightening global citizens about the essential attributes of democracy" (249). Unfortunately, the role of translation and the resultant mixture of constructs does not enter into his discussion. As such, he attributes error to respondents that may be better attributed to design choices.

14. Postcolonial MENA governments used extensive public-sector employment as a large-scale jobs program until the structural adjustments of the late twentieth century. The expectation of employment and the cost of fulfilling it placed political and socioeconomic burdens on their societies, which contributed to the Arab Spring and contemporary issues (Hong 2019; Bishara 2021b).

15. Islamists may particularly struggle with this dimension. Liberalism is often an assertion of individual rights. Islamists' assertions of group rights, such as the protection of Muslims' sensibilities in a Muslim-majority society, argue that individual freedoms could undermine the group's freedoms (Khanani 2021). It is an argument for an illiberal democracy. More work is needed on this point, but it is beyond the scope of this book.

16. The Middle East is not unique in this regard. Schaffer (2000, 145) proposes that Western scholars have struggled to understand political behavior in Senegal because the Senegalese are responding to the "different sets of values and concerns" in *demokaraasi* than the scholars envision for *democracy*. He argues that the consensus/solidarity focus of *demokaraasi* leads the Senegalese to engage differently with the concept of voting. In this case, Arab Barometer results indicate that conception of *dimuqratiyya* is linked to the likelihood of engaging in many political behaviors—the PCD are more participatory—but voting is the exception.

2

Defining Democracy

I know it when I see it.
—Potter Stewart (*Jacobellis v. Ohio*, 1964)

The concept of democracy has a complicated history. The frameworks encompassed by it have morphed remarkably since the ancient Athenians "invented" democracy. Even now, political scientists— who, if anyone, might be expected to have a mutual understanding of what democracy is—have variegated ideas about what can be appended to this term. A brief—and certainly not exhaustive—discussion of the proposed descriptions and analytics of democracy is instructive in identifying the key patterns in how political scientists think about democracy as a construct. They range from minimalist conceptions that focus tightly on competitive elections to expansive visions that enumerate various freedoms, political parties, free markets, or socioeconomic equalities that could accompany those institutions. At core, though, political science has chosen to highlight electoral competition as the sine qua non of democracy.

This chapter juxtaposes the meaning(s) ascribed to the word *democracy* with the multiple meanings attached to *dimuqratiyya* in the Arab world. To identify the conception of *dimuqratiyya*, the chapter examines the features that make Middle East/North Africa (MENA) citizens call a country *dimuqratiyya*. Democracy and *dimuqratiyya* are distinct constructs. *Dimuqratiyya* may incorporate those elections and freedoms that political science measures to chart regime types, but it is most crucially marked by the socioeconomic outcomes it generates. *Dimuqratiyya* states are states with regimes that work—even if they may not be regimes of or by the people.

27

28   *Defining Democracy*

These two sets of meanings have only intermittent overlap. Neither group is wrong in defining its terms. Recognizing this distinction, though, is a requisite first step to examining how these terms can relate to each other in public opinion, social movements, and processes of democratization. Subsequent chapters will lay out the political ramifications of MENA citizens' holding these competing views of *dimuqratiyya* for their political beliefs and behavior.

For Political Science

At its broadest, we could think of democracy as a government by the people, of the people, and for the people. This is what Stasavage (2020, 4) aims at when he takes "seeking consent as a basic ingredient of democracy" that is "natural among humans." He argues that early democracy was invented independently at multiple points throughout history by a series of communities that developed inclusive political institutions. It is to this ideal that Sklar (1983, 11) appeals when he asserts, "Democracy stirs and wakens from the deepest slumber whenever the principle of accountability is asserted by members of a community or conceded by those who rule."

Athenian democracy, though, would not be recognized as democracy by a modern public. Athenian democracy dates to Cleisthenes's introduction of equality before the law (*isonomia*), although the word *democracy* itself was not used for Cleisthenes's reforms. His reforms were laid over Solon's earlier reforms, which created a system for popular participation. Athens featured the boule, in which five hundred wealthy Athenians would draft an agenda for the *ekklesia*, an assembly in which adult, male Athenian citizens could vote on laws and decrees. Citizenship was allotted to the offspring of Athenian citizens. Personal freedoms were more limited, especially for women and foreigners. Slavery was legal. Substantial class differences prevailed. An orthopraxic religion was embedded in the state and culture. Many government offices were assigned by lottery rather than election. The demos was represented in this system through the opportunity to speak in the *ekklesia* and the equal chance of being selected from the lottery, at least among the citizenry, for certain government offices. Nonetheless, Athens is counted as the birthplace of democracy. It is a government of (some of) the people that theoretically worked for (some of) the people, although those people were not necessarily chosen by any of the people.

Political scientists' identifications of democracy focus on modern democracy, the kind that has spread since the American revolution.

Modern democracy is "a political system in which representatives are chosen in competitive elections under universal suffrage" (Stasavage 2020, 5). That democracy is an expression of the "freedoms that entitle people to self-determine their private lives and to have a voice and vote in the public sphere of which they are a part" (Welzel 2021a, 1012). Many institutional structures fall within this paradigm. Political scientists have spilled a great deal of ink to define democracy and still more on how to adequately measure the construct for empirical analyses. These meanings can be divided into minimalist and maximalist conceptions of democracy.

Minimalist conceptions focus on political institutions. This means that, at a fundamental level, democracy is understood as a system of competitive elections in which the governed population chooses its leaders by majoritarian rule. Przeworski (1991, 10) puts the matter pithily: "Democracy is a system in which parties lose elections." In other renderings of his definition, Przeworski substitutes incumbents for parties and requires that they leave office after defeat. To identify countries as democracies, Przeworski et al. (2000) specify that democracies are systems in which the chief executive and legislators are elected in popular elections for which the outcome is *ex ante* uncertain, more than one party competes, and power has been successfully transferred from one administration or officeholder to another. Their classification is binary. Any system not fulfilling all of these requirements is a "dictatorship."

Schumpeter (2008 [1942], 271) characterizes democracy as a set of political institutions—namely, "the electoral method"—for the selection of representatives, including the removal of other leaders. He does not valorize democracy for its own sake: "Democracy is a political method, that is to say, a certain type of institutional arrangement for arriving at political—legislative and administrative—decisions and hence incapable of being an end in itself" (242). In practice, Schumpeter argues, the "the democratic method does not necessarily guarantee a greater amount of individual freedom than another political method would permit in similar circumstances. . . . But there is still a relation between the two" (271–272). Democracy plus freedom is liberal democracy.[1]

Dahl (2008 [1971]) frames democracy as an ideal type rather than an existing government. It is "a political system one of the characteristics of which is the quality of being completely or almost completely responsive to all its citizens" (2). He identifies "eight institutional guarantees" to make it possible: (1) the freedom to form and join organizations, (2) freedom of expression, (3) the right to vote, (4) eligibility for public office, (5) the right of political leaders to compete for support (votes), (6) multiple sources of information, (7) free and fair elections,

30 *Defining Democracy*

and (8) government policy formation dependent on votes and expressions of public preference. From these, Dahl formed his measure of country democratization, *polyarchy*. In forming his list of necessary institutions, Dahl incorporated some liberal values, such as freedom of speech and assembly. All of these are political inputs rather than socioeconomic outcomes. Sartori (1987, 156) argues that democracy is the system that generates this ideal type: "Large-scale democracy is a procedure and/or a *mechanism* that (a) generates an *open polyarchy* whose *competition* on the electoral market (b) attributes *power to the people* and (c) specifically enforces the *responsiveness* of the leaders to the led." Within the scope of polyarchy, states have a wide range of institutional structures they can enact. See Schmitter and Karl (1991) for discussion of the choices they can consider.

Maximalist frameworks append additional features to the electoral institutions that define the minimal conception of democracy. Linz and Stepan (1996) argue that the free and fair elections must be accompanied by institutional guarantees of political rights, the ability of the government to make major public policy, and obedience to a democratic constitution, the rule of law, and human rights.[2] They argue that polyarchy is insufficient for institutionalized democracy "because no matter how free and fair the elections and no matter how large the government's majority, democracy must also have a constitution that itself is democratic in that it respects fundamental liberties and offers considerable protections for minority rights" and must "rule within the confines of its constitution and be bound by the law and by a complex set of vertical and horizontal institutions that help to ensure accountability" (Stepan 2000, 39).

A still more expansive take on the concept of democracy introduces economic circumstances. These can include both "liberal" and "socialist or social-democratic" economic models (Schmitter and Karl 1991, 77). It is not possible to state truly that either economic policy is more or less democratic than the other. Even Papacharissi (2021, 105), who is hunting for the system that should replace democracy while bestowing that title on the as-yet-to-be-invented system, acknowledges, "Democracy is a system of governance, not of financial management."[3] Incorporating either liberal or social economic models into the term *democracy* makes the results of the political process, which is how an economic policy would be determined, definitional of the process itself.

Diamond and Morlino (2004) attempt to thread the needle between a maximalist and minimalist conception of democracy by looking at the additional elements as a means of gauging the "quality" of the democracy, which is defined as polyarchy. They establish eight dimensions on which to assess the quality of the democracy: rule of law, participation, competition, vertical accountability, horizontal accountability, freedom, equality, and responsiveness. They nonetheless introduce socioeconomic considerations through the backdoor. They note that "democracy does not demand a certain set of substantive social or economic policies" but appeal to "'social' rights" to "certain goods (health, education, a minimal income, and perhaps others)" while also saying that democracy "presuppose[s] a degree of political equality that is virtually impossible if wealth and status inequalities become too extreme" (27). State control over such socioeconomic outcomes is decidedly an expansive view of the state, let alone democracy.

This minimalist-maximalist distinction is sometimes called the procedural and substantive distinction. The meaning of substantive democracy, though, is muddy. For instance, Mattes and Bratton (2007) treat "substantive" as the obverse of "procedural." Wedeen (2007, 80) uses the language of "substantive representation" as a necessary component of "definitions of democracy," into which she includes "citizen participation, modes of continual accountability, and informed publics whose participants engage in lively deliberation and criticism." Such informed publics could result from private choice or government policies. Though Wedeen (2007) does not offer an affirmative definition for democracy, she argues that the minimalist framework she identifies with Przeworski and Schumpeter allows scholars to ignore other forms of political contestation; they "evacuate politics of the messy stuff of contestation—of initiative, spontaneity, self-fashioning, revelation, ingenuity, action, and creativity—which often occurs outside the domain of electoral outcomes" (63).[4] Collier and Levitsky (1997) also employ the "substantive policies" and "procedures" language. Democracies that feature liberal socioeconomic policies, provide services like education and health care for all, and/or have a small income gap are then considered the substantive democracies as opposed to democracies that do not have such generous social policies. In other usages, the labels distinguish democracies that have elections but do not possess the accompanying rights, culture, and public participation that would facilitate the system's operating as a representation of the public will—"procedural democracies"—from "substantive democracies," which do have the other elements that work together to make the democratic government work well (Magone 2014).

Researchers have also identified deficient versions of democracies to describe particular states. Collier and Levitsky (1997) dub these the "democracies with adjectives." We should recognize nondemocratic states that have lurched toward democracy and incorporated some of its

32   Defining Democracy

elements. However, when the adjectives describe the failure to embody democracy (e.g., authoritarian democracy or neopatrimonial democracy) rather than the type of democracy (e.g., presidential democracy), this is a question of precision in exclusion rather than inclusion. They should be considered subtypes of authoritarianism or nondemocracy, not subtypes of democracy. "Improved description, in turn, is essential for assessing the *causes* and *consequences* of democracy, which is a central goal" of the scholars engaging in this "precising" of definitions (Collier and Levitsky 1997, 431–433). These questions should not be defined away.

The minimalist framework is central to how political scientists measure democracy for the study of those causes and consequences. Arguably the most common measurement of democracy is the Polity score system. In it, "democracy is conceived as three essential, interdependent elements": (1) "the presence of institutions and procedures through which citizens can express effective preferences about alternative policies and leaders," (2) "institutionalized constraints on the exercise of power by the executive," and (3) "the guarantee of civil liberties to all citizens in their daily lives and in acts of political participation" (Marshall and Gurr 2020, 14). While the "rule of law, systems of checks and balances, freedom of the press, and so on are means to" these objectives, they are not coded into the score. Autocracies are states in which "chief executives are chosen in a regularized process of selection within the political elite, and once in office they exercise power with few institutional constraints" (Marshall and Gurr 2020, 16). Treier and Jackman (2008) draw on the same features using a latent trait modeling approach to score democracies.[5]

The Varieties of Democracy Project has created a polyarchy index based on Dahl's description. It is called the "electoral democracy index" (Coppedge et al. 2020, 42). Boix, Miller, and Rosato (2013) also draw on Dahl's polyarchy concept. A country is coded as democratic if "the executive is directly or indirectly elected in popular elections and is responsible either directly to voters or to a legislature," the legislature and/or executive "is chosen in free and fair elections," and a "majority of adult men" have "the right to vote" (1530). Failure on one of these points means classification as a nondemocracy.

Alvarez et al. (1996, 4) hew closely to the point that a democracy is "a regime in which some governmental offices are filled as a consequence of contested elections." They require that the chief executive and legislature be elected and there be more than one party. Cheibub, Ghandi, and Vreeland (2010) extend the Alvarez et al. (1996) metric to develop the democracy-dictatorship dichotomy measure. They require that the executive be elected or chosen by an elected body, that the legislature be directly elected, that there be more than one party, and that an alternation in power has occurred.

The purpose of this project is not to provide a comprehensive list of measures of democracy. For lists of additional metrics, see Munck and Verkuilen (2002). Rather, the purpose of this discussion has been to highlight the centrality of political institutions to political scientists' understanding and evaluation of democracy as a construct.

The maximalist construction is challenging empirically.[6] The first challenge is the perennial problem of not having a shared sense of the construct when only some researchers append these points to the term. Methodological challenges can be introduced by these maximalist definitions because "the sheer overburdening of a concept may decrease its usefulness by making it a concept that has no empirical referents" (Munck and Verkuilen 2002, 9). Additionally, there are theoretical issues caused by tensions between these appendages. For one thing, liberal values can be difficult to incorporate and sustain in a majoritarian system. The necessary fear of the tyranny of the majority as well as a disagreeable popular will could lead to voting against some of these values. Papacharissi (2021) bemoans the perpetual rebalancing act between freedom and equality, which she identifies as the fundamentals of "democracy" and as always in tension with each other. Schaffer (2000, 13) does the same, although he identifies "three dimensions" that vie for importance: "participation, equality, and choice." Diamond and Morlino (2004) cite additional tension between popular sovereignty, in the form of participation, competition, and vertical accountability, and freedom and equality. Sklar (1983, 11) fears that appeals to "freedom," namely "freedom from want," would be the "deadly agent" that would (try to) kill African democracy in the third wave of democratization.[7] If one appends a diversity of viewpoints to the idea of democracy, the challenge is even greater. The majoritarianism in democracy stifles the "democratic premise of plurality" by "enforc[ing] a homogeneity of public opinion through voting" (Papacharissi 2021, 73). Thus, maximalism faces ongoing tension.[8]

To the extent that liberalism and democracy are all but fused in the Western worldview—making the term *liberal democracy* practically redundant—it is understandable that researchers elide these concepts. Democratic culture theory explicitly and causally links liberal values and democratization. For more on this, see Inglehart (2003) and Welzel (2021a, 2021b). Incorporating these additional features poses a particular problem when discussing Middle East democratization. This is beyond

34 Defining Democracy

the fact that the Middle East—in addition to having relatively low levels of democratization—experiences great restrictions on many human rights and civil liberties. For many in the Middle East, attitudes toward liberal values and electoral governance are not inherently linked. There are liberal democrats, liberal nondemocrats, and less-than-liberal respondents of varying relationships with democracy (Ridge 2022a, 2022b). Fusing liberalism and democracy in a definition obscures this variation in public opinion.

Incorporating the economic outcomes that a state generates into the definition is not consistent with how researchers typically think about democracy. Democracy scores do not plummet by default during recessions, nor do scholars argue that they should—even when they might propose such expansive definitions of democracy. While democratization is often associated with economic development, whether democratization is the cause or consequence of that development is still an area of debate (Przeworski et al. 2000). The relationship between gross domestic product (GDP) and democracy is particularly inconsistent in Arab countries (Stepan and Robertson 2003). The vast literature debating the cause-and-effect relationship between democratization and economic development would be entirely redundant if democracy were defined by economic policies or products. The same is true of any economics-regime linkage studies.

The fundamental challenge in identifying democracies then is including what must be included at minimum, while ensuring that the bar is not so low that everything fits into the category. Researchers must not obviate the actual research question by assuming the answer into the definition or forsake a coherent meaning. Functionally, "the most popular definition of democracy equates it with regular *elections*, fairly conducted and honestly counted" (Schmitter and Karl 1991, 78). Neither a liberal nor a conservative economic policy is "intrinsically more democratic than the other—just *differently*. . . . Both, if carried to extremes, could undermine the practice of democracy" (77). To this end, elections are taken by political scientists to be the fundamental characteristic of democratic governance.

In the Arab World

The meaning ascribed to *dimuqratiyya* is quite different from the meaning ascribed to *democracy*. This is not because the citizens are inherently wrong or confused. Rather, it is because these are different things.

This chapter identifies how Arab citizens understand *dimuqratiyya* following the method of American justice Potter Stewart. Even if he could not explain what something was (hardcore pornography, in that case), he knew people could identify it. We see Arabs refer to different regimes as *dimuqratiyya* or not. They know it when they see it. What features make them see it?

Dimuqratiyya draws on the same Greek words—people (*demos*) and rule (*kratos*) for δημοκρατία (*dēmokratiā*)—as the English word *democracy*. Mernissi (1992), in *Islam et démocratie*, bemoans the lack of an original Arabic word for the concept democracy. She notes, "We say *dimuqratiyya*, which is to say we use the Greek word. Two Arabs who speak of democracy are obliged to speak Greek to each other, all while remembering that the Greek patrimony is forbidden to us under the pretext that it is foreign to us" (113).[9] She defends adopting the foreign import, like telephones and cars were adopted: the "French colonial army" brought democracy among "other equally foreign things" (113).[10]

Mernissi may be right that contemporary understandings of democracy entered Middle East political discourse and political institutions via colonialism. This claim itself is subject to contestation. Some Arab writers, for instance, argue that the early Islamic practice of consultation (*shūrā*) provides an Arab basis for democratic governance.[11] For a systematic unpacking of arguments that Islamic theology is compatible with democracy, see Ciftci (2021).

The word and concept, however, had a much earlier—though still foreign—entrance into Arabic and Arab political thought. Arab philosophers had access to several of the same Greek sources that were used in developing European political thought. By the tenth century, "most of Plato, Aristotle and their late Greek commentators had been translated [into Arabic] (partly by Eastern Christians via Syriac). Aristotle's *Politics* was an exception; only its existence, and possibly a version of Books I and II, were known" (Black 2011, 57). Aristotle's *Nichomachian Ethics* and Plato's *Republic* were informative from a practical politics perspective. Philosophers like al-Farabi were greatly influenced in their depictions of virtuous cities and ideal rulers. However, the absence of Aristotle's *Politics* meant that Arab philosophers could not draw on his discussions of a constitutional democracy. As an institutional framework, democracy thus retained the deficient status it had for several Greek philosophers as a function of mass will. Ibn Rushd characterized "democracy" as a "defective" and "non-virtuous" government (Black 2011, 127). Not long after Ibn Rushd's time, Christian European philosophers, including Thomas Aquinas, acquired Aristotle's *Politics* via Byzantium.

36 *Defining Democracy*

While Greek philosophy was expansive, only certain domains made the transition into Arab philosophy. The nature of political institutions received less attention. Instead, the focus was on right action, happiness/ the good life via right action, and the philosopher-king-lawgiver. This included the development of Advice to Kings and arguments about circles and cycles of justice. It also included, to some extent, philosophy of religion. Philosophical topics were interpreted within the boundaries of Islam, and certain domains, like ethics and existence, were only to be interpreted in the religious frame. The "Muslim Philosophers thought it was their task to restate and interpret the Platonic-Aristotelian body of knowledge and transmit it to the Islamic world for future generations. All that was needed was to fill it out at certain points, especially where the appearance of Islam had fundamentally changed things, as it clearly had in social moeurs and political organizations" (Black 2011, 60). Ultimately, Greek ideas did not penetrate so far in the Arab world as they did in Europe. Hellenistic philosophy declined there after the eleventh century.

Bodies both devoutly religious and secularly power seeking preferred a system more favorable to religious obedience to a lawgiver. Drawing on Persianate political philosophy was more amenable to absolutist monarchy.[12] These less-democratic philosophical notions included principles such as the Circle of Justice, which was invoked in empires from the post-Abbasid sultanates to the Ottoman Empire to claim that social hierarchies were legitimate and behooved society as a whole (Şiviloğlu 2018). The sultan's status was unquestionable in this philosophy, although philosophers might question particular acts or issue advice. Endorsing this philosophy was then a move away from the adoption of democratic, republican, or consultative principles.

The king was not wholly removed from public will, either by the philosopher or by practice. After all, the regime was constrained by what the public or the subsidiary lords would bear. Although the sultan might hold himself apart from the public, he was by necessity cognizant of the limits that popular will and the threat of rebellion, even by those close to the throne, placed on his power (Şiviloğlu 2018). Contemporary Arab kings arguably face similar constraints. More will be said on a "democratic" sheen on monarchy in Chapter 6. Ultimately, despite a mutual source in Greek philosophy, democracy and *dimuqratiyya* took different paths into the early modern period and beyond.

To unpack what shapes Arabs' construal of *dimuqratiyya*, I draw on the Arab Barometer. In these surveys (as well as in surveys like the World Values Survey and the Afrobarometer), citizens of countries, both democracies and nondemocracies, are asked to what extent their countries are "democratic."[13] In this case, they are literally asked the extent to which the country is *dimuqratiyya* on a 0–10 scale. If democracy and *dimuqratiyya* were one and the same, then we would expect MENA countries to score very low. After all, sources from Polity to Freedom House assure us that these countries are not democracies, even by the minimalist standard.

The 2018 Arab Barometer results entirely contradict the expert assessments (Table 2.1). On a 0–10 scale from no democracy at all to democratic to the highest degree, 33.4 percent of the respondents rated their country 6 or higher in the 2018 survey; 10 percent rated Kuwait 4 or lower, which would align with the expert ratings. However, 43.5 percent rated Tunisia 4 or lower on this scale, which would be in direct opposition to the expert classification at the time. In the same survey, nearly half rated Yemen as *dimuqratiyya*, and more than a third did so for Jordan.

Table 2.1 Extent of *Dimuqratiyya* in the Country Rating (Arab Barometer V) (percentage)

Rating Country (Mean, Median)	0	1	2	3	4	5	6	7	8	9	10
Algeria (3.9, 4)	12.8	5.1	9.4	15.1	15.6	18.8	10.5	6.9	4.3	1.3	0.6
Egypt (5.2, 5)	12.6	0.9	2.0	5.0	13.2	16.9	13.9	15.8	11.5	3.1	5.0
Iraq (3.9, 4)	22.2	3.9	5.8	10.8	9.7	23.8	6.1	5.7	3.2	1.0	7.7
Jordan (5.4, 5)	7.0	3.2	4.0	6.5	7.6	25.8	10.4	14.7	10.9	4.4	5.5
Kuwait (7.0, 7)	1.2	1.1	1.7	2.6	3.5	11.1	14.6	21.3	18.3	11.8	12.9
Lebanon (4.3, 4)	7.5	5.3	11.8	13.0	12.6	15.9	14.0	12.4	5.4	1.8	0.3
Libya (2.4, 2)	43.9	5.4	7.4	11.3	7.6	13.3	3.7	2.3	1.8	0.7	2.7
Morocco (4.1, 4)	13.1	4.3	11.5	13.5	13.4	12.5	13.3	9.2	4.7	1.7	2.8
Palestine (3.9, 4)	12.1	7.2	9.5	12.9	12.2	19.9	10.8	8.8	3.7	1.9	0.9
Sudan (2.6, 2)	30.3	10.0	13.4	14.4	10.1	9.1	4.1	2.5	1.9	1.3	3.0
Tunisia (4.6, 5)	14.2	3.9	5.0	9.7	10.4	22.8	8.6	8.4	7.4	1.7	7.9
Yemen (5.1, 5)	8.3	5.4	7.1	7.0	7.6	16.0	15.0	15.5	6.3	4.0	7.7

38   Defining Democracy

Some residents are expressly aware that their countries are not democratic. The ongoing democratization movements speak to that. A forty-plus-year-old man from Marrakech, who defined *dimuqratiyya* primarily in terms of low corruption and law and order, noted, "Any contact with reality is completely different from what is on paper under the heading The Democracy [*al-dimuqratiyya*]."[14]

The difference between democracy and *dimuqratiyya* explains this discrepancy between how researchers rate the countries and how the citizens do. After all, the recent surveys from Egypt and Morocco indicate that citizens will identify several nondemocratic systems as *dimuqratiyya*.[15] Respondents were asked "How *dimuqratiyya* is a country if . . . ," from "very *dimuqratiyya*" to "not *dimuqratiyya* at all." For 17.3 percent of Egyptians and 18.2 percent of Moroccans, it was somewhat or very *dimuqratiyya* for an elected leader to remain in power for decades. This is possible in many democracies and is not inherently undemocratic. The respondents might understandably be skeptical about how that is accomplished, particularly given the tenure of some Arab-state leaders (e.g., Hosni Mubarak, Zine El Abidine Ben Ali, Muammar Gaddafi). For 16.4 percent of Egyptians and 13.2 percent of Moroccans, a country is somewhat or very *dimuqratiyya* if "the elected leader is never challenged by another candidate for office." For 13.2 percent of Egyptians and 11.2 percent of Moroccans, a country that bans some parties from participating in elections is somewhat or very *dimuqratiyya*. The Muslim Brotherhood was famously banned from Egyptian politics, and Ennahda was banned in Tunisia. Moroccan elections do not include parties that will not recognize the king's constitutional role as *amir al-mu'minin* (commander of the faithful).

Entirely undemocratic systems were not viewed as entirely contrary to *dimuqratiyya*. For 20.5 percent of Egyptians and 11.3 percent of Moroccans, it is somewhat or very *dimuqratiyya* for the military to be in charge of the government. Egyptians' political tolerance for military involvement is discussed in Chapter 5; the military has played a substantial role in Egyptian politics over many decades, including a coup some Egyptians identified as a *dimuqratiyya* course of action. A military regime is at odds with democratic precepts. For 19.6 percent of Egyptians and 17.0 percent of Moroccans, it was somewhat or very *dimuqratiyya* to require that elected leaders "be approved by religious leaders." The Islamic Republic of Iran, for instance, requires candidates to be approved by religious leaders. Such constraints on competition violate some theories of democracy. Neither Egypt nor Morocco has an equivalent veto authority, and at least a sizeable majority of the population indicates that it would not be *dimuqratiyya* to have one.

Furthermore, 79.3 percent of Egyptians and 86.7 percent of Moroccans said a country is only slightly or not at all *dimuqratiyya* if "the government is elected but there are high levels of poverty." Thus, even when presented with a democratic system, *dimuqratiyya* is heavily down-weighted by socioeconomic outcomes. This demonstrates that *dimuqratiyya* has a strong economic valence that is not part of how researchers are measuring democracy. Per the democracy metrics discussed above, the level of poverty in a country is not a factor in its democracy classification, and it may or may not be a function of the level of democracy in the country. Moroccans also answered a question about a system that "includes both elected and unelected offices that take an active part in decision-making and policy." Morocco has a king who is actively involved in the government of the country; 40 percent of Moroccans indicated that it is somewhat or very *dimuqratiyya* to include unelected offices in decisionmaking.[16] The nontrivial associations between some of these systems and *dimuqratiyya* indicates that this construct does not map onto how political scientists recognize democracy.

This linkage between *dimuqratiyya* and the lack of poverty is evident in Khanani's (2021, 88–90) interviews with Moroccan Islamists. He recounts individuals telling him that *dimuqratiyya* is *khubz*, which literally means "bread." Figuratively the word refers to having access to necessities or living a life with dignity. A country may have democratic institutions, like freedom of expression, but, he quotes a taxi driver as saying, "there's no meaning to *dimuqrāṭiyya* if the economic and social conditions of citizens don't change. . . . [D]*imuqrāṭiyya* must contribute to some extent to social justice, justice, in the distribution of national resources, and not in an angelic way, but to achieve the minimum" (90). Thus, the meaning of *dimuqratiyya*, for some citizens at least, can be quite expansive and distinct from the common empirical metrics.

What, then, to make of Arab citizens' *dimuqratiyya* ratings? To answer this question, I turn to citizens' *dimuqratiyya* ratings for their countries in five waves of the Arab Barometer (2007, 2011, 2013, 2016, 2018).[17] These are the ratings depicted in Table 2.1. On the face of it, citizens' evaluations of their countries' *dimuqratiyya* do not align with the countries' Polity2 scores (Table 2.2). The Polity2 scores are expert ratings of democratization based on competitive recruitment and selection of the executive. It rates countries from autocracies (-10 to -6) to democracies (6 to 10). Failed and occupied states (0) are classed with the anocracies (-5 to 5).[18] In Waves 1, 3, and 4, there is a significant negative correlation between respondents' ratings and the Polity score. In Waves 2 and 5, the relationship is negative but not significant. This does not bode well for the idea that the terms *dimuqratiyya* and *democracy* represent

40   Defining Democracy

Table 2.2   Correlation of *Dimuqratiyya* and Democracy Ratings

Wave	Correlation
Wave 1	-0.227***
Wave 2	-0.013 ($p = 0.16$)
Wave 3	-0.066***
Wave 4	-0.052***
Wave 5	-0.009 ($p = 0.22$)

Notes: ***$p < 0.001$; **$p < 0.01$; *$p < 0.05$.

the same construct. In any case, the correlations are quite low, which also bespeaks differences in meanings, at least for some.

What factors do correlate with countries' *dimuqratiyya* ratings? If respondents are conceiving of *dimuqratiyya* as a system of political institutions in the way that researchers are measuring democracy, then elements of strong institutional performance should predict high *dimuqratiyya* ratings. If, however, they are intermingling extrapolitical considerations, such as economic policy, in their conception of *dimuqratiyya*, then nonpolitical factors will also be influential.

OLS regression with country fixed effects and clustered standard errors is used, as the surveys are conducted within countries. The Arab Barometer includes survey weights for the representativeness of the samples.[19] The reference country for the fixed effects is Algeria.

Several metrics tap into the institutional features of democracy. A binary variable identifies viewing the country's elections as "completely free and fair" or "free and fair, but with minor problems" as opposed to "free and fair, with major problems" or "not free or fair." Free elections are definitive features of democracy and should be a strong and positive indicator of *dimuqratiyya* to the extent that it tracks with democracy. Other features tap into whether citizens have the freedom to criticize the government and whether the government cares about the people's needs. For more information on the coding of these variables, see Appendix C.

Other variables relate to services or outcomes, which do not fit with the typical democracy ratings. Respondents indicate how satisfied they are with their government's performance on a scale from "completely unsatisfied" (1) to "completely satisfied" (10). They could also rate the corruption in their country and whether the government was cracking down on it, their difficulty accessing state services, and the national economy. They were also asked if they felt safe where they lived.

Defining Democracy **41**

Citizen-specific items were also included. Variables are included for age, gender, tertiary education, religion and religiosity, membership in a civil society organization, public-sector employment, interpersonal trust, institutional trust, and income sufficiency. Living, working, or studying in the West in the last five years is also noted.

Three items are included from outside the Arab Barometer dataset. One is the World Bank–reported GDP per capita ($1,000 increments) for each country for the year of the survey. The other is the Polity2 score for the country for the year of the survey. If respondents' understanding lines up with the empirical treatment of democracy, this would be a strong and positive predictor of *dimuqratiyya*. As Palestine does not receive a Polity2 rating, the models are shown with and without this variable in order to preserve Palestine in the sample. A country-level variable is included for the former colonial occupiers of these states. In Middle East history, the predominate players in this domain were England and France via their empires, protectorates, and mandates. Italy was implicated through Libya.

The results present limited support for a relationship between the elected-government construct of democracy and *dimuqratiyya* (Table 2.3). In the two most recent waves, the Polity rating is positively associated with the respondents' *dimuqratiyya* ratings, which is what would be expected if they were the same construct. However, for two of the earlier waves, the Polity rating is negatively associated with the *dimuqratiyya* ratings. This does not speak to a strong connection between *dimuqratiyya* and democracy, at least as Polity measures it.

Some countries take votes—sometimes referred to as holding elections—in order to advise unelected political leaders, to choose the members of parliaments or advisory councils of questionable power, or to fill subnational government offices. Others hold elections that truly determine who will be in government. In either case, ideally the results translate into representation. Still, even in established and widely recognized democracies, citizens can feel that an election served no purpose. Papacharissi (2021, 103) describes "the *invisible citizen*, a citizen summoned to vote and then abandoned, a citizen wanting to speak but not listened to, a citizen looking to contribute to the local community and finding that one's efforts are undervalued and not counted as civic duty." Holding elections, convincing the world they were valid, and convincing the citizenry they were effective are not one and the same process.

Citizens are aware that elections vary in quality, which is demonstrated in their choices to participate in or abstain from the contests and public discussion of them. Where elections are free and fair, there is

Table 2.3 How *Dimuqratiyya* Is the Country? (OLS)

	Wave 1	Wave 1	Wave 2	Wave 2	Wave 3	Wave 3	Wave 4	Wave 4	Wave 5	Wave 5
Intercept	1.22*** (0.25)	0.80 (0.67)	5.01*** (0.57)	1.78*** (0.16)	0.01 (0.21)	0.04 (0.19)	8.00*** (0.45)	5.60*** (0.45)	2.94*** (0.41)	2.09*** (0.38)
Political institutions										
Free elections	0.46** (0.22)	0.44* (0.25)	0.59*** (0.14)	0.62*** (0.15)	0.58*** (0.09)	0.60*** (0.09)	0.44*** (0.07)	0.47*** (0.08)	0.48*** (0.10)	0.49*** (0.11)
Care about needs	0.10 (0.22)	−0.15 (0.18)	0.26*** (0.10)	0.23** (0.10)			0.27*** (0.04)	0.24*** (0.05)	0.31** (0.13)	0.32** (0.14)
Criticize the government	0.35*** (0.10)	0.23*** (0.08)	0.50*** (0.11)	0.47*** (0.11)	0.57*** (0.11)	0.59*** (0.12)	0.65*** (0.14)	0.61*** (0.17)		
Socioeconomic outcomes										
Government performance	0.24*** (0.07)	0.32*** (0.08)	0.40*** (0.03)	0.41*** (0.03)	0.41*** (0.03)	0.42*** (0.04)	0.34*** (0.03)	0.34*** (0.04)	0.32*** (0.04)	0.32*** (0.04)
Crackdown on corruption	0.31* (0.18)	0.44** (0.24)	0.05 (0.07)	0.08 (0.08)	0.28** (0.13)	0.31** (0.14)	0.23*** (0.04)	0.26*** (0.04)	0.35*** (0.08)	0.35*** (0.09)
Corruption	−0.27 (0.17)	−0.02 (0.11)	−0.09*** (0.03)	−0.08* (0.04)			−0.19*** (0.06)	−0.23*** (0.06)	−0.16 (0.17)	−0.16 (0.19)
Service difficulties	−0.04 (0.07)	−0.12** (0.05)	−0.07 (0.07)	−0.09 (0.08)	−0.13 (0.09)	−0.09 (0.08)			0.20** (0.09)	0.19** (0.09)
Safe area	0.08 (0.14)	0.02 (0.21)	0.40*** (0.11)	0.41*** (0.12)	0.23*** (0.07)	0.24*** (0.07)	0.56*** (0.12)	0.59*** (0.15)	0.27* (0.15)	0.32** (0.17)
National economy	0.40*** (0.11)	0.45*** (0.19)	0.25*** (0.06)	0.24*** (0.07)	0.17* (0.10)	0.14 (0.10)	0.14 (0.13)	0.10 (0.15)	0.34* (0.17)	0.31 (0.19)
Demographic										
Institutional trust	−0.20 (0.13)	−0.13 (0.15)	−0.16*** (0.05)	−0.16*** (0.05)	0.21** (0.10)	0.21* (0.11)	0.32*** (0.10)	0.36*** (0.12)	−0.29*** (0.06)	−0.30*** (0.06)
Interpersonal trust	0.30*** (0.10)	0.33* (0.18)	−0.10 (0.14)	−0.08 (0.15)	0.18* (0.10)	0.17* (0.10)	0.09 (0.10)	0.08 (0.11)	0.04 (0.09)	0.05 (0.10)
Time in West	−0.24 (0.16)	−0.11 (0.18)	−0.16 (0.22)	−0.21 (0.25)	−0.10 (0.13)	−0.08 (0.13)				

continues

Table 2.3 Continued

	Wave 1	Wave 1	Wave 2	Wave 2	Wave 3	Wave 3	Wave 4	Wave 4	Wave 5	Wave 5
Age	−0.01**	−0.00	−0.01**	−0.01**	−0.01**	−0.01***	−0.01	−0.01	−0.01**	−0.01***
	(0.00)	(0.00)	(0.00)	(0.00)	(0.00)	(0.00)	(0.00)	(0.00)	(0.00)	(0.00)
Male	−0.10	−0.17	−0.12	−0.07	−0.02	−0.03	−0.30***	−0.32***	−0.13	−0.13
	(0.09)	(0.13)	(0.09)	(0.08)	(0.07)	(0.08)	(0.05)	(0.05)	(0.18)	(0.19)
College education	−0.24**	−0.18	−0.04	−0.02	0.06	0.06	−0.10	−0.09	0.14**	0.17**
	(0.10)	(0.13)	(0.09)	(0.10)	(0.10)	(0.10)	(0.08)	(0.10)	(0.07)	(0.07)
Religion: Christian	0.34***		0.20	0.21	−0.08	−0.19***	−0.06	−0.18	−0.18	−0.20*
	(0.07)		(0.14)	(0.15)	(0.15)	(0.06)	(0.12)	(0.11)	(0.14)	(0.12)
Religion: other									−0.14*	−0.13
									(0.08)	(0.08)
Religion: none	0.75***		1.35**	1.36*					0.01	0.02
	(0.07)		(0.69)	(0.71)					(1.18)	(1.17)
Religion: not clear/ declined	−0.70***		−0.59	−0.68					−0.39	−0.36
	(0.18)		(0.67)	(0.88)					(0.30)	(0.29)
Religious: in between	−0.27	0.45***	0.03	0.04	0.18	0.15	0.12	0.13	0.15	0.16
	(0.20)	(0.10)	(0.09)	(0.10)	(0.16)	(0.17)	(0.09)	(0.11)	(0.09)	(0.10)
Religious	0.19**	0.20***	0.02	−0.02	0.15	0.16	0.04	−0.01	0.32**	0.37***
	(0.08)	(0.07)	(0.10)	(0.10)	(0.19)	(0.20)	(0.13)	(0.14)	(0.13)	(0.13)
Civil society member	0.06	−0.25***	0.06	0.01	0.24***	0.21**	−0.03	−0.04	0.18*	0.24***
	(0.26)	(0.08)	(0.12)	(0.13)	(0.08)	(0.09)	(0.06)	(0.08)	(0.09)	(0.09)
Public employee	0.23	0.10	−0.00	−0.00	−0.04	−0.03	0.24***	0.25***	0.13	0.15
	(0.16)	(0.17)	(0.10)	(0.10)	(0.10)	(0.11)	(0.08)	(0.09)	(0.10)	(0.11)
Country										
Colony (France)	−2.87**	0.16	0.30***	0.44***	−2.38***	−2.39***	0.60***	−1.70***	1.10***	−4.34***
	(1.25)	(0.46)	(0.06)	(0.08)	(0.26)	(0.22)	(0.13)	(0.06)	(0.14)	(0.60)
Colony (Italy)					−8.02***	−8.06***			0.04	−6.82***
					(0.65)	(0.56)			(0.20)	(0.64)
GDP per capita	1.34***	0.61***	−0.53***	0.10	0.94***	0.94***	−1.57***	−0.39***	−0.19***	0.78***
	(0.37)	(0.10)	(0.07)	(0.06)	(0.07)	(0.06)	(0.15)	(0.05)	(0.04)	(0.07)

continues

Table 2.3 Continued

	Wave 1	Wave 1	Wave 2	Wave 2	Wave 3	Wave 3	Wave 4	Wave 4	Wave 5	Wave 5
Polity2		-0.42*** (0.04)		-0.22*** (0.05)		-0.01 (0.01)		0.06*** (0.01)		0.42*** (0.04)
Bahrain	-26.98*** (7.28)	-14.64*** (2.02)								
Egypt			-0.92*** (0.17)		-1.63*** (0.19)	-1.73*** (0.18)	-0.42*** (0.06)	-1.93*** (0.07)		
Iraq					-4.95*** (0.39)	-4.95*** (0.34)			0.80*** (0.15)	-6.27*** (0.69)
Jordan	-0.69 (0.49)				-1.46*** (0.15)	-1.53*** (0.14)	2.31*** (0.15)		1.36*** (0.12)	-0.78*** (0.22)
Kuwait					-44.28*** (3.32)	-44.39*** (2.76)				
Lebanon	-3.48*** (0.26)		1.73*** (0.11)	1.24*** (0.09)	-2.45*** (0.22)	-2.37*** (0.20)			1.10*** (0.19)	-2.91*** (0.23)
Morocco					0.76*** (0.13)	0.68*** (0.10)	-1.58*** (0.19)		-1.28*** (0.08)	3.49*** (0.50)
Palestine			-1.92*** (0.11)						-0.14 (0.13)	
Sudan			-2.85*** (0.27)	-1.49*** (0.14)					-1.64*** (0.15)	
Tunisia			-1.07*** (0.14)	0.12 (0.10)						
Yemen			-1.29** (0.55)	0.65 (0.89)						
N	3,147	2,160	6,760	6,158	7,327	6,803	5,129	4,323	8,151	7,424
Adjusted R²	0.2983	0.412	0.288	0.2993	0.4163	0.4245	0.3963	0.4023	0.3592	0.365

Notes: ***$p < 0.01$; **$p < 0.05$; *$p < 0.1$.

Defining Democracy **45**

greater democracy. It is then a positive sign for overlap between the constructs that where elections are free and fair, citizens see more *dimuqratiyya*. On the ten-point measure of *dimuqratiyya*, however, this binary indicator for free elections is not shifting ratings all that much. The same is true for having the right to speak freely about the government and the sense that the government cares about the public's needs. The parameters that factor into political science measures of democracy are related to *dimuqratiyya*. However, they are not equivalent.

Instead, socioeconomic outcomes are more consistent predictors of the *dimuqratiyya* rating. Government performance is the single strongest predictor of how *dimuqratiyya* the regime is rated. Furthermore, the effect size, given that performance is a rated on a 0–10 scale, dwarfs that of the other predictors. The regime that pleases the citizens is *dimuqratiyya*. *Dimuqratiyya* is recognized by its impact, not its inputs.

To a lesser extent, the strength of the economy and the circumstances of corruption also matter. A good economy and low—or at least counteracted—corruption are also *dimuqratiyya*. Those living in safe areas gave significantly higher ratings, although the effect size of this binary, on a ten-point rating scale, is not too large. This pattern is intriguing because it inverts a common narrative about authoritarian regimes. Subjects of authoritarian governments are often accused of supporting or tolerating authoritarian government because it offers them security. In this case, it seems that creating stability is creating the impression of *dimuqratiyya*. Although democracy and *dimuqratiyya* are not the same, this connection between a sense of safety and perceiving *dimuqratiyya* could shield nondemocratic regimes from citizen agitation, not by pushing them to make the democracy-authoritarianism trade-off but by making them think "mission accomplished." All told, however, it seems that the government performance and socioeconomic outcomes measures are the strongest drivers of citizens' *dimuqratiyya* ratings.

Implications

This chapter has focused on the discontinuity between democracy and *dimuqratiyya*. To do so, it has compared how political scientists assess a country's level of democracy and how MENA residents rate *dimuqratiyya*. In the face of a scholarly consensus that the region is not democratic, *dimuqratiyya* ratings range even to the topmost end of the scale in each country. The non-*dimuqratiyya* ratings, while prevalent, far undershoot expectations. This result is in sharp contrast with Papacharissi's (2021, 35) description of her conversations about democracy. She describes how

46 *Defining Democracy*

many people assert that their countries are not democracies—even in ones that researchers deem democratic—and reports, "Everyone seems to understand what democracy is, but nobody appears to think that it exists." These results indicate that people think they know what *dimuqratiyya* is, and they may even know where it is. It just is not, it seems, democracy.

While the most common metrics in political science focus on institutional parameters, such as competitive elections and civil liberties, the factors that define *dimuqratiyya* are primarily socioeconomic outcomes. On one hand, the central feature of democratization—free and fair elections—is a significant predictor of perceived *dimuqratiyya*. The same is true for recognizing a protection for free expression, including expression that is critical of the state. Expert ratings would expect, if not demand, these elements in order to identify democratization. Their influence on *dimuqratiyya* indicates some overlap in the constructs.

At the same time, nondemocratic (though not antidemocratic) features are also significant predictors of *dimuqratiyya* scores. Policy outcomes, like low corruption, a strong economy, and public safety, are significant predictors. Most importantly, the strongest and most consistent predictor is satisfaction with regime performance. Governments that are working, in the respondents' opinion, are *dimuqratiyya*. This is true even in the face of a regional paucity of democracy. By necessity, then, *dimuqratiyya* ratings are not evaluating democracy. Although political institutions are influencing the ratings, socioeconomic or outcome-specific features are dominating the popular conception.

These results could indicate that *dimuqratiyya* is identifying governments that are working for the people even if those are not governments by the people. Government by the people helps too. In this way, *dimuqratiyya* seems to embody part of the root of the word by expecting the government to enact the public's will for an effective state. It just seems to be doing that sometimes in a nondemocratic context.

An additional point should be noted. Even with all of these factors taken into consideration, only about 40 percent of the variance in respondent country ratings is explained. These indirect measures can only provide so much insight into how citizens conceive of *dimuqratiyya*, especially given the likelihood that multiple conceptions of *dimuqratiyya* are at work here. More direct questions can provide additional information. This will be the focus of the next chapter, which will also discuss who is likely to ascribe these various meanings to *dimuqratiyya* and the relationship of these diverse understandings to citizens' attitudes toward democracy.

To characterize democracy for this book—especially as it broaches questions of support for democracy (as opposed to *dimuqratiyya*)—I rely on a minimalist definition of democracy. Arguably the minimalist conception provides the most favorable assessment possible of Middle East support for democracy. Citizens who reject elections do not support the central institutional requirement of modern democracy, so they are not democrats. However, rejecting elements of a maximalist framework might lead respondents to seem antidemocratic when they were instead squeamish of parties or secularism. Thus, this choice poses greater risk of overestimating support than underestimating it. That the surveys reveal—as Chapters 5 and 6 will show—that the publics are endorsing minimalist-definition democracy at a lower rate than they do *dimuqratiyya* (the democracy-*dimuqratiyya* gap) indicates that the identification of a distinction in the constructs is withstanding the harder test. By either framework, democracy and *dimuqratiyya* are held distinct.

Notes

1. Regardless of his definition, Schumpeter (2008) is not necessarily a democrat. He states, "There are ultimate ideals and interests which the most ardent democrat will put above democracy," and thus any person who expresses "uncompromising allegiance" to democracy "feels convinced that democracy will guarantee those ideals and interests" (242). His suggested ideals are liberal values, like justice. However, it takes no great command of history to see economic points that would hold this place for some individuals. These could range from the idealistic (e.g., a commitment to communism) to the quotidian (e.g., the cost of daily bread). Schumpeter thus provides an example of an individual who understands democracy as a political construct but is not *thereby* a committed democrat. This distinction will be relevant in Part II of this book.

2. Collier and Levitsky (1997, 434) describe their conception as the "procedural minimum" while including "fully contested elections with full suffrage and the absence of massive fraud, combined with effective guarantees of civil liberties, including freedom of speech, assembly, and association."

3. In her search for Democracy 2.0, she advocates for suppressing capitalism into "soft capitalism" to remove money's influence on politics. She notes, "There is no recipe for soft capitalism that works for all countries. Each context calls for its own solution" (Papacharissi 2021, 106).

4. Wedeen (2007) suggests the scholars who focus on contested elections replace the word *democracy* in their research agenda with the term *contested elections*. She even suggests that political science "avoid thinking about democracy as a thing at all, or a label that we affix to a state, and focus instead on the existence or absence of democratic practices" (81). I endorse being specific with terminology.

5. That political scientists recognize the central role of electoral institutions in the construct does not mean that scholars cannot understand the misuse to which elections can be put. Some scholars identify a "fallacy"—"electoralism"—that merely holding elections is sufficient, "even ones from which specific parties or candidates are excluded, or in which substantial portions of the population cannot freely participate" (Schmitter and Karl 1991, 78). The constraints coders will accept on the franchise or on participants is a subject of both theoretical and empirical decision.

48   Defining Democracy

Philosophers have argued that it is necessary and right to exclude certain parties for the sake of democracy (Kirshner 2010). The scope of elections and political institutions within a democracy or democratizing regime is worthy of consideration.

6. Some empirical techniques have attempted to incorporate a maximalist framework. Freedom House rates states on two dimensions for the Freedom in the World assessment: political rights and civil liberties (Freedom House 2021). The political rights scale includes the electoral processes, political pluralism, participation, functionality, transparency, and corruption. The civil liberties scale includes personal autonomy; freedom of expression, belief, and association; and the rule of law. V-Dem also offers indexes that weight the polyarchy score by other traits. These indexes weight by minority rights status, direct democracy opportunities, deliberation, and material and immaterial inequalities. They acknowledge these alternatives exist to satisfy "uneasiness about a bedrock practice of electoral democracy: delegating authority to representatives," which tacitly recognizes elections as the core of democracy (Coppedge et al. 2020, 43).

7. For Sklar (1983, 14), accountability is the key feature, so he was willing to bestow the title "democracy" on several nondemocracies in Africa. For instance, he called "the type of government by guardians of the public weal who insist upon uniformity" a "guided democracy" while at the same time calling it a "developmental dictatorship" because it accepted "accountability" to the public by unspecified means. The application of the appellation *democracy* to regimes that are *for the people* without being *of* or *by the people* will be discussed more in the final chapter.

8. All metrics for measuring democracy must grapple with issues of time. Huntington (1991) identifies three chunks of democratization that have occurred in human history. In these periods and beyond them, the expectations that have accompanied "democratization" have expanded greatly. This is particularly true with respect to matters like the scope of the franchise, civil liberties, and economic relativity. This expansion complicates cross-temporal measures. Adcock and Collier (2001, 535) point out that "one problem in establishing equivalence across these two eras lies in the fact that the plausible agenda of 'full' democratization has changed dramatically over time." They note that researchers can create indicators that take the context into account ("context-specific indicators"). However, these are not immune to problems of data availability and comparability. They propose that researchers' "use of such indicators should match the analytic goal of the researcher" and stress that content validation "is central to determining whether and how measurement needs to be adjusted in particular contexts" (536). This book could be construed as an exercise in such validation.

9. "Nous disons *demoqratiya*, c'est-à-dire que nous utilisons le mot grec. Deux Arabes qui parlent de démocratie sont obligés de se parler grec, tout en rappelant que le patrimoine grec nous est interdit sous prétexte qu'il nous est étranger."

10. Schaffer (2000) makes a similar assertion about the movement from French *démocratie* into the Wolof *demokaraasi*. He says that because there were "no direct equivalents in Wolof," the "political elite have attempted to convey their views of *démocratie* by projecting traditional Wolof words into new political contexts or by using metaphors to bridge the gap between the familiar and unfamiliar" (52). This resulted in the Wolof *demokaraasi* being "related in meaning" but also "refer[ring] to a wider range of institutions and situations" (85).

11. For a nuanced discussion of the historicity and present-day viability of this assertion, see An-Na'im (2008), Esposito (1998), or El Fadl (2015).

12. Stasavage (2020) also assigns some credit to the Sasanian bureaucratic system that Umayyad and Abbasid caliphs were able to draw on after absorbing eastern

lands in the Arab conquests. The Sasanians were the last Persianate empire before the Arab conquests. At the same time, he casts an early democratic shine over the Circle of Justice ideology that was also incorporated from the Sasanians, although it was used to justify an autocratic system of governance, because it encouraged the king to think of the common people's interests.

13. By some lights, they should not be scoring "democracy" at all. Sartori argues that "regimes must be classified as democracies or nondemocracies. Then, only as a second step, a further set of criteria can be applied to those regimes deemed democratic by the initial dichotomy. Only with regard to these cases should we inquire as to how democratic they are" (Collier and Adcock 1999, 548), or "the oxen may well wreck the cart rather than pull it" (Sartori 1987, 156). That protocol is not observed in these surveys.

14. ʿalā ayy al-iḥtikāk bal-wāqiʿ yakhtalif tamāmān ʿalā mā yuwjid fī al-waraq taḥt ʿanwān al-dimuqrāṭiyya.

15. These surveys, conducted in August 2019 (Egypt) and January 2020 (Morocco) by YouGov MENA, will be discussed at greater length in subsequent chapters. The percentages shown here adjust for the survey weights for age and gender representativeness. For information on the methodology and content of these surveys, consult Appendices A and B.

16. For more information on the decision not to ask directly about the king, see Chapter 6 and Appendix A.

17. In the first wave, respondents were given a scale of one to ten instead of zero to ten.

18. NB: If these two cases (Yemen and Libya during the conflicts) are dropped because failed states and warring states are not rated in other Polity codings, then Wave 3 remains negative and significant and Wave 5 becomes significant; also, in both cases, the negative correlation becomes stronger. As such, the Polity2 coding is the more conservative coding.

19. The dataset does not include survey weights for Wave I, so weights are not included in those models.

3

Defining *Dimuqratiyya*

Such notions as modernity, enlightenment, and democracy are by no means simple and agreed-upon concepts that one either does or does not find, like Easter eggs in the living room.
—Edward Said, *Orientalism*

The previous chapter established that the way democracy is used in political science and the way *dimuqratiyya* is identified among Middle East/North Africa (MENA) populations are not the same. Although political scientists cast nets of varying size—minimalist to maximalist—in scoping out democracies, the most common empirical indicators rely on competitive elections and civil liberties to classify regimes. Arabic speakers rely heavily on regime efficacy to identify *dimuqratiyya*. Free and fair elections inform that identification, but they are not determinative.

This chapter approaches the question "What is *dimuqratiyya*?" in a descriptive fashion. What features do citizens explicitly identify as central components of *dimuqratiyya*? Several waves of the Arab Barometer ask respondents to examine a list of features that are potential characteristics of a regime and identify the most important feature for a *dimuqratiyya*. These direct questions show how citizens conceive of *dimuqratiyya*.

The first part of the chapter identifies what features are essential to *dimuqratiyya*. There are two main blocs, each of which makes up about half the survey population. The first is a political-institutional conception of *dimuqratiyya* (PCD). This is highly similar to the sense of democracy measured by the Polyarchy and Polity indicators. The second is based on socioeconomic outcomes (SECD). This *dimuqratiyya* is quite different, then, from how researchers usually define democracy.

51

52   *Defining Democracy*

The remainder of the book addresses the knock-on effects of these diverging views for citizens' attitudes toward democracy—which is to say, electing their governments—and their political participation.

The second section of the chapter uses regression analysis to identify patterns within citizen responses. It draws on the 2018 Arab Barometer surveys and the surveys of Egypt and Morocco that form the basis of Chapters 5 and 6. Are there groups that are more likely to hold political or economic conceptions of *dimuqratiyya*? Are these patterns consistent across countries? To preview the results, the multiple surveys demonstrate that there are not consistent predictors of conceptions of *dimuqratiyya* across countries. There is far more variation within countries—differences among the citizens—than between the countries. The variation is not overtly driven by forces such as country history or individual education. Basically, who holds what conception of democracy is highly idiosyncratic.

A Note on the Method

The questions at work here ask respondents which features of a regime, from a closed list, are the most essential for a country to be a *dimuqratiyya*. This structure forces them to make a choice. Choosing one comes at the expense of choosing others. While many characteristics may be considered important—or even essential—for a state to be a *dimuqratiyya*, only one could be the *most* essential.

Asking which features are the most important is distinct from asking how important a feature is to a democracy.[1] That structure is employed in the World Values Survey and, by dint of that, is used in most studies. That style encourages cheap talk; it is easy for the respondents to just say that everything is essential or that all the options are equal. That is evident, for instance, in Oser and Hooghe's (2018a) work, which finds that in three clusters the same score—high, medium, or low, respectively—was given to each item. As will be demonstrated below, it is easy for respondents to claim that all the features are essential (Figures 3.1 and 3.2). They are not required to make choices, so their answers do not reveal what they actually view as important, let alone most important. By addressing the most essential features, the Arab Barometer question structure is better able to identify the crucial institutions or outcomes.

This analysis inverts Schaffer's (2000) focus in his study of Senegal. Schaffer examined the electoral institutions in place in Senegal and asked the public what words in French and Wolof they used to describe

Figure 3.1 Importance of Elements of *Dimuqratiyya* in Egypt

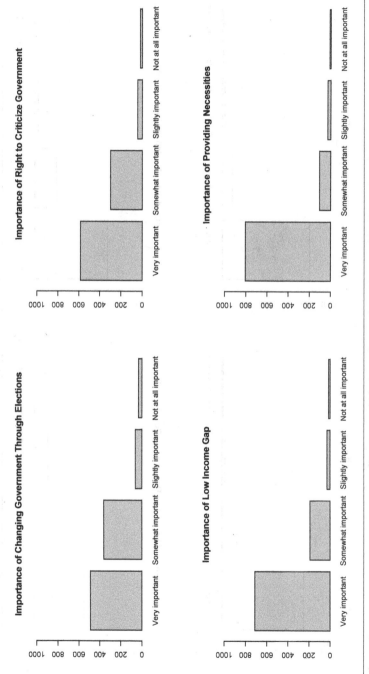

continues

Figure 3.1 Continued

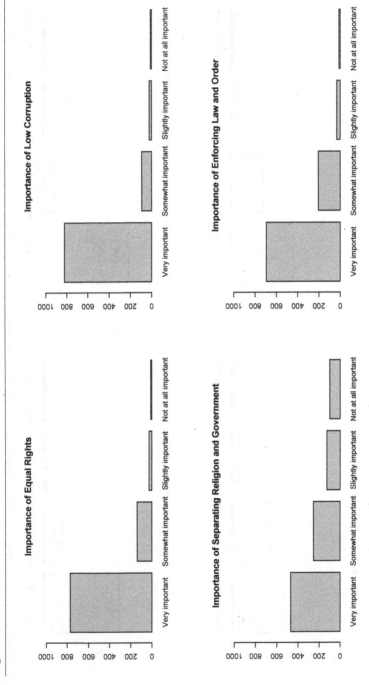

Figure 3.2 Importance of Elements of *Dimuqratiyya* in Morocco

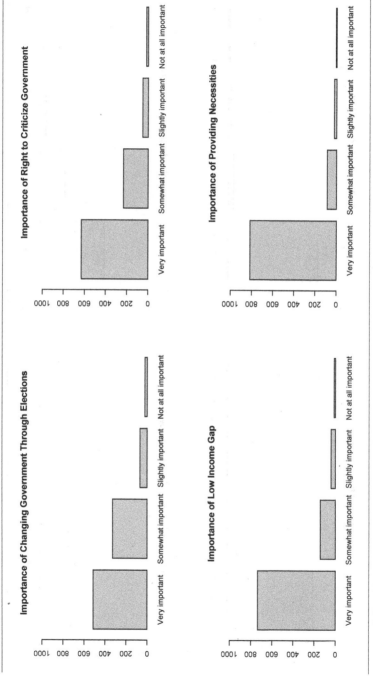

continues

Figure 3.2 Continued

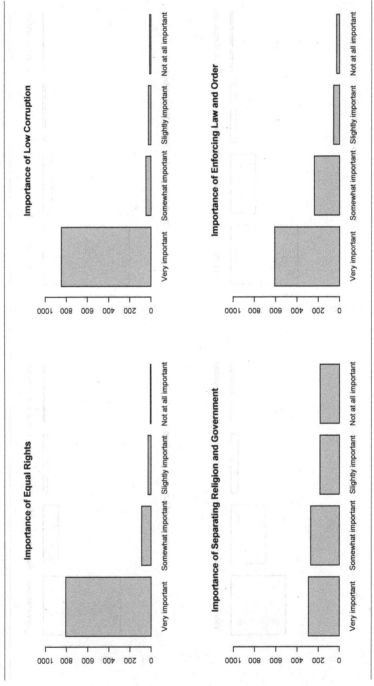

Defining Dimuqratiyya   **57**

those systems. In his study, the institutional system was held fixed, while the response words were open. In this case, the word *dimuqratiyya* is held fixed, and the corresponding institution(s) are sought.

Khanani (2021, 12) engaged in the type of qualitative exercises that Schaffer (2014) endorses by looking at how Moroccan *ilsāmiyūn* ("non-violent, socially conservative political actors who draw upon the Muslim tradition") use the word *dimuqratiyya*. He looks at how they use the word and probes, in conversation, its boundaries and linkages. These *ilsāmiyūn* do not present a more united front on this construct's meaning than other Moroccans. These discussions invoked concepts like freedom, justice, accountability, sovereignty, dignity, economic programs, and equality. They appealed to political-institutional frameworks, like elections and civil liberties. The invocations of these features, even while advocating for expansive and outcomes-based meanings, Khanani suggests, "bridges" democracy and *dimuqratiyya* as constructs (70). The *ilsāmiyūn* also appealed extensively to socioeconomic outcomes, like low unemployment rates and access to daily necessities. Their *dimuqratiyya* "is also predicated on a series of substantive outcomes (e.g., an equitable distribution of wealth, government provision of welfare, etc.)" without which "free and fair elections, the autonomy and authority of elected officials, freedom of expression, and the presence of an independent media" are not enough (73). This would be very much in line with the results in Chapter 2. This variation is in keeping with what is shown in other parts of the Arab world.

It is crucial to remember that saying that a characteristic, policy, or institution is an essential element of a democracy (or *dimuqratiyya*) does not mean that the identifier endorses or supports that policy or institution. In turn, saying something is not essential to democracy is not the same as opposing that characteristic. Definition and commitment are separate. The assumption of their equivalence has pervaded the conceptions of democracy literature. Oser and Hooghe (2018b), for instance, buy into this fallacy. The same is true for AlAzzawi and Gouda (2017, 15), who describe respondents' beliefs about the essentialness of different state characteristics as expressions of "higher preference" or "lower preference" for these notions of "democracy." This is inaccurate. Citizens' policy and program preferences are distinct from their understanding of democracy. Both of these elements, in turn, are related separately to citizens' preferences for or against a system of government. That nexus is the focus of this book.

The conflation of these points invokes circular logic based on the normative value of democracy. Researchers who value democracy conflate

58 Defining Democracy

viewing something as part of democracy as an endorsement. A characteristic is good *because* it is part of democracy; at the same time, democracy is good *for* having these good things. They also assume respondents are engaging in this practice. For instance, a respondent would benefit from equitable treatment of minorities, so the respondent puts that idea onto democracy; then the respondent is also assumed to like democracy because it would provide the equitable treatment. The construct—democracy itself—never exists in this argument; it is merely a continual source and receptor of preferred institutions and policies.

When interpreting statements about conceptions of democracy (or *dimuqratiyya* in this case), it is necessary to note that the individuals responding may not be democrats. They may even be actively opposed to democracy. In fact, far from endorsing the system or the characteristic because of a link to democracy, some respondents may oppose democracy on the basis of its inclusion of this characteristic. For example, citizens who desire a role for religion in government and believe that democracy is necessarily a secular system may not support democracy because of that. Indicating on a survey that secularism is an essential component of democracy does not indicate respondents' support for either—in fact, in this hypothetical, they are opposed to both. In turn, indicating that a welfare structure or economic policy is not an essential feature of democracy does not indicate support for or opposition to a democracy or that economic policy. It merely recognizes that economic programs and outcomes are not structural elements of democracy and not necessarily something that a democratic government would introduce or would be able to guarantee. Whether they are an essential part of *dimuqratiyya* is part of the examination of this chapter.

What Is *Dimuqratiyya*?

In 2018, the Arab Barometer asked residents in twelve countries, "If you had to choose only one of the statements below, which one would you choose as the most essential characteristic of a [*dimuqratiyya*]?" They selected the option from a closed list. The responses to this question are used to classify respondents by their conception of *dimuqratiyya*.

In the 2018 Arab Barometer, the choices were "Government ensures law and order," "Media is free to criticize the things government does," "Government ensures job opportunities for all," and "Multiple parties compete fairly in the election." Each respondent could choose one. The final option embodies what common democracy indexes are measuring.

Defining Dimuqratiyya   59

The freedom of the press option also recognizes the liberties and freedoms often invoked in discursive descriptions of democracy. The other two options are government objectives; they are socially and economically valuable, and a democracy could choose to pursue those goals or not. Nondemocracies could too. Both might fail.

What options do the Arab Barometer respondents identify with *dimuqratiyya*? The social policy outcome responses dominate. Overall, 31.1 percent chose law and order, and 35.7 percent, the largest bloc, chose job guarantees. Only 15 percent focused on freedom of the press. Holding multiparty elections was the least common response, with only 13.6 percent of the responses.[2]

Only in Sudan and Yemen did elections receive more than a quarter of the votes. The jobs guarantee was the most chosen option in almost every case; it even received a majority in Tunisia and Iraq as well as 48.4 percent in Jordan. Iraq and Tunisia both received "democracy" ratings from Polity in recent years, and after the Arab Spring Tunisia was considered a regional democratic success story until a coup in July 2021 called that reputation into question. Even in these supposed democracies, *dimuqratiyya* is focused on employment. In each country, the most commonly chosen answer was one of the socioeconomic outcome options. Arabs' construct of *dimuqratiyya* is quite distinct from the construct to which researchers appeal when using the word *democracy*. *Dimuqratiyya* may well involve elections, but they are not obligatory. It is primarily understood based on the socioeconomic outcomes that the regime generates.

Earlier waves of the Arab Barometer also showed divisions. For instance, in 2007, 18.9 percent selected choosing the government by election, and 13 percent selected having the right to criticize the government. In the same wave, 20.1 percent selected popular access to basic necessities, while 15 percent chose a small income gap.[3] In Wave 2, during the Arab Spring, 26 percent chose elections, 13.9 percent chose freedom to criticize the government, and 12.5 percent chose equality of political rights. At the same time, 11.6 percent chose narrowing the income gap, 16.9 percent chose access to basic necessities, and 18.5 percent indicated eliminating corruption. The results were similar after the Arab Spring. In 2013, 21.2 percent chose elections, 11.2 percent chose freedom to criticize the government, and 11.9 percent chose equality of political rights. At the same time, 19.8 percent chose narrowing the income gap, 17.2 percent chose access to basic necessities, and 18 percent indicated eliminating corruption. Over time, the survey results show consistent divides in meanings, not a growing PCD consensus.

60 Defining Democracy

Notably the statement refers specifically to political rights. More recent theories of human rights have appealed to conceptions of social rights, such as health care and education (Chapter 2). Protests in the Middle East have asserted a "right" to employment, which would be a social right. Beinin (2016) highlights a protest chant from Gafsa, Tunisia, in 2008: "A job is a right, you pack of thieves." Such programs would be a socioeconomic outcome of the political process, whereas political rights are part of the more minimalist, institutional framework. They were previously common in the Arab world, which may have established this expectation.

That the key features of a *dimuqratiyya* are mixed across countries and across the multiple waves of the Arab Barometer suggests that ascribed meaning is not merely a function of living under a particular regime or regime type. If regime type were causing the citizens to conceive of *dimuqratiyya* in a particular way, then there would be substantial transformation with the Arab Spring revolutions or more unity in the more democratic states.

In 2021, Arab Barometer VI used the essentialness question style on a subset of features: 54.6 percent said elections were absolutely essential to *dimuqratiyya*; 23.5 percent said they were somewhat essential; 18.6 percent said they were either not very or not at all essential. This is entirely at odds with the literature on democracy. Equal rights regardless of religion or ethnic group were seen as absolutely or somewhat essential by 57.5 percent and 22 percent, respectively, whereas 17.5 percent found them not very or not at all essential to *dimuqratiyya*. In contrast, 47.8 percent and 29.2 percent, respectively, said that providing basic necessities was absolutely or somewhat essential to *dimuqratiyya*. *Dimuqratiyya* may not be democracy at all, and it certainly is not liberal democracy.

This point is also examined in the more recent surveys in Egypt (2019) and Morocco (2020).[4] These surveys gave respondents more options for essential features of *dimuqratiyya*. They were also asked how important these items were to *dimuqratiyya*, in the style of the World Values Survey. These responses demonstrate how easy it is for respondents to claim that any item is important. They also establish how relatively unimportant some essential features of democracy are to *dimuqratiyya*.

In these studies, Egyptians and Moroccans were asked to identify the first and second most important characteristics of *dimuqratiyya*. They were presented with a list of eight characteristics: (a) the opportunity to change government by election, (b) freedom to criticize the government, (c) narrowing the gap between the rich and the poor, (d) providing basic items (such as food and housing) to every individual, (e) equality of polit-

Defining Dimuqratiyya   **61**

ical rights between citizens, (f) eliminating financial and administrative corruption, (g) separation of religion and the government, and (h) the government ensures law and order.[5]

The respondents who identified a, b, e, or g as the most essential characteristic were considered to have identified a political or procedural characteristic of *dimuqratiyya*. Individuals who indicated c, d, f, or h were considered to have identified a socioeconomic or outcome-based conception. To sort the respondents, four groupings are made based on the first and second choices the respondents identified. In the first group are those who identified political elements for both. For this book, individuals holding this political conception of *dimuqratiyya* will be called PCD. The second group includes those who chose a political item as the most important feature and a socioeconomic characteristic as the second most important. The third group includes those who chose a socioeconomic characteristic as the most important, followed by a political element. The fourth group chose socioeconomic elements for both. For this book, individuals holding this socioeconomic-outcomes-based conception of *dimuqratiyya* will be called SECD. Those who hold mixed conceptions will be referred to by the trait they indicated first, so Mixed PCD and Mixed SECD. A crosstabulation of the variables is shown below. The results for Egypt are shown in Table 3.1, and the results for Morocco are shown in Table 3.2.

In Egypt, SECD are the most common. They make up 36.2 percent of the sample. PCD, by contrast, comprise 16.1 percent. Mixed SECD are 18.7 percent, and Mixed PCD are 29.1 percent. In Morocco, the SECD population is even larger: 42.0 percent are SECD. Only 11.9 percent are PCD. Mixed SECD are 13.6 percent, and Mixed PCD are 32.4 percent. These patterns are in line with the 2018 Arab Barometer surveys.[6]

The most commonly selected primary element in Egypt is political: changing the government by election. The most frequently chosen second feature is economic: the elimination of financial and administrative corruption. The most commonly selected pairing is economic: having a small income gap between the rich and the poor and the elimination of corruption. The second most common pairing is also economic: government provision of personal necessities and the elimination of corruption.

The most commonly selected primary element in Morocco is political: the opportunity to change the government by election. The most frequently chosen second feature is economic: the elimination of financial and administrative corruption. The most commonly selected pairing is economic: providing necessities for every individual and the elimination of corruption. The second most common pairing is also economic:

Table 3.1 Crosstabulation of *Dimuqratiyya* Characteristics in Egypt (unweighted)

	The opportunity to change the government through elections	Freedom to criticize the government	Narrowing the gap between the rich and the poor	Providing basic items to every individual	Equality of politica rights between citizens	Eliminating financial and administrative corruption	Separation of religion and the government	Government ensures law and order	Total Choice first
The opportunity to change the government through elections		3.9 (n = 37)	3.6 (n = 34)	3.1 (n = 29)	2.4 (n = 23)	6.1 (n = 58)	0.8 (n = 8)	1.1 (n = 10)	21.0 (n = 199)
Freedom to criticize the government	0.84 (n = 8)		1.5 (n = 14)	2.5 (n = 24)	2.4 (n = 23)	3.9 (n = 37)	1.3 (n = 12)	0.8 (n = 8)	13.3 (n = 126)
Narrowing the gap between the rich and the poor	1.0 (n = 9)	1.0 (n = 9)		3.3 (n = 31)	2.3 (n = 22)	8.9 (n = 84)	1.6 (n = 15)	0.6 (n = 6)	18.6 (n = 176)
Providing basic items to every individual	1.4 (n = 13)	1.1 (n = 10)	3.6 (n = 34)		2.9 (n = 27)	6.8 (n = 64)	1.3 (n = 12)	1.5 (n = 14)	18.4 (n = 174)
Equality of political rights between citizens	1.7 (n = 16)	1.1 (n = 10)	1.6 (n = 11)	0.6 (n = 6)		2.0 (n = 19)	0.7 (n = 7)	1.1 (n = 10)	8.4 (n = 79)

continues

Table 3.1 Continued

	The opportunity to change the government through elections	Freedom to criticize the government	Narrowing the gap between the rich and the poor	Providing basic items to every individual	Equality of politica rights between citizens	Eliminating financial and administrative corruption	Separation of religion and the government	Government ensures law and order	Total Choice first
Eliminating financial and administrative corruption	1.6 (n = 15)	1.2 (n = 11)	4.3 (n = 41)	2.7 (n = 26)	0.6 (n = 6)		0.8 (n = 8)	2.0 (n = 19)	13.3 (n = 126)
Separation of religion and the government	0.1 (n = 1)	0.1 (n = 1)	0.2 (n = 2)	0.4 (n = 4)	0.6 (n = 6)	0.7 (n = 7)		0.2 (n = 2)	2.4 (n = 23)
Government ensures law and order	0.4 (n = 4)	0.4 (n = 4)	0.5 (n = 5)	0.7 (n = 7)	1.0 (n = 9)	1.2 (n = 11)	0.3 (n = 3)		4.5 (n = 43)
Total second choice	7.0 (n = 66)	8.7 (n = 82)	14.9 (n = 141)	13.4 (n = 127)	12.3 (n = 116)	29.6 (n = 280)	6.9 (n = 65)	7.3 (n = 69)	

Table 3.2 Crosstabulation of *Dimuqratiyya* Characteristics in Morocco (unweighted)

	The opportunity to change the government through elections	Freedom to criticize the government	Narrowing the gap between the rich and the poor	Providing basic items to every individual	Equality of politica rights between citizens	Eliminating financial and administrative corruption	Separation of religion and the government	Government ensures law and order	Total Choice first
The opportunity to change the government through elections		3.3 (n = 31)	2.9 (n = 27)	2.9 (n = 27)	1.7 (n = 16)	6.7 (n = 62)	0.6 (n = 6)	0.9 (n = 8)	19.0 (n = 177)
Freedom to criticize the government	1.1 (n = 10)		2.3 (n = 21)	2.0 (n = 19)	1.5 (n = 14)	6.0 (n = 56)	0.6 (n = 6)	0.4 (n = 4)	14.0 (n = 130)
Narrowing the gap between the rich and the poor	0.4 (n = 4)	0.9 (n = 8)		4.9 (n = 46)	2.8 (n = 26)	8.3 (n = 77)	0.4 (n = 4)	1.0 (n = 9)	18.7 (n = 174)
Providing basic items to every individual	1.1 (n = 10)	0.3 (n = 3)	4.2 (n = 39)		1.7 (n = 16)	9.6 (n = 89)	0.3 (n = 3)	0.8 (n = 7)	18.0 (n = 167)
Equality of political rights between citizens	0.6 (n = 6)	0.5 (n = 5)	1.0 (n = 9)	1.4 (n = 13)		3.8 (n = 35)	1.1 (n = 10)	1.0 (n = 9)	9.4 (n = 87)

continues

Table 3.2 Continued

	The opportunity to change the government through elections	Freedom to criticize the government	Narrowing the gap between the rich and the poor	Providing basic items to every individual	Equality of politica rights between citizens	Eliminating financial and administrative corruption	Separation of religion and the government	Government ensures law and order	Total Choice first
Eliminating financial and administrative corruption	1.1 (n = 10)	1.6 (n = 15)	4.4 (n = 41)	6.1 (n = 57)	1.7 (n = 16)		0.9 (n = 8)	1.5 (n = 14)	17.3 (n = 161)
Separation of religion and the government	0.2 (n = 2)	0.1 (n = 1)	0.1 (n = 1)	0.5 (n = 5)	0.4 (n = 4)	0.3 (n = 3)		0.2 (n = 2)	1.9 (n = 18)
Government and order	0.2 (n = 2)	0.0 (n = 0)	0.2 (n = 2)	0.4 (n = 4)	0.1 (n = 1)	0.6 (n = 6)	0.1 (n = 1)		1.7 (n = 16)
Total second choice	4.7 (n = 44)	6.8 (n = 63)	15.1 (n = 140)	18.4 (n = 171)	10.0 (n = 93)	35.3 (n = 328)	4.1 (n = 38)	5.7 (n = 53)	

66 Defining Democracy

having a small gap in incomes between the rich and the poor and the elimination of corruption.

Because the survey also asked about the nonrelative importance of these characteristics to *dimuqratiyya*, we can compare respondents' choice of the most important to the answers they gave when they could say everything was important. As noted in Chapter 1, many studies use the "What is essential in a democracy" question based on the World Values Survey structure. De Regt (2013, 40) does this in her study of Egypt, Iraq, Jordan, and Morocco. She identifies three "different notions of democracy": procedural democracy, instrumental democracy, and authoritarian democracy. While the first term embodies democracy as political scientists use the term, the second term conflates supporting democracy for economic gain with supporting a regime type, and the third term is inherently contradictory. De Regt does not, however, recognize from this finding that the construct being addressed in these responses has migrated far from democracy itself.

Figures 3.1 and 3.2 show the level of importance, from very important to not at all important, that the respondents in each country assigned to each item on the list. The figures reveal what is important in the eyes of the public. The importance ratings are next juxtaposed with the "most important feature" responses. This comparison has not been possible in previous studies, which have only incorporated one question style or the other. It shows an important disjuncture of measurement.

In both countries, for every attribute, "very important" to *dimuqratiyya* is the most commonly selected rating. None of the characteristics included here would be antithetical to democracy. Several of them, however, are optional for democracies, while others are not. This highlights that potentially important elements of *dimuqratiyya* are characteristics that are extraneous to democratic classification.

Transitioning power via election is, compared to its definitional role in democracy, quite flat for *dimuqratiyya*; elections do not seem so fundamental to *dimuqratiyya* for many of the respondents. This is in sharp contrast to features like the provision of individual necessities and the absence of corruption, which are strikingly identified with *dimuqratiyya* in both sets of surveys. Compared to the other traits, the relative importance placed on elections in a *dimuqratiyya* is weak. In both Egypt and Morocco many more people recognize economic outcomes, like provision of private necessities, as important to *dimuqratiyya* than recognize holding elections as being very important. Equality of political rights is more a part of *dimuqratiyya* than elections or the right to criticize the government.

Defining Dimuqratiyya   67

A democratic government does not have to have any particular relationship to religion, although many theories of democracy assume overt separation. Gouda and Hanafi (2020) expressly blame the incorporation of Islam or Islamic law into state constitutions for the paucity of democracy in the Middle East. Nonetheless, research on the Middle East has questioned whether the citizens are imagining an expressly not-secular version of democracy when they endorse *dimuqratiyya* (Ciftci 2013; Tessler 2002). The graphs for the separation of religion and government are the flattest of all. Of all the traits, secularism is the least important for recognizing *dimuqratiyya* in both Egypt and Morocco. The Moroccan regime has long been connected to Islam; Maliki Sunni Islam is the official religion of the country. In this case, the connection to Islam, including involvement of Islamist parties in elections and, until recently, in government itself, makes this acceptance of comingling reasonable. However, for Egypt, where turbulent relations with the Muslim Brotherhood have defined politics, placing so little import on secularism is interesting. It suggests that opposition to Islamist parties relates not to a theory of democracy but rather to objection to those players. Muslim societies are not "less 'secular'" than non-Muslim societies, but this concept is distinguished from citizens' understanding of *dimuqratiyya* (Fish 2002, 5).

How, then, do respondents' "most important" items compare to their "importance" ratings? On one hand, Tables 3.3 and 3.4 show that respondents were quite likely to say that the characteristic they rated as most important for a country to be *dimuqratiyya* was very important or at least somewhat important in the importance question. On the other hand, "very important" was the most common answer for each characteristic. Thus, it is not necessarily a sign of a special connection.

These tables show that for each category, respondents rated their "most important" category highly; however, that rating was not unique. Tables 3.5 and 3.6 show the percentage of individuals labeling a category "very important" based on which characteristic they said was the most important. Respondents regularly rated their "most important" feature as very important. However, they also regularly identified other features as also very important too. "Very important" and "Most important" are clearly quite distinct categories for respondents. This is further evidence that the World Values Survey question format is not the best indicator of what citizens view as crucial for a democracy or a *dimuqratiyya*. Lots of features can be very important, and it is certainly too easy to answer that they all are. Objectively, though, only one could be the most important.

68 Defining Democracy

Table 3.3 Relationship Between Most Important Characteristic and Characteristic Importance in Egypt (percentage)

Characteristic Labeled Most Important	Rated the Characteristic Very Important	Rated Characteristic Somewhat Important	Rated Characteristic Slightly Important	Rated Characteristic Not at All Important
The opportunity to change the government through elections	72.4	26.1	0.5	1.0
Freedom to criticize the government	74.6	19.8	5.6	0.0
Narrowing the gap between rich and poor	81.8	15.9	1.7	0.6
Providing basic items to every individual	86.8	9.8	2.3	1.1
Equality of political rights between citizens	89.8	7.6	0	2.5
Eliminating financial and administrative corruption	90.5	6.3	1.6	1.6
Separation of religion and the government	87.0	13.0	0	0
Government ensures law and order	79.1	11.6	2.3	7.0

Predicting Conceptions of *Dimuqratiyya*

We can now turn to identifying which individuals are more likely to conceive of *dimuqratiyya* in the political sense and which individuals are more likely to conceive of *dimuqratiyya* in socioeconomic terms. As Canache (2012, 1133) notes, "How citizens form their views of democracy is likely the result of a multiplicity of factors operating at the individual and societal levels." In fact, there are not clear and cross-country predictors for or against a PCD. They appear to be highly idiosyncratic and personalized.[7]

Table 3.4 Relationship Between Most Important Characteristic and Characteristic Importance in Morocco (percentage)

Characteristic Labeled Most Important	Rated the Characteristic Very Important	Rated Characteristic Somewhat Important	Rated Characteristic Slightly Important	Rated Characteristic Not at All Important
The opportunity to change the government through elections	63.3	28.2	6.8	1.7
Freedom to criticize the government	80.0	16.2	2.3	1.5
Narrowing the gap between rich and poor	86.8	10.9	1.7	0.6
Providing basic items to every individual	92.8	6.0	0.6	0.6
Equality of political rights between citizens	86.2	9.2	4.6	0.0
Eliminating financial and administrative corruption	96.9	1.9	1.2	0.0
Separation of religion and the government	94.4	5.6	0	0
Government ensures law and order	81.3	6.3	0	12.5

As researchers become increasingly cognizant of the diverse meanings publics are casting onto the "d-word"—or whatever word is used in the language of these multinational studies—they have started plumbing the antecedents of those diverse views. Marcus, Mease, and Ottemoeller (2001) examine demographic predictors of understanding of democracy in sub-Saharan Africa. The majority of people in their studies define *democracy* in terms of freedom, specifically social freedoms, as opposed to defining it in terms of elections, participation, independence, or economic development. Economic development receives only a few

Table 3.5 Relationship between Most Important Characteristic and Very Important Characteristics in Egypt (percentage)

Characteristic Labeled "Most Important"	Characteristics Labeled "Very Important"							
	Opportunity to change the government through elections	Freedom to criticize the government	Narrowing the gap between rich and poor	Providing basic items to every individual	Equality of political rights between citizens	Eliminating financial and administrative corruption	Separation of religion and the government	The government ensures law and order
The opportunity to change the government through elections	72.4	70.4	73.9	83.9	82.4	84.5	46.7	74.9
Freedom to criticize the government	50.0	74.6	80.1	84.9	84.9	85.7	54.0	74.6
Narrowing the gap between rich and poor	46.0	53.4	81.8	85.2	80.7	87.5	48.3	68.8
Providing basic items to every individual	47.1	54.6	70.7	86.8	79.3	86.8	52.9	72.4
Equality of political rights between citizens	45.6	60.8	75.9	91.1	89.9	93.7	45.6	75.9
Eliminating financial and administrative corruption	46.8	59.5	75.4	84.9	77.0	90.5	44.4	73.0
Separation of religion and the government	34.8	69.6	60.9	73.9	82.6	87.0	87.0	82.6
Government ensures law and order	41.9	51.2	62.8	79.1	76.7	79.1	41.9	79.1

Table 3.6 Relationship Between Most Important Characteristic and Very Important Characteristics in Morocco (percentage)

Characteristic Labeled "Most Important"	Characteristics Labeled "Very Important"							
	Opportunity to change the government through elections	Freedom to criticize the government	Narrowing the gap between rich and poor	Providing basic items to every individual	Equality of political rights between citizens	Eliminating financial and administrative corruption	Separation of religion and the government	The government ensures law and order
The opportunity to change the government through elections	63.3	67.8	71.2	80.2	80.8	84.2	32.2	65.5
Freedom to criticize the government	55.4	80.0	79.2	87.7	87.7	91.5	31.5	58.5
Narrowing the gap between rich and poor	46.6	63.8	86.8	87.4	83.3	90.2	29.3	67.8
Providing basic items to every individual	51.5	62.3	77.2	92.8	89.2	96.4	2.69	58.7
Equality of political rights between citizens	49.4	576.3	71.2	82.8	86.2	83.9	33.3	66.7
Eliminating financial and administrative corruption	59.6	73.3	84.5	93.2	93.8	96.9	27.3	70.2
Separation of religion and the government	72.2	83.3	88.9	88.9	88.9	94.4	94.4	94.4
Government ensures law and order	62.5	56.3	75.0	93.8	81.3	93.4	56.3	81.3

72 Defining Democracy

percentage points in their samples. As such, they are mostly looking at diversity within a PCD.[8] Baviskar and Malone (2004) look at Argentina, Brazil, Chile, and Guatemala. They divide conceptions of democracy into means-and-ends systems, with some acknowledgment that people can have mixed views. They classify civil liberties, political rights, elections, and accountability under means. Ends include "equality of opportunity and outcome, social rights, policy, responsiveness, public safety, and corruption" (9). Lagos (2008) examines definitions in the Latinbarometer and citizens' propensity to link the concept of *democracia* to liberty, to elections, or to an economy that ensures a fair income for all citizens. Alvarez and Welzel (2017, 5) divide World Values Survey respondents into "four different notions of democracy"—liberal, social, populist, and authoritarian—based on "essentialness."[9] These researchers probe gender, age, income, and level of education. Consistent predictors have not been identified within or across sociolinguistic contexts.

The surveys of the Middle East do not demonstrate this same predominance of PCD identified in these studies. SECD understandings are prevalent, even the most prevalent, there. Few studies have broached this topic in the region.

Doherty and Mecellem's (2013) working paper focuses on conceptions of *dimuqratiyya* in four countries from the first wave of the Arab Barometer: Algeria, Jordan, Lebanon, and Palestine. They divide their predictions into two camps. The first focuses on elements related to a factual knowledge of democracy; they predict the respondent will provide a political-institutional response because of education and/or political interest, which would inform them that that answer is correct. (Note, this book does not posit that any response is inherently incorrect.) The second relates to a propensity to "project" desired outcomes onto the concept *dimuqratiyya* (4). They argue that the poor, the religious, and women would favor redistribution, so they would take this tact.

Mohamad-Klotzbach and Schlenkrich (2016) make the most rigorous pursuit of this point. They use the third wave of the Arab Barometer to consider the "input-oriented" and "output-oriented" views of *dimuqratiyya* and the "preference for varying democracies in Arab societies" (404).[10] They argue that all conceptions of *dimuqratiyya* are focused on political demands, even if they are economic issues, so they dislike a political-versus-economic distinction. Their dependent variable is based on what the respondent believes is the most important characteristic of *dimuqratiyya*. Holding elections, the freedom to criticize the government, and equal political rights are considered input-oriented characteristics; narrowing the gap between rich and poor, providing basic items, and reducing corruption are considered output-oriented characteristics.

Mohamad-Klotzbach and Schlenkrich (2016) take a circular approach to citizens' conception of *dimuqratiyya*. Their study uses theories that predict democratic stability to predict how people understand the word *democracy* in authoritarian regimes. They assume that if something makes people more democratic, then it will make them "input-oriented." They thus assume a definition rather than try to uncover one. Furthermore, the language of "the preference [*die Präferenz*] for the input-oriented concept of democracy" indicates that they are concerned with what the respondent would like the government to focus on rather than what he thinks the system is (408).[11] While this is arguably a linguistic point, citizens' aspirations for their government are distinct from their understanding of the nature of a government. Arguably, the results of their study are sufficient, save some methodological reservations with their modeling strategy.[12] However, it is useful to present more recent Arab Barometer survey findings in conjunction with the results from the Egypt and Morocco studies.

This chapter examines what factors, both attitudinal and demographic, are associated with an increased propensity to hold a political rather than a socioeconomic understanding of *dimuqratiyya*. Several items are included in the analyses based on the findings from previous research and potential influences on individuals' beliefs. The prior scholarship appeals to modernization theory (Lerner 1958; El Badawi and Makdisi 2007), social capital and civic political culture theory (Almond and Verba 1963; Jamal 2007), diffusion theory, and Islamic culture theory (Huntington 2000). Based on these prior studies, education, income, civil society membership, religion and religiosity, and urbanity are included in the models. Demographics used in these studies, such as age and gender, are included. For this study, no generalized theory is proposed, especially as the prior research in this arena has largely come up dry. The results will be considered first for the fifth wave of the Arab Barometer. For results broken down by country, consult Appendix F. Next the results are presented for the surveys in Egypt and Morocco. The variation across these models demonstrates the individuated nature of citizens' conception of *dimuqratiyya*.

The fifth wave of the Arab Barometer included only the most essential characteristic of *dimuqratiyya*. The options were "Government ensures law and order," "Media is free to criticize the things government does," "Government ensures job opportunities for all," and "Multiple parties compete fairly in the election." Those choosing the freedom of the press or the elections option are counted as choosing a political element; those choosing the law and order or jobs option are coded as identifying a socioeconomic element. In these analyses, binary logistic

74 Defining Democracy

regression models with country fixed effects are used, and population weights are included. The reference country is Algeria. Standard errors are clustered by country. When dealing with the Egypt and Morocco data, the four-group classification is available because respondents were asked about the first and second most essential characteristics. In this case, the responses are organized in order from SECD to PCD. Ordered logistic regression models with survey weights are used. For information on the coding for the variables, see Appendix C. Table 3.7 shows the results based on the Arab Barometer surveys from 2018. Table 3.8 shows the results from the Egypt and Morocco survey studies.

Table 3.7 Conception of *Dimuqratiyya* (Arab Barometer V)

	Full Sample		Full Sample
Intercept	−0.52***	Age	−0.00
	(0.10)		(0.00)
Government	0.02	Civil society	0.27***
evaluation	(0.06)	member	(0.05)
Political interest	0.28***	Colony (France)	−0.16***
	(0.08)		(0.04)
Gender	0.03	Colony (Italy)	−0.82***
traditionalism	(0.12)		(0.06)
Secularist	0.02	Egypt	−0.23***
orientation	(0.05)		(0.04)
Unemployed	−0.13**	Iraq	−0.65***
	(0.06)		(0.04)
Sufficient income	0.12**	Jordan	−0.65***
	(0.06)		(0.02)
Male	0.14**	Lebanon	0.02
	(0.06)		(0.09)
College education	0.06	Morocco	−0.34***
	(0.09)		(0.04)
Christian	−0.12	Palestine	−0.21***
	(0.17)		(0.03)
No religion	−0.45	Sudan	0.34***
	(0.48)		(0.04)
Other religion	−0.05	Tunisia	−0.74***
	(0.09)		(0.04)
No response	−0.21	AIC	27,293.11
	(0.40)	Log likelihood	−13,620.56
Daily prayer	−0.14*	N	22,716
	(0.07)		

Notes: ***$p < 0.01$; **$p < 0.05$; *$p < 0.1$.

Table 3.8 Conception of *Dimuqratiyya*

	Egypt	Morocco
Government evaluation	−0.08	0.13*
	(0.07)	(0.07)
News consumption: daily	−0.06	0.20
	(0.14)	(0.13)
Prayer: daily	−0.26*	0.02
	(0.14)	(0.15)
Interested in politics	0.36***	−0.00
	(0.14)	(0.13)
Gender traditionalism	−0.08	0.06
	(0.09)	(0.08)
Secularist orientation	−0.23***	0.12
	(0.08)	(0.08)
Male	0.39***	0.21
	(0.14)	(0.14)
Unemployed	0.10	−0.05
	(0.14)	(0.14)
Religion: Christianity	0.21	1.00
	(0.22)	(1.19)
Religion: none	0.15	0.49
	(0.64)	(0.43)
Income: covers expenses	0.48***	0.27**
	(0.13)	(0.13)
College education	0.14	−0.42***
	(0.16)	(0.13)
Urban	−0.20	−0.02
	(0.16)	(0.16)
Spend time in the West	0.12	0.06
	(0.20)	(0.18)
25–29	−0.31	0.02
	(0.20)	(0.23)
30–34	−0.50**	−0.14
	(0.23)	(0.24)
35–39	−0.70***	0.24
	(0.25)	(0.27)
40+	−0.08	0.19
	(0.19)	(0.20)
Region: Canal Zone	0.17	
	(0.29)	
Region: Upper Egypt	−0.11	
	(0.18)	

continues

76   Defining Democracy

Table 3.8   Continued

	Egypt	Morocco
Region: Delta	0.25	
	(0.17)	
Region: Alexandria	0.05	
	(0.18)	
Region: Other	−0.06	
	(0.40)	
Region: Agadir		−0.09
		(0.27)
Region: Marrakech		−0.12
		(0.25)
Region: Rabat		0.23
		(0.29)
Region: Fès		0.61**
		(0.26)
Region: Salé		−0.41
		(0.37)
Region: Tangier		0.09
		(0.30)
Region: Kenitra		1.01**
		(0.43)
Region: Other		0.46**
		(0.19)
0|1	−0.20	0.06
	(0.31)	(0.32)
1|2	0.58*	0.64**
	(0.31)	(0.32)
2|3	2.10***	2.49***
	(0.31)	(0.34)
AIC	2,515.50	2,333.75
Log likelihood	−1,231.75	−1,137.87
N	946	930

Notes: ***$p < 0.01$; **$p < 0.05$; *$p < 0.1$.

All told, the models show that there is very little that regularly predicts individuals' propensity to conceive of *dimuqratiyya* in political-institutionalist terms. The country fixed effects show that countries have different baseline propensities in their populations to hold this belief. Also, residents of former French and Italian colonies are less likely than those of former British colonies to conceive of *dimuqratiyya* in political terms. The causal chain for this pattern, however, cannot be determined. Additionally, the difference is not substantial.

Defining Dimuqratiyya   77

At the personal level, the results are also distinct across the country samples. Political interest is associated with PCD. This is consistent with Doherty and Mecellem's (2013) and Mohamed-Klotzbach and Schlenkrich's (2016) findings. Again, the causal nature of this relationship cannot be discerned from observational data. It is possible that political interest caused individuals to become aware of democracy's focus on political institutions. It is also possible that elections- and freedom-focused people are more invested in politics. Civil society members are also more likely to hold a political conception of *dimuqratiyya* in most of the countries. This is consistent with Mohamed-Klotzbach and Schlenkrich's (2016) findings.

Men are more likely to conceive of *dimuqratiyya* politically, which is consistent with Doherty and Mecellem (2013) and Mohamed-Klotzbach and Schlenkrich (2016). Research on women in the West, for instance, has found that women are more likely to focus on social service provision (Kaufmann 2004). They might see social service provision as an essential component of any government structure. Notably, this is inconsistent with other assumptions that have been made with regard to women. Previous studies have implied women are prone to PCD by arguing that women's relatively lower support for democracy is because MENA women, in forming their support for *dimuqratiyya*, are focused on how the electoral processes will lead to their having fewer rights and losing the cultural constraints that Islam places on men (Jamal 2006; Ciftci 2013). These conclusions assume that women are understanding *dimuqratiyya* politically. The results suggest otherwise.

The differential does not reveal that women are less democratic. Ridge (2022a) finds that women are not distinguished from men in their support for elections once the relative liberalness of the regime is taken into account. The preference patterns would be a rational response to a perceived threat.

College education is not a significant predictor in the full sample; this likely reflects the fact that it has diverging relationships depending on the country. In some of the Arab Barometer countries, it is associated with a political view of *dimuqratiyya*; in other countries and in the YouGov Morocco surveys, college education is associated with a socioeconomic conception. The Arab Barometer data also shows uneven effects of government evaluation on conception of *dimuqratiyya* across countries. Evaluation of the extant nondemocracy's performance is positively associated with *dimuqratiyya* rating—identified in Chapter 2—but the performance evaluation does not drive what people think *dimuqratiyya* is. Gender traditionalism and secularist orientation also have an inconsistent

78 Defining Democracy

effect across the country contexts, leading to a nonsignificant finding in the pooled Arab Barometer sample.

There is some predictive capacity in individuals' economic circumstances. In the Arab Barometer pooled data and in several country subsamples, those who are unemployed are more likely to hold a socioeconomic-outcomes-focused view of *dimuqratiyya*. Having an income sufficient for household expenses is significantly associated with PCD across multiple surveys. These findings are consistent with other studies. Baviskar and Malone (2004), Doherty and Mecellem (2013), and Mohamed-Klotzbach and Schlenkrich (2016) find that richer respondents in their respective studies are more likely to express PCD.

Religion is associated with a socioeconomic perspective, though there is not a clear cross-national denominational pattern. In some countries, Christians are more likely to hold a political understanding than Muslims, and in some countries they are less likely to do so. Religiosity is a more reliable predictor. Arabs who pray daily are more likely to hold a socioeconomic understanding. Surveys in Egypt and Tunisia have suggested that religious Muslims are more sensitive to social justice issues and unequal treatment of people in their communities (Hoffman and Jamal 2012). The social justice focus that religion makes salient in their lives may be transferring onto their construction of *dimuqratiyya*, or any government form for that matter. Whether the patterns proposed for religiosity and for gender with respect to issue salience and conception are unique to *dimuqratiyya* or would show in respondents' view of what is essential to any system of government is necessarily left to other research.

The Egypt and Morocco surveys had two additional items. One is a marker for urban residence. It is significantly associated with a socioeconomic understanding of *dimuqratiyya* in the Egyptian study but not in the Moroccan study. Exposure to established Western democracies via living, working, or studying in the United States, Canada, or Europe in recent years is not a significant predictor in either of the YouGov studies. While this is not proof of a null effect, it is noted insofar as it suggests that Western democracy is not instilling a notion of itself on *dimuqratiyya* through these cross-cultural experiences.

Conclusion

The cross-national studies indicate that there is no consensus in the Arab world about the defining features of *dimuqratiyya*. Approximately half the population ascribes political-institutional attributes to *dimuqratiyya*. This

Defining Dimuqratiyya   **79**

population's conception is consistent with the meaning political scientists intend when they use the word *democracy* in studies. The other half of the population, however, has an understanding of *dimuqratiyya* grounded in socioeconomic outcomes that democracy as a political system does not and cannot guarantee. There is a schism between the constructs of *dimuqratiyya* and democracy. It is evident, then, that researchers and subjects are talking past each other with this translation.

This chapter has examined these survey responses to identify predictors of these diverse conceptions of *dimuqratiyya*. Ultimately citizens' conception of *dimuqratiyya* is highly idiosyncratic. Even Khanani's (2021, 97) qualitative treatment reports an interlocutor's assessment that "the concept of *dimuqrāṭiyya* is broad and comprehensive, and everyone uses it from their own perspective." While it would be intriguing to point to a specific factor (e.g., colonialism, education, or the Arab Spring) that could drive the public conception, the data do not bear this out. Nonetheless, some features predict citizens' propensity to understand *dimuqratiyya* in political-institutional or socioeconomic terms. Namely, political interest, income, unemployment status, and religiosity are significantly associated with the conception of *dimuqratiyya* in several of the populations. Even these factors, though, do not perform uniformly across country cases.

Few of these factors are amenable to external influence. Changing citizens' evaluations of their regimes' performance is challenging in its own right, and it would be an inefficient and indirect route to influence attitudes toward democracy. The change in regime sentiment would also have additional knock-on effects that would be difficult to predict, particularly in a volatile region. Furthermore, what it means to think highly of the regimes when they are often undemocratic and whether citizens should do so, or should be encouraged to do so, are questions of substantial theoretical and ethical weight. Addressing this matter is beyond the scope of this book. However, it would be an appropriate area for additional future consideration.

Citizens' levels of religiosity, interest in politics, and interest in involving religion in politics do not offer clear levers for manipulation. Other features, like economic circumstances and education, are already the subject of substantial effort. Governments, nongovernmental organizations, and international organizations foreign and domestic already support policies and programs that would help Middle Eastern publics have incomes sufficient to their needs and further access to education. There is normative value to this work regardless of its relationship to *dimuqratiyya* and the impact of that understanding on support for democracy (the subject of the remainder of this text) because of the direct benefits anticipated for the aid recipients and their communities.

80 Defining Democracy

Development, however, is hard to achieve and a roundabout way to support democratization. It is particularly fraught given the questionable relationship between economic development and democratization. The abuse of such foreign aid by autocrats for regime sustainability further complicates the question (Snider 2022). Other features subject to policy influence and foreign assistance, like living or studying in the West, are not strong or significant influences on citizens' understanding of democracy.

Why does this matter? The interest in how citizens understand *dimuqratiyya* is not merely academic. It matters both for practical politics and for survey research. The consequences for political preferences and political behavior will be discussed in the next chapter. Namely, PCD and SECD are linked with unequal levels of political participation and different regime-type preferences. From a research perspective, the multiple conceptions of *dimuqratiyya* impede our ability to understand survey responses and social movements that rely on this word. In both cases, it drives our (mis)understanding of calls for democratization—or *dimuqratization*—in the Middle East and the propensity for democratic durability. This relationship will be the subject of the next several chapters.

Notes

1. The question style is also preferable to asking whether any particular policy "should definitely happen in a democracy" (Jacobsen and Fuchs 2020). Things that do or do not happen in a democracy are not necessarily happening *because* those things are or are not constitutive elements of democracy. The presence of a robust welfare system, for instance, is not a feature of democracy, and whether or not a country should have one is a matter of opinion, maybe even a matter for public debate, but it does not address the core question of regime type. The normative bent of this "should happen" question cannot address the positive element of the state structure question.

2. 4.7 percent of respondents skipped the question.

3. The question was not asked in two of the countries, leading to substantial missingness.

4. For more information on these surveys, see Appendix A.

5. It is acknowledged that when survey takers are provided a list of potential government "characteristics," rather than being required to produce up to three meanings from nothing, they more readily identify economic interests (Bratton 2009). However, in comparing the Middle East with other regions, in which he identified a common political understanding of "democracy," Bratton anticipates that 15 percent of Middle East respondents "associate democracy with the fulfillment of basic needs" (7), and he concludes that "citizens prioritize electoral choice above the provision of basic needs in terms of what they expect from democracy" (8). This is not what the Arab Barometer exposes in the Middle East. Unlike other regions, based on the above characterizations, half of the respondents identify an economic characteristic as the first most important feature of *dimuqratiyya*. To

Defining Dimuqratiyya   81

avoid Schaffer's (2014) legitimate concerns about compressing open-ended answers, a closed-response choice list is used here. The respondents could have been asked to rank third or more place statements, but that would increase the cognitive burden of the task, and it would assume that the respondents were making nuanced rankings among the lower-ranked items, which may not be the case.

6. In those studies, 40 percent of Egyptians said that ensuring law and order was most important, followed by 25.9 percent identifying providing jobs as most important. Of the procedural features, media's being allowed to criticize the government and holding multiparty elections received 15 and 13.6 percent, respectively. A similar distribution appeared in Morocco, with 38.1 percent focusing on law and order, 29.6 percent identifying providing jobs, 13.9 percent identifying press freedom, and 12.1 percent citing elections.

7. Looking ahead, Chapter 7 links some citizens' conception of *dimuqratiyya* to their ideal state structure.

8. Marcus, Mease, and Ottemoeller (2001) conclude that there is "a strong current of liberal political values in Africa" (115) and that "the normative assumption that democracy is imbued with meaning not by the processes and procedures of the state, but by the personal freedoms that it offers" (130). They conclude that the potential for African democratization is thus high.

9. Alvarez and Welzel allow that a social notion could coexist with a liberal understanding of "democracy" but aver that populist and authoritarian notions are necessarily nonliberal and antiliberal respectively. Their study is a prelude to ascribing the development and persistence of liberal democracies to the combination of emancipative values—support for free choice and equality—and theoretical support for democracy. While liberal values and democratic support are distinct in the Middle East (Ridge 2022a), the second half of the book demonstrates that PCD is linked to greater democratic commitment.

10. "Input- und outputorientierter demokratievorstellungen" "die Präferenz variierender Demokratievorstellungen in arabischen Gesellschaften."

11. "Die Präferenz für die inputorientierte Demokratievorstellung."

12. For their study, they employ hierarchical logit models using subnational regions (i.e., provinces or districts) as the second level, instead of countries; this is purportedly due to the local ethnic differences and concentrations within the countries. It is used to generate a large enough number of cases at the second level to permit a hierarchical modeling approach. The inclusion of other variables is unsound. Crucially, it is backward to predict the definition a respondent holds for *dimuqratiyya* based on his support for *dimuqratiyya* in theory—the thing that is as yet undefined. Additionally, participation in the Arab Spring is included based on an argument that considers the uprising as both a cause and a consequence of conception of *dimuqratiyya*. In considering the Arab Spring, they model it as though only Egypt and Tunisia experienced the Arab Spring, even though the whole region witnessed the movements that spread beyond those two countries. At the same time, only about a seventh of respondents actually participated in the Arab Spring demonstrations.

4

Dimuqratiyya and Political Behavior

Decisions are made by those who show up.

—Unknown

This chapter marks the turn to the second section of the book. The preceding chapters focused on the meanings of democracy and (the two meanings of) *dimuqratiyya*. They answered the question "What do Arabs think of when encountering the word *dimuqratiyya* and what do they mean when they say it?" This section begins the consideration of the implications of thinking of *dimuqratiyya* in political-institutional terms (PCD) as opposed to socioeconomic terms (SECD). Does it matter, for politics in practice, that citizens conceive of *dimuqratiyya* differently? In a word, yes.

First, this chapter demonstrates the connection between conceptions of *dimuqratiyya* and political participation. Democratic governance is based on citizen participation. Although democracy is thin on the ground in the Middle East, there are opportunities for political action. These range from the institutional (e.g., voting) to the noninstitutional (e.g., protesting). Recent Arab Barometer data demonstrates the diverging patterns of political participation between these blocs.

Second, this chapter commences the analysis of the relationship between *dimuqratiyya* and democratic commitment. Do citizens who understand *dimuqratiyya* differently have different preferences for democracy? This difference in constructs between democracy and *dimuqratiyya* imposes challenges in using extant surveys to study opinion and attitudes toward democracy. To address this domain, it draws on the earliest waves of the Arab Barometer.

84 Defining Democracy

In theory, citizens' conception of *dimuqratiyya* could be entirely unrelated to their political participation and their attitudes toward democracy. If the democratic attitudes and conceptions are unrelated, then this project could be focusing on a distinction without a difference. That is to say, members of the public might have different understandings of this core political construct than political scientists do and different understandings even from each other, but so what? There would be no empirical ramifications. The differences in understanding of *dimuqratiyya* would be merely an academic point. In that case, the distinction could not facilitate scholars' understanding of the democracy paradox or democracy deficit. It would not shed light on the myriad objectives of pro-*dimuqratiyya* social movements. That situation would not mean that the old questions were entirely reliable. Arguably other differences that could be particularly pertinent could still exist. However, for the focus here on democratic commitment, they would not pertain.

Alternatively, citizens' conceptions of *dimuqratiyya* could be substantively related to their politics. In that case, differences identified in these surveys based on this distinction in meanings of *dimuqratiyya* would demonstrate the necessity of accounting for citizens' understandings of *dimuqratiyya* in qualitative and quantitative analyses of public opinion and social movements. This is true both because of the central role it serves as a political construct and because of the normative importance placed on political participation and democratization and the multiple movements foreign and domestic for political development in the Middle East.

This chapter provides preliminary insight into the implications of PCD and SECD for Middle East/North Africa (MENA) politics using several waves of the Arab Barometer. Overall, the second half of the book shows that PCD evince greater levels of political participation. This includes positive practices, like signing petitions, and negative practices, like engaging in political violence. It also demonstrates that citizens' who hold different conceptions of *dimuqratiyya* also express different levels of interest in choosing the government by election and openness to different regime types. PCD are more likely to be democrats.

Dimuqratiyya and Political Engagement

Do people who conceive of *dimuqratiyya* as a system of political institutions (PCD) and those who think of it in terms of a series of socioeconomic outcomes (SECD) perform politics differently? On one hand, engaging in politics in certain ways is associated with democracies. Joining parties, petitioning the government for redress of grievances, and voting are often considered democratic behaviors. On the other hand, these citizens would be engaging with politics in less-than-fully-democratic systems. This has knock-on effects. For instance, parties occasionally boycott elections to demonstrate their attitudes toward the ruling party. Citizens may, then, be strategic in how they participate in politics. Political participation, even in noninstitutionalized forms, serves an important role in the "formation of democratic persons," including in nondemocratic contexts, by developing citizens' sense of themselves as "deliberative persons" (Wedeen 2007, 61). Political participation cannot be ignored merely because it is participation in a non-democratic setting.

Political participation can be construed quite broadly. Institutional forms of political participation include joining a party and voting in a referendum or election. There are also noninstitutional mechanisms by which citizens express their political preferences and attempt to shape the decisions and actions that their leaders take. For instance, they may join protests or demonstrations, contact elected officials, or sign petitions to express themselves politically.

People engage in these forms of political expression to varying degrees based on personal characteristics, like their interest in politics or level of education, and the circumstances of their country. There are many reasons that citizens vote or abstain, for example. They may desire to express their opinions on and to influence public policy. They may advance a group interest, obtain material rewards in exchange for voting, or make a statement by boycotting an election. They may view participation as costly, capitulate to peer pressure to participate or not, or just not believe it matters.

Voter turnout in the Middle East is lower than turnout in advanced democracies but not profoundly so. The 2016 Arab Barometer shows that nearly half of the respondents reported voting in the most recent election; the rates ranged from 34.4 percent in Algeria to 54.7 percent in Jordan. This puts MENA electoral participation on par with Switzerland (36.1 percent of the voting-age population in 2019) and the United States (55.7 percent of the voting-age population in 2016) (Desilver 2020). This is despite the questionable importance and caliber of some regional elections. In that same 2016 survey, while 50.1 percent said the elections were free and fair or free and fair with minor problems, 11.7 percent reported major problems, and 20.6 percent said the elections were not free or fair. Within-country variation is also possible; lower-level elections may be

86 Defining Democracy

fair, while the highest offices are not (freely) elected. For instance, the monarchical leaders of Jordan and Morocco would not appear on a ballot although parliamentary seats or mayoralties are elected. Citizens can factor that potentiality into their participatory calculus.

MENA residents are less likely to report attachment to political parties than they are to vote. In the 2018 Arab Barometer, 43.1 percent of respondents stated that they did not feel close to any political party. Palestinians were an exception, with only 5.5 percent reporting a lack of affiliation. Voting does not require partisanship, especially in countries where candidates run independently. Not feeling close to any party is far less common in western Europe; for instance, only 13 percent of French citizens and 10 percent of Dutch nationals did not feel close to a party. Eastern Europeans are more likely to feel unaffiliated; for instance, 32 percent in Poland and 37 percent in Hungary did not. It is quite common in South America, though, where 60 percent of Brazilians and 78 percent of Chileans reported no such attachment (Fetterolf 2018).

In Arab Barometer V, only 20.5 percent of respondents reported joining a protest, march, or sit-in in the previous three years. The nature of the protest is not specified and likely varied across countries and movements. Participation rates were highest in Yemen (40.3 percent) and Palestine (30.1 percent) and lowest in Jordan (6.6 percent) and Tunisia (11.8 percent). A protest requires many people to participate, so it is not just one person's decision. Protest behavior can also be contagious, so even a small initial movement can grow (Kuran 1997). For instance, in the 2013 Arab Barometer, 13 percent reported participating in Arab Spring demonstrations; a sixth of those who reported having participated in the Arab Spring protests stated that they did so not because they were convinced of the goals but "because everyone was participating in these demonstrations." Most participants, however, would be expressing a political position by participating in protests. These are not necessarily antiregime protests. Protesting, petitioning the government, and community organizing on external causes, such as Palestinian liberation, are a breeding ground for political agency (Kurd 2022). The skills honed in demonstrating for foreign causes, though, can be turned toward domestic mobilization given the right spark. Mass mobilization occurred in Iran in 2022, for instance, after Mahsa Amini died at the hands of the morality police.

Meeting attendance and petition signing also vary by country. Attending a meeting to discuss a topic or sign a petition in the previous three years was nearly as common as protesting (18.7 percent). The behavior was most common in Yemen (38.2 percent) and Sudan (33.7

percent) and least common in Iraq (9.2 percent) and Jordan (6.2 percent). Each country would have its own impetuses for participation and engagement, but the within-country differences in participation are a reflection of individuals' choices with respect to organizing or pursuing such avenues of political participation.

Reported engagement in political violence was rare (8.3 percent). It was most common in Yemen (19.2 percent) and Sudan (18 percent) and least common in Tunisia (1.5 percent) and Jordan (1.2 percent). Unfortunately, the Arab Barometer does not contextualize how violence should be construed for this question. Research in the United States suggests that support for political violence is dependent on the type of violence involved. Researchers estimate that up to 6.3 percent of Americans would support political violence, though some researchers put the estimate even higher, especially when they do not define the term *violence* to respondents (Westwood et al. 2022; Kalmoe and Mason 2022). The Arab Barometer respondents are admitting to actually having used violence—as opposed to just endorsing it theoretically—so the low rate is quite reasonable. Between-country variation is certainly understandable. Recurrent civil conflict in some MENA states, such as the Yemeni Civil War, is consistent with higher rates of political violence. However, the ultimate decision to engage in political violence is highly individual.

Political Behavior

Due to the perceived global agreement on the meaning of *democracy* in cross-national studies, the impact of the diverging views on political behavior has not been heavily canvased. Where individuals have different conceptions in mind for key political constructs, they may engage with politics differently. For stance, Schaffer (2000, 99) posits that voting motivations in Senegal reflected different concepts of the state: "What Dahl sees as incompetence in the service of democracy may be perfectly competent in the service of *demokaraasi*." If these different conceptions of *dimuqratiyya* reflect different views of the function of the state—as Chapter 7 will touch on—then these citizens may well engage in politics differently.

Some work has examined variations in participation in Europe. Oser and Hooghe (2018a) identify five classes of democracy interpretation in Europe based on the European Social Survey's "How important [do] you think it is for democracy in general that . . ." question battery. They focus their discussion on two of the five clusters: one emphasizes

88   Defining Democracy

political rights (16 percent), and one emphasizes social rights (20 percent). They conclude that those who are focused on political rights are "highly active in all types of political behaviour, while the social rights group is less active overall" (712). Those who are focused on social rights have high rates of participation in noninstitutionalized political participation (e.g., signing a petition or boycotting a product), but they are less likely to engage in institutionalized politics (e.g., contacting or joining a party). Thus, "while this group emphasizes protection from inequality and poverty as important for the functioning of democracy, apparently this normative ideal does not lead to more political participation" (712).

Canache's (2012) work on Latin America posits that individuals' protest behavior and attitudes toward protests can be linked to their definition of *democracia*. Respondents could give up to three definitions, but the most common category of definitions was "liberty." Those who used a definition other than liberty for one of their responses (compared to a hypothetical respondent whose every answer fit the liberty category) were more likely to report participating in a political protest; they were also more approving toward illegal protests. Conception of *democracia* was not significantly linked to voting behavior.

If MENA residents follow a similar tendency to that identified by Oser and Hooghe, then PCD should be more likely than SECD to vote or to join parties. High rates of SECD participation in the noninstitutional features might mean the groups are not significantly distinguished in their propensities for participation. However, MENA residents, both PCD and SECD, could follow an entirely different pattern of political participation.

For instance, Ciftci's (2022, 7) work on conceptions of justice (*'adl/adalet*) in Islam anticipates that the "political" dimension of Islamic justice, if underpinned by a sense of free will, would lead to protest participation and a demand for governmental accountability; if underpinned by a belief in predestination, it would lead to political quietism. The "social" dimension could lead to a preference for order over freedom or rights. In that case, those citizens may disengage, especially from protest behavior. If the dimensions of *dimuqratiyya* are akin to the dimensions of *'adl*, it would make sense for PCD to be more politically engaged than SECD. However, the tendency toward quietism would predict a null effect. PCD then could just be more politically engaged on all fronts.

To examine this point, I return to the fifth wave of the Arab Barometer. Only the most essential characteristic of *dimuqratiyya* was measured in that wave. A binary indicator identifies PCD: those who selected "Media is free to criticize the things government does" or "Multiple parties compete fairly in the election." SECD were those who chose "Government ensures law and order" or "Government ensures job opportunities for all." For covariate measurement information, consult Appendix C.

Respondents were asked about both institutional and noninstitutional forms of political participation.[1] The institutional forms were voting and feeling close to a political party. Respondents were asked whether they voted in the most recent parliamentary election. Party membership itself is not as common in the Middle East as it is in many Western countries, so respondents are not asked if they are party members. Instead, the study makes "Which party if any do you feel closest to?" a binary marker for feeling close to any party.

The noninstitutional participation codings draw from questions about the frequency of participation. Respondents could indicate that in the previous three years they had once, more than once, or never attended a meeting to discuss a subject or sign a petition; participated in a protest, march, or sit-in; and used force or violence for a political cause. A binary indicator marks having engaged in the activity either once or more than once in the previous three years.

As noted above, participating at all in any of these activities was a minority position. Political participation is something of a syndrome. Those who engage in some of these behaviors likely engage in others as well. The items are almost all significantly correlated, although the correlations are weak with respect to voting and the other behaviors (Table 4.1). Protesting is best correlated with attending meetings/signing petitions and with using violence for political reasons. This could reflect meetings about the cause or planning a march. Violence could also be used during a demonstration. Partisanship is also correlated, though to a lesser degree, with these behaviors—understandable given that parties too can organize petitions and demonstrations. Partisanship is better linked to voting.

Table 4.1 Political Behavior Correlations

	Close to a Party	Protest	Petition	Use Violence
Voting	0.267	0.041	0.088	−0.004***
Close to a Party		0.162	0.177	0.117
Protest	0.162		0.413	
Petition	0.177	0.487		0.372
Use Violence	0.117	0.413	0.372	

Notes: ***Correlations not significant ($p > 0.05$).

90 Defining Democracy

To examine propensities for political engagement, logistic regression models are used. The models include country fixed effects and survey weights. Errors are clustered by country.

PCD are more likely than the SECD to sign a petition; participate in a protest, march, or sit-in; and feel close to a political party (Table 4.2). They are even more likely to report having used violence or force for political reasons. This means that when social movements and social actions in the Middle East occur, they are more likely being done by individuals who construe *dimuqratiyya* in the way outsiders construe democracy. It does not mean that democracy is always what those social movements are calling for, even when they use the word *dimuqratiyya*.

Table 4.2 *Dimuqratiyya* and Political Behavior

	Model 1	Model 2	Model 3	Model 4	Model 5
Intercept	0.91***	1.08***	5.18***	1.07**	−6.11***
	(0.14)	(0.19)	(0.28)	(0.43)	(0.38)
PCD	0.24***	0.21***	0.26***	0.32***	0.01
	(0.09)	(0.06)	(0.09)	(0.08)	(0.07)
Government	0.14	−0.14	−0.00	0.49***	0.34***
evaluation	(0.13)	(0.16)	(0.18)	(0.08)	(0.09)
Most people	0.13	0.16	0.19	0.05	0.10
can be trusted	(0.12)	(0.15)	(0.13)	(0.12)	(0.07)
Pray daily	−0.19	−0.21**	−0.75***	0.08	0.31***
	(0.12)	(0.10)	(0.18)	(0.12)	(0.10)
Political interest	1.03***	0.96***	0.87***	0.67***	0.66***
	(0.10)	(0.11)	(0.09)	(0.06)	(0.09)
Gender 0.22***	0.26***	0.60***	−0.01	−0.15*	
traditionalism	(0.08)	(0.09)	(0.16)	(0.05)	(0.08)
Secularist	0.08	0.06	0.26**	0.11*	−0.01
orientation	(0.06)	(0.05)	(0.11)	(0.07)	(0.02)
Male	0.57***	0.68***	0.58***	0.08	0.18***
	(0.11)	(0.12)	(0.17)	(0.08)	(0.07)
Unemployed	−0.12	0.02	0.11	−0.28***	−0.07
	(0.12)	(0.07)	(0.14)	(0.09)	(0.12)
Religion: Christian	0.37	0.29	0.03	0.47***	0.56***
	(0.30)	(0.23)	(0.31)	(0.17)	(0.07)
Religion: none	1.00***	0.90	1.85***	0.00	−1.20*
	(0.26)	(0.60)	(0.27)	(0.43)	(0.63)
Religion: other	−1.10***	−1.27***	−1.22**	0.74	0.72***
	(0.31)	(0.37)	(0.58)	(1.65)	(0.08)
Sufficient income	0.09	−0.02	−0.11	0.02	−0.04
	(0.08)	(0.07)	(0.08)	(0.06)	(0.08)

continues

Table 4.2 Continued

	Model 1	Model 2	Model 3	Model 4	Model 5
College education	0.54***	0.43***	0.01	0.08	0.30***
	(0.11)	(0.10)	(0.11)	(0.12)	(0.10)
Age	−0.00**	−0.02***	−0.01***	0.01*	0.04***
	(0.00)	(0.00)	(0.00)	(0.01)	(0.01)
Colony (France)	5.11***	3.52***	18.20***	4.17***	−12.01***
	(0.20)	(0.20)	(0.32)	(0.46)	(0.46)
Colony (Italy)	16.41***	12.57***	55.18***	11.71***	−33.29***
	(0.66)	(0.74)	(1.13)	(1.47)	(1.41)
GDP per capita	−2.55***	−1.94***	−8.03***	−1.90***	4.62***
	(0.10)	(0.11)	(0.16)	(0.21)	(0.20)
Egypt	3.10***	1.87***	12.50***	2.61***	−8.93***
	(0.17)	(0.19)	(0.26)	(0.36)	(0.36)
Iraq	10.14***	7.70***	36.22***	8.59***	−20.96***
	(0.42)	(0.47)	(0.72)	(0.96)	(0.92)
Jordan	6.59***	4.44***	25.01***	2.97***	−15.86***
	(0.33)	(0.36)	(0.52)	(0.73)	(0.67)
Lebanon	11.69***	8.90***	38.55***		−20.75***
	(0.50)	(0.57)	(0.77)		(0.93)
Morocco	0.23***	0.61***	−0.01	0.57***	0.68***
	(0.03)	(0.06)	(0.10)	(0.04)	(0.05)
Palestine	6.35***	4.78***	21.49***	22.57***	−12.69***
	(0.24)	(0.25)	(0.40)	(1.18)	(0.53)
Sudan	−0.30***	−0.82***	−0.07	−0.17***	0.13***
	(0.10)	(0.11)	(0.10)	(0.06)	(0.05)
AIC	18,922.17	19,989.48	10,650.61	17,222.18	27,343.97
Log likelihood	−9,435.09	−9,968.74	−5,299.30	−8,586.09	−13,645.98
Deviance	18,684.35	19,681.63	10,591.53	16,833.14	26,630.02
N	22,447	22,457	22,380	16,208	22,375

Notes: ***$p < 0.01$; **$p < 0.05$; *$p < 0.1$. Model 1: Petition. Model 2: Protest. Model 3: Use violence. Model 4: Feel close to a party. Model 5: Vote.

The only avenue of political participation in which the groups are not statistically distinguished is voting. The absence of a significant relationship does not necessarily demonstrate that there is no difference. However, in this case, the fact that the effect is miniscule suggests that there is credibly no difference between these groups in their propensity to vote in parliamentary elections.

This chapter is not focused on the covariates. However, some significant relationships are identified. Unsurprisingly, those who are interested in politics are more likely to engage in all forms of political participation. Men and college-educated respondents are broadly more likely to report

92   *Defining Democracy*

participating. Gender traditionalists are more likely to engage in the noninstitutional forms of participation, while older respondents are less likely to have done so.

Secularists are more likely to report using violence. Those who pray daily are less likely to protest or use violence but more likely to vote. Christians are more likely to vote than Muslims, while atheists are more likely to engage in noninstitutional forms of politics. Other religious minorities are also more likely to vote, while they are less likely to engage in noninstitutional political behavior.

Dimuqratiyya and Democratic Commitment

In addition to engaging in politics differently, these groups can have different state-structural preferences. Few data sources allow for this kind of analysis. It is now well-established that democracy and *dimuqratiyya* are not mutually interchangeable in meaning. Thus, understanding public support for democracy requires careful selection of public opinion questions.

By and large it is not possible to use the extant multinational surveys to study support for democracy. The World Values Survey, Arab Barometer, and Afrobarometer employ a variety of questions that specifically ask citizens about their support for *dimuqratiyya*. Is *dimuqratiyya* the best form of government? Is *dimuqratiyya* appropriate for their country? Is it important to them to live in a *dimuqratiyya* society? By using this word with multiple meanings, the surveys introduce two problems in understanding support for *democracy*.

First, the questions are not asking about democracy. How the respondents feel about *dimuqratiyya* is not a clear barometer of their attitudes toward democracy. Second, the disparities in citizen understandings confound the results because the respondents are not understanding the question equivalently among themselves. Some respondents are providing their opinions about a system of political institutions; some respondents are providing their opinions about a system of socioeconomic outcomes. These are responses are to functionally distinct items—opinions about apples and oranges.

It is thus necessary to account for this distinction by using survey questions that focus on democracy. That is to say, researchers should ask the question that they want to be asking with explicit reference to the institutions they mean to address.[2] This book approaches this method in two ways. The first uses a question from early waves of the Arab Barometer that presented respondents with both the word *dimuqratiyya* and a description of regime features associated with a maximalist conception of democracy. It thus presents an in-between style of question that appeals to both constructs. The second method is to employ novel survey data incorporating questions specifically addressing the central feature of democracy: elections. The following two chapters will present the new data.

A Good Idea

In the vast majority of survey questions invoking *dimuqratiyya*, the word goes undefined and uncontextualized. For instance, the World Values Survey features questions such as how important an individual deems living in a "democratically" governed country or how "democracy" is developing in the individual's country. All such questions rely on the word *dimuqratiyya*. The Arab Barometer regularly addresses *dimuqratiyya* without a definition, despite the fact that multiple waves of the Arab Barometer have identified heterogenous public conceptions of *dimuqratiyya*. In the three earliest waves of the Arab Barometer, however, the word was presented in conjunction with a context.

In Wave 1 (2006–2009), after more than a dozen questions about *dimuqratiyya* without contextualization or definition, respondents were asked to rate "various types of political systems" as a way of governing the country on a scale from "very good" to "very bad." Together the questions form the democracy-autocracy preference (DAP) battery (Ariely and Davidov 2011).[3] For the Arab Barometer, the democracy part of that democracy-autocracy preference draws on the evaluation of a "[*dimuqratiyya*] political system (public freedom, equal political and civil rights, balance of power, accountability and transparency)." Notably the central feature of democracy—elections—is not specifically included in this description. The other regime types the respondents were asked to rate were decidedly undemocratic.

Typically, the DAP asks opinions on having a strong leader who can ignore parliament and elections, expert-based government, and military rule. Wave 1 replaced the typical question about military rule with a description of a regime that mixes elections, a strong leader, and expert rule under one leader. Wave 2 (2010–2011) asks these questions as well, but it omits the final question about a mix of systems, and Wave 3 (2012–2014) only includes the strongman alternative. The DAP battery identifies individuals who identify *dimuqratiyya* as (very) good while also marking the alternatives (very) bad. These are singular democrats; more is said on singular democrats in Chapters 5 and 6.

94   Defining Democracy

Waves 1 to 3 followed the DAP battery by asking citizens to consider the governments of several MENA countries with the names removed: "Parliamentary system in which nationalist, left-wing, and Islamic political parties all compete in elections"; "A parliamentary system in which only Islamic political parties and factions compete in elections"; "A system with a strong president and military in which elections and competition among political parties are not important"; and "A system governed by Islamic law in which there are no political parties or elections." Waves 2 and 3 add a fifth option: "parliamentary system in which only non-religious parties compete in parliamentary elections." Waves 2 and 3 also include "right-wing" parties in the description of the multi-party-elections regime.

The definition paired with *dimuqratiyya* in the DAP battery should constrain respondents' conception of the construct somewhat in their answers. This question follows the respondents' opportunity to define the term themselves, which many did in ways that are not consistent with that definition. Thus, several of them are being asked in this question, by means of the incorporated definition, to answer about a system that is different from their understanding of the principal components of *dimuqratiyya*. SECD, for instance, have already indicated that the central components of *dimuqratiyya* are socioeconomic outcomes not featured in this question wording. As the specified elements are shared for all respondents, it reduces the likelihood that the responses have the apples-to-oranges comparison problem discussed in the first half of the book.

The question wording takes a maximalist view of democracy. As discussed in Chapter 2, maximalist conceptions can incorporate extra-electoral features, such as the rule of law. They may also include liberal values. This book is not arguing that a maximalist view of democracy is wrong insofar as the definition is constrained to political-institutional elements. As noted in Chapter 2, some people attempt to elevate social democracy—one of the forms of democracy with adjectives—to the status of democracy writ large by incorporating economic policy and economic success into the definition. This book does not incorporate economic policies and outcomes—the results of, among other things, political choices—into the definition of political institutions, nor does it otherwise assume liberal democracy.[4]

In this case, the respondents are asked about *dimuqratiyya* and the coterie of additional features. These elements may be driving some of the response behavior. Freedom broadly construed may incorporate for the respondent some freedoms that they would not endorse, and it is not necessarily clear whether those are the freedoms the researchers intended.

Equality of civil and political rights, also included in the definition, may be construed as opposing Islamic law. Conversely, respondents may be open to elections or constraints on the executive but not eager to broach areas of law where popular will would formalize an inequality. Surveys in Egypt and Tunisia have found that support for liberal values and electoral democracy coexist to varying degrees (Ridge 2022a, 2022b). There are liberal democrats, illiberal democrats, and liberal nondemocrats in the Middle East. This question cannot account for such nuanced positions. The inclusion of these descriptors thus places frames around the interpretation of the question and may place additional sway on the responses. The Arab Barometer question, by formulation, focuses on the liberal democrats.

The question is also country specific. It asks if the described regimes would be good or bad for that country. Chapter 5 will discuss further the limitations of questions that present a regime type as specific to a country with respect to understanding democratic commitment. For now, suffice it to say it is not the same as addressing support for democracy in itself or for identifying committed democrats in the population. Reasonable actors, after all, can distinguish a good idea per se from a good idea for them or a good idea for the moment.

This question still underscores the concern about *dimuqratiyya* addressed in the previous chapters. That the uncontextualized word taps into a different construct is again demonstrable in the limited correlation between the answers to this question and the answers to the survey findings for whether a "[*dimuqratiyya*] system may have problems, yet it is better than other systems" and whether the "citizens in your country are not prepared for a [*dimuqratiyya*] system." For comparison, the question from the second battery, which describes multiparty elections for parliament, is also included. The latter two questions are included to account for the country-specific framing of the *dimuqratiyya*-with-context question.

In each case, the question answers are significantly correlated (Table 4.3). The correlations, however, are rather weak. There is a weak correlation between belief that a "[*dimuqratiyya*] political system (public freedom, equal political and civil rights, balance of power, accountability and transparency)" is good or very good for the respondents' countries and belief that *dimuqratiyya* is the best form of government. Democracy and *dimuqratiyya* are not one and the same; however, one can draw on a standard often set for committed democrats—believing that democracy is both good and appropriate for one's country—as a point of consideration. In this case, the dual believers would be "committed *dimuqrats*." Belief in these two statements does not move in

96 Defining Democracy

Table 4.3 Correlation of Meanings

Survey Wave	Correlation with "*Dimuqratiyya* Is Best"	Correlation with "Citizens Are Not Prepared for *Dimuqratiyya*"	Correlation with "A Parliamentary System in Which Nationalist, Left-Wing, Right-Wing, and Islamist Parties Compete in Parliamentary Elections Is Appropriate"
I	0.149***		0.161***
II	0.161***	−0.049***	0.187***
III	0.181***	−0.083***	0.225***

Note: ***$p < 0.001$.

lockstep, even though both are broadly endorsed: 79.5 percent of the respondents in Wave 1 agree or strongly agree with both statements, 76.7 percent in Wave 2, and 74.2 percent in Wave 3. The populations that endorse only one of those characteristics, however, are also important for potential institutionalization.

There is almost no correlation between thinking that *dimuqratiyya* is good for the country and thinking that the people in the country are (un)prepared for *dimuqratiyya*. If the system would be good for the country, the public would be expected to be prepared for it. In theory, then, a strong negative correlation should be identified between supporting *dimuqratiyya* for the country and believing the citizens are unprepared for it. This minimal correlation could reflect disparities in the understanding of *dimuqratiyya* across the questions based on the introduction of this maximalist definition in one of the questions.

Another style of question can address democratic institutions where they exist. Bratton (2003) is able to circumvent the "d-word" problem in a comparison of Muslim and non-Muslim support for democracy in French- and English-language Uganda, Mali, Tanzania, and Nigeria by using a question about "our present system of government with free elections and many parties." This phrasing emphasizes the preeminence of these institutions in how researchers view the system. He found no difference between Muslims and non-Muslims. This wording, however, requires a democratic regime, which would not apply to most of the Middle East.

The correlation is even weak when juxtaposing the belief that a "[*dimuqratiyya*] political system (public freedom, equal political and civil rights, balance of power, accountability and transparency)" is good

Dimuqratiyya *and Political Behavior* **97**

for the respondent's country and the belief that a "parliamentary system in which nationalist, left-wing, and Islamic political parties all compete in elections" is good for the country. That is arguably a democratic state. Although the country is unnamed, it sounds like Tunisia, which was for years considered to be the functioning, if fragile, democracy of the Middle East and the success story of the Arab Spring. Supporting *dimuqratiyya*, even with the contextualizing appendages, is not the same thing as supporting democracy for many respondents. It cannot be determined to which part of the description they object, but they are held distinct.

Ultimately, it is evident that *dimuqratiyya* as a term, in isolation, is not drawing on the same parameters featured in the definition in this question. It also demonstrates that survey questions using the term *dimuqratiyya*, especially without a contextualizing definition that influences respondents' understanding, are not good approximators of democratic commitment. Nonetheless, this maximalist formulation that focuses on a subset of liberal democratic institutions is better than other available questions for reducing the apples-to-oranges comparison problem that is introduced by the undefined word. It is a start.

Accounting for Conceptions of Dimuqratiyya

In each of the survey modules, respondents were asked about their understanding of *dimuqratiyya*. The survey stated, "People often differ in their views on the characteristics that are essential to [*dimuqratiyya*]. If you have to choose only one thing, what would you choose as the most important characteristic, and what would be the second most important?" In the first module, the respondents could choose among four options; in the second and third wave, they were presented with six choices.

These modules allowed respondents to indicate a first and second characteristic. Thus, the respondents can be divided into four groups based on their choices. The following three choices are coded PCD: the opportunity to change the government by election, the freedom to criticize the government, and equal political rights among the citizens. The following options are coded SECD: narrowing the gap between the rich and the poor, providing basic items (such as food, housing, and clothing) to all individuals, and eliminating financial and administrative corruption. As before, those who chose a political option for both are PCD, those who chose a socioeconomic outcome for both are SECD, and those who chose one of each are mixed. The share of the sample in each

98 Defining Democracy

of the categories across the waves can be seen in Table 4.4. In each case, approximately half the sample views *dimuqratiyya* primarily as political, and half view it as socioeconomic.

These are statements about the essential features of *dimuqratiyya*. They are reminiscent, though, of the two types of Islamic justice identified by Ciftci (2022), described above. Ciftci argues that social penetration of political justice could promote or suppress democratic behavior under certain circumstances. Social justice, on the other hand, especially if focused on order, security, and the common good, would favor benevolent authoritarian rule. It could, though, be turned into a democratizing appeal if the authoritarian regime failed to deliver. In parallel logic, different conceptions of *dimuqratiyya* could be linked to different engagements with democracy.

A handful of researchers have attempted to incorporate understanding of the construct into their analyses. For instance, Canache (2012) finds that Latin American individuals who associate the word *democracia* with liberalism are more likely to say they support *democracia*, whereas Kiewiet de Jonge (2016) concludes that understanding of *democracia* does not significantly distinguish Latin Americans' democratic commitment. Mattes and Bratton (2007) construct indexes for "procedural" and "substantive" views of "democracy" based on how important potential regime features are for a society to be called democratic. They suggest that individuals rating higher on the procedural index are more likely to support "democracy" and oppose alternatives. Substantive index ratings are not significant predictors of "demand" for "democracy." Mattes and Bratton also find political, rather than economic, indicators are better predictors of perceived "supply" of "democracy." They interpret this as citizens' endorsing a "separate and correct" distinction between economic and political goods. These studies are hamstrung by the fact that the dependent variables nonetheless use the same word that they are analyzing. Thus, the apples-and-oranges problem impinges on interpreting their findings.

Table 4.4 Conception of *Dimuqratiyya* per Wave

Wave	PCD	Mixed PCD	Mixed SECD	SECD
I	17.8	30.0	20.1	32.1
II	25.4	32.7	12.2	29.7
III	19.1	29.2	20.0	31.7

Conception of *Dimuqratiyya* and Support for *Dimuqratiyya*

Support for *dimuqratiyya* is assessed based on respondents' attitudes toward a "[*dimuqratiyya*] political system (public freedom, equal political and civil rights, balance of power, accountability and transparency)." A binary indicator is created for agreeing that the described system of government is good or very good as opposed to bad or very bad. Binary logistic regression, including additional covariates from the Arab Barometer, is then employed. The models include country fixed effects and clustered standard errors. For more information on the coding of the covariates, see Appendix C.

The relations are analyzed compared to PCD and SECD (Table 4.5). In these questions, limited relationships are identified between citizens' conceptions of *dimuqratiyya* and their attitudes toward *dimuqratiyya* as a system. The models also demonstrate some connection between conception of *dimuqratiyya* and the democracy-autocracy preference binary (Table 4.6). In the earliest wave, individuals with a mixed PCD are less likely to endorse *dimuqratiyya* while rejecting the alternatives than either SECD or PCD. The relationships do not reach significance in the other modules. However, the items included in the battery changed across the waves; the difference across time could reflect changing public opinion or the different alternative regimes included in the battery.

Secularists, those who live in safe areas, and religious minorities are more likely to endorse a "[*dimuqratiyya*] political system (public freedom, equal political and civil rights, balance of power, accountability and transparency)." Gender traditionalists are less likely to say it is good for the country. Also, secularists and the college educated are more likely to endorse *dimuqratiyya* to the exclusion of other regime types. Religious minorities are less likely to approve singularly of *dimuqratiyya*. This is consistent with studies showing that concerns about the installation of illiberal regimes under popular choice dampens minorities' support for democracy (Ridge 2022a; Rizzo, Abdel-Latif, and Meyer 2007). As such, though the minorities may like the idea of democracy, especially liberal democracy, they may be open to less-than-democratic regimes as well. The largely null effects of organizational membership on democratic attitudes are consistent with Jamal's (2007) argument that civil society will only build democratic commitment in certain contexts.

The country suitability of the nondemocratic regime types was also assessed. The aforementioned questions about the suitability of multiparty parliaments also considered the appropriateness of parliaments

Table 4.5 *Dimuqratiyya* Is Good (Binary)

	Model 1	Model 2	Model 3	Model 4	Model 5	Model 6
Intercept	-13.67***	-13.45***	-0.35	-0.44	1.09***	0.85***
	(1.56)	(1.72)	(0.56)	(0.46)	(0.22)	(0.22)
SECD		-0.21		0.09		0.25
		(0.27)		(0.16)		(0.26)
Mixed SECD	0.03	-0.19***	-0.06	0.03	0.06	0.30
	(0.28)	(0.05)	(0.10)	(0.11)	(0.14)	(0.22)
Mixed PCD	0.01	-0.21	0.16*	0.26*	-0.36	-0.12
	(0.12)	(0.16)	(0.10)	(0.15)	(0.37)	(0.18)
PCD	0.21		-0.09		-0.25	
	(0.27)		(0.16)		(0.26)	
Government	0.06**	0.06**	0.00	0.00	0.07*	0.07*
performance	(0.03)	(0.03)	(0.07)	(0.07)	(0.04)	(0.04)
National	0.14	0.14	0.25***	0.25***	0.26*	0.26*
economy	(0.09)	(0.09)	(0.10)	(0.10)	(0.13)	(0.13)
Time in West	0.12	0.12	-0.23***	-0.23***	-0.27	-0.27
	(0.39)	(0.39)	(0.07)	(0.07)	(0.23)	(0.23)
Religion:	0.15***	0.15***	0.13	0.13	0.03	0.03
Christianity	(0.05)	(0.05)	(0.20)	(0.20)	(0.23)	(0.23)
Religion:	9.73***	9.73***	-0.19	-0.19		
not clear	(1.21)	(1.21)	(0.74)	(0.74)		
Religion: other	-3.80***	-3.80***	10.36***	10.36***		
	(0.13)	(0.13)	(0.75)	(0.75)		
Pray daily	-0.42*	-0.42*	-0.13	-0.13	0.21	0.21
	(0.25)	(0.25)	(0.14)	(0.14)	(0.16)	(0.16)
Interpersonal	-0.07	-0.07	-0.01	-0.01	-0.22	-0.22
trust	(0.13)	(0.13)	(0.19)	(0.19)	(0.27)	(0.27)
Safe area	0.12	0.12	0.49***	0.49***	0.69***	0.69***
	(0.15)	(0.15)	(0.09)	(0.09)	(0.13)	(0.13)
Age	-0.00	-0.00	0.01	0.01	0.01**	0.01**
	(0.00)	(0.00)	(0.00)	(0.00)	(0.00)	(0.00)
Male	-0.10	-0.10	0.01	0.01	-0.13	-0.13
	(0.15)	(0.15)	(0.14)	(0.14)	(0.15)	(0.15)
College	0.22	0.22	0.23	0.23	0.22	0.22
education	(0.13)	(0.13)	(0.15)	(0.15)	(0.14)	(0.14)
Civil society	-0.09	-0.09	0.14	0.14	-0.17*	-0.17*
member	(0.13)	(0.13)	(0.14)	(0.14)	(0.10)	(0.10)
Follows the	0.27	0.27	0.20*	0.20*	0.19**	0.19**
political news	(0.22)	(0.22)	(0.12)	(0.12)	(0.09)	(0.09)
Political interest	-0.00	-0.00	-0.18	-0.18	-0.06	-0.06
	(0.10)	(0.10)	(0.16)	(0.16)	(0.12)	(0.12)
Gender	-0.16	-0.16	-0.40**	-0.40**	-0.26	-0.26
traditionalism	(0.13)	(0.13)	(0.17)	(0.17)	(0.18)	(0.18)
Secularist	0.13	0.13	0.30***	0.30***	0.35	0.35
orientation	(0.15)	(0.15)	(0.10)	(0.10)	(0.28)	(0.28)

continues

Dimuqratiyya *and Political Behavior* 101

Table 4.5 Continued

	Model 1	Model 2	Model 3	Model 4	Model 5	Model 6
Colony: France	−31.75***	−31.75***	−1.01***	−1.01***	−0.40	−0.40
	(3.26)	(3.26)	(0.07)	(0.07)	(0.25)	(0.25)
Colony: Italy					−2.08***	−2.08***
					(0.76)	(0.76)
GDP per capita	9.32***	9.32***	0.51***	0.51***	0.21**	0.21**
	(0.94)	(0.94)	(0.05)	(0.05)	(0.09)	(0.09)
Bahrain	−179.20***	−179.20***				
	(18.13)	(18.13)				
Egypt			2.58***	2.58***	−0.70***	−0.70***
			(0.08)	(0.08)	(0.17)	(0.17)
Iraq					−0.90**	−0.90**
					(0.44)	(0.44)
Jordan	−9.60***	−9.60***			−1.18***	−1.18***
	(0.99)	(0.99)			(0.19)	(0.19)
Kuwait					−10.30***	−10.30***
					(3.96)	(3.96)
Lebanon			−0.32***	−0.32***	−0.09	−0.09
			(0.12)	(0.12)	(0.30)	(0.30)
Morocco					−0.25	−0.25
					(0.18)	(0.18)
Palestine			0.08	0.08	−0.51***	−0.51***
			(0.11)	(0.11)	(0.14)	(0.14)
Saudi Arabia			−10.56***	−10.56***		
			(1.06)	(1.06)		
Sudan			0.69***	0.69***	0.08	0.08
			(0.12)	(0.12)	(0.07)	(0.07)
Tunisia			2.82***	2.82***		
			(0.07)	(0.07)		
Yemen			1.01	1.01		
			(0.77)	(0.77)		
AIC	2,170.42	2,170.42	5,229.37	5,229.37	5,865.24	5,865.24
Log likelihood	−1,060.21	−1,060.21	−2,584.68	−2,584.68	−2,902.62	−2,902.62
Deviance	2,120.42	2,120.42	4,959.73	4,959.73	5,875.11	5,875.11
N	3,573	3,573	9,469	9,469	10,110	10,110

Notes: ***$p < 0.001$; **$p < 0.01$; *$p < 0.05$. Wave 1: Models 1 and 2. Wave 2: Models 3 and 4. Wave 3: Models 5 and 6.

with only Islamic parties, parliaments without any religious parties allowed, strongman rule, and unelected Islamic rule. PCD were less likely to find Islamic rule, parliaments banning religious parties, or strongman rule suitable for their countries in the early waves of the Arab Barometer (see Appendix G). By Wave 3, when more countries

Table 4.6 *Dimuqratiyya* and DAP (Binary)

	Model 1	Model 2	Model 3	Model 4	Model 5	Model 6
Intercept	13.48***	13.66***	−0.33	−0.33	−0.60***	−0.96***
	(1.69)	(1.67)	(0.37)	(0.23)	(0.22)	(0.15)
SECD		−0.18		0.00		0.36*
		(0.17)		(0.23)		(0.21)
Mixed SECD	0.15	−0.03	0.00	0.01	−0.16	0.20
	(0.23)	(0.32)	(0.19)	(0.17)	(0.11)	(0.17)
Mixed PCD	−0.31**	−0.49***	0.03	0.04	−0.37	−0.01
	(0.14)	(0.17)	(0.20)	(0.12)	(0.22)	(0.15)
PCD	0.18		−0.00		−0.36*	
	(0.17)		(0.23)		(0.21)	
Government	0.00	0.00	−0.04*	−0.04*	0.02	0.02
performance	(0.04)	(0.04)	(0.03)	(0.03)	(0.03)	(0.03)
National	−0.23***	−0.23***	−0.22	−0.22	−0.21	−0.21
economy	(0.07)	(0.07)	(0.17)	(0.17)	(0.23)	(0.23)
Time in West	−0.20	−0.20	−0.11	−0.11	−0.06	−0.06
	(0.15)	(0.15)	(0.19)	(0.19)	(0.37)	(0.37)
Religion:	−0.31***	−0.31***	−0.72***	−0.72***	0.39*	0.39*
Christianity	(0.06)	(0.06)	(0.10)	(0.10)	(0.21)	(0.21)
Religion:	−13.82***	−13.82***	−0.12	−0.12		
not clear	(1.12)	(1.12)	(0.56)	(0.56)		
Religion: other	−15.22***	−15.22***	−11.29***	−11.29***		
	(1.12)	(1.12)	(0.81)	(0.81)		
Pray daily	−0.21	−0.21	−0.15	−0.15	0.33	0.33
	(0.15)	(0.15)	(0.12)	(0.12)	(0.20)	(0.20)
Interpersonal	−0.06	−0.06	0.06	0.06	−0.12	−0.12
trust	(0.18)	(0.18)	(0.17)	(0.17)	(0.17)	(0.17)
Safe area	−0.04	−0.04	0.13	0.13	0.47***	0.47***
	(0.23)	(0.23)	(0.11)	(0.11)	(0.14)	(0.14)
Age	0.00	0.00	0.00	0.00	0.01**	0.01**
	(0.00)	(0.00)	(0.00)	(0.00)	(0.00)	(0.00)
Male	0.20	0.20	−0.02	−0.02	0.06	0.06
	(0.20)	(0.20)	(0.07)	(0.07)	(0.09)	(0.09)
College	0.38***	0.38***	0.18**	0.18**	0.15**	0.15**
education	(0.14)	(0.14)	(0.09)	(0.09)	(0.07)	(0.07)
Civil society	0.27	0.27	0.15	0.15	−0.32***	−0.32***
member	(0.18)	(0.18)	(0.11)	(0.11)	(0.05)	(0.05)
Follows the	0.01	0.01	−0.10	−0.10	0.07	0.07
political news	(0.14)	(0.14)	(0.12)	(0.12)	(0.08)	(0.08)
Political interest	0.41***	0.41***	−0.03	−0.03	−0.02	−0.02
	(0.13)	(0.13)	(0.08)	(0.08)	(0.09)	(0.09)
Gender	−0.22	−0.22	−0.02	−0.02	−0.58***	−0.58***
traditionalism	(0.24)	(0.24)	(0.18)	(0.18)	(0.15)	(0.15)
Secularist	−0.09	−0.09	0.34**	0.34**	0.53***	0.53***
orientation	(0.09)	(0.09)	(0.15)	(0.15)	(0.15)	(0.15)

continues

Dimuqratiyya *and Political Behavior* 103

Table 4.6 Continued

	Model 1	Model 2	Model 3	Model 4	Model 5	Model 6
Colony: France	35.76***	35.76***	−0.28***	−0.28***	−2.03***	−2.03***
	(3.18)	(3.18)	(0.04)	(0.04)	(0.39)	(0.39)
Colony: Italy					−7.80***	−7.80***
					(1.16)	(1.16)
GDP per capita	−9.77***	−9.77***	−0.17***	−0.17***	0.86***	0.86***
	(0.90)	(0.90)	(0.03)	(0.03)	(0.14)	(0.14)
Bahrain	190.38***	190.38***				
	(17.32)	(17.32)				
Egypt			0.36***	0.36***	−1.38***	−1.38***
			(0.09)	(0.09)	(0.26)	(0.26)
Iraq					−3.63***	−3.63***
					(0.69)	(0.69)
Jordan	10.73***	10.73***			−2.73***	−2.73***
	(0.98)	(0.98)			(0.28)	(0.28)
Kuwait					−41.21***	−41.21***
					(6.21)	(6.21)
Lebanon			1.31***	1.31***	−2.68***	−2.68***
			(0.06)	(0.06)	(0.51)	(0.51)
Morocco					0.79***	0.79***
					(0.23)	(0.23)
Palestine			−0.21**	−0.21**	−1.69***	−1.69***
			(0.09)	(0.09)	(0.21)	(0.21)
Saudi Arabia			3.39***	3.39***		
			(0.69)	(0.69)		
Sudan			−1.21***	−1.21***	0.43***	0.43***
			(0.12)	(0.12)	(0.05)	(0.05)
Tunisia			0.53***	0.53***		
			(0.06)	(0.06)		
Yemen			−0.52	−0.52		
			(0.55)	(0.55)		
AIC	2,321.72	2,321.72	10,505.90	10,505.90	9,053.61	9,053.61
Log likelihood	−1,135.86	−1,135.86	−5,222.95	−5,222.95	−4,496.81	−4,496.81
Deviance	2,271.72	2,271.72	10,046.72	10,046.72	9,101.18	9,101.18
N	3,508	3,508	9,256	9,256	10,121	10,121

Notes: ***$p < 0.001$; **$p < 0.01$; *$p < 0.05$. Wave 1: Models 1 and 2. Wave 2: Models 3 and 4. Wave 3: Models 5 and 6.

were redesigning their structures due to the Arab uprisings, the groups were not significantly different in their assessments. Nonetheless, these results provide further indication that these populations hold different political preferences. Again, the suitability questions are limited by their focus on a particular country rather than general support.

104 *Defining Democracy*

Implications and Limitations

This Arab Barometer data is an opening for considering the connection between citizens' understanding of *dimuqratiyya* and the potential for democratic commitment. It is evident even in these regressions that this is not an issue of a distinction without a difference. These groups have different conceptions of *dimuqratiyya*, and they engage with politics differently.

PCD are more likely to participate in politics, both institutional and not. That extends to political violence. This means that social movements—including democratization movements—are more likely to be made in their image. To understand social movements, their motivations, and their objectives, researchers must hear from participants. However, they cannot be confused with a representative subsection of the population and its opinions. If—as this chapter has probed and the rest of the book will discuss—they have different political preferences, then these groups can tell only part of the story of MENA opinion.

The only exception to this is voting. PCD are no more or less likely to vote than SECD. This is true even though they show different rates of party affiliation. This could be because about half of MENA respondents indicated that they voted, which means it is a much more common form of political participation than the others considered here. Although the other forms of participation may be aimed at politicians, voting directly engages the government. The votes are cast and counted. It is expected that something will happen based on a parliamentary election—namely, that seats will be allocated based on the result; whether this occurs is part of electoral fairness. The other forms of participation, although they can have observable outputs and influence state actors and actions, are not express means of controlling part of the state. It thus appears that SECD use fewer of the opportunities they might have to impact the state. They have not, however, entirely ceded the field.

The divergence extends also to differences in ideals. These citizens express different levels of support for institutionalizing democracy in the fuzzy form implied by the questions by mixing the word *dimuqratiyya* and these maximalist liberal democracy descriptors. This difference is empirically informative for understanding both how citizens understand the words researchers, politicos, and policy professionals are using and how citizens feel about democracy.

These data, however, have inexorable limitations. First, the data are dated. The first three waves of the Arab Barometer are not fundamentally that old; even the oldest only turns the clock back fifteen years.

Dimuqratiyya *and Political Behavior*   105

However, given the youth bulge in the Middle East, fifteen years represents nontrivial population turnover. More pertinently, though, the survey sample may be politically extinct. The first wave predates the Arab Spring entirely. The subsequent waves occurred during or shortly after the Arab uprisings. The Egyptian data in all three waves predate the July 2013 military coup against the elected government of Mohamed Morsi. Libya's second civil war was not yet underway. Multiple waves of protests, such as the Rif and Hogra movements, had not yet taken place in Morocco. Countries, including Morocco and Tunisia, have held elections. States have rewritten constitutions. Researchers may dispute the extent to which the Arab uprisings were truly transformative for the region. They, as well as the many other movements that have happened since, however, ought not to be ignored with respect to citizens' political opinions.

A second limitation is the more pressing methodological concern: the questions. First, the question phrasing folds the problematic word *dimuqratiyya* into the descriptor. The apples-to-oranges problem cannot be entirely excised. Forces that drive respondents' relative *dimuqratiyya* evaluations of their own countries, like feeling they live in a safe area, are also influencing their support for the described institutions here. This can cloud the results. Furthermore, it leaves open the central question: How do they feel about *democracy*?

Second, the question of how good or bad the described regime would be for the country cannot speak to respondents' democratic commitment more broadly. Do they consider it the best form of government? Is it the only game in town? To answer these questions, more fine-grained questioning is required. Such questions and their relationship to citizens' understanding of *dimuqratiyya* will be addressed in the following chapters.

To understand MENA public opinion, particularly as it relates to democratic politics, new studies are required. The next chapters continue the examination of the implications of these diverse views of *dimuqratiyya*. These groups both want different states and propose different means to acquire them.

Notes

1. Researchers are often concerned that respondents will misreport political behavior. Voting behavior, for instance, is often assumed to be overreported because citizens believe that they are supposed to vote or that survey evaluators would want them to vote. It is thus theoretically possible that these studies are a generous estimate of political engagement. The voting reports in the Arab Barometer, though, are

106 *Defining Democracy*

consistent with the turnout metrics identified for these countries during the elections. This is good news for data reliability. Furthermore, there is no reason to believe that PCD and SECD would be systematically different in terms of a likelihood to report political behaviors *inaccurately*. Thus, there is not substantial concern that falsification would bias the result.

2. Doorenspleet (2015) goes in the completely opposite direction in this regard. In designing what he calls a "people-centered" democracy scoring system, he objects to the view that some citizens are "incorrect" about the meaning of democracy or that they "have a 'lack of awareness' and still need time to 'learn'" (479). He argues that the definition should be allowed to deviate in each country while continuing to compare the results across countries: "While people-centered measures might compare 'apples' with 'oranges,' this approach at least acknowledges that there are different types of fruit; better to accept those differences than to focus only on the apples, or—even worse—believe that fruit consists only of apples, so that we study only those apples" (487). The intention of this book is to take people's understandings into account while acknowledging that those difference create functional incomparability. Empirically and theoretically, it is unreasonable to compare apples to oranges and to pretend that they are the same foods.

3. Ariely and Davidov (2011, 274) evaluate the DAP using the World Values Survey. They claim the battery "taps support for democratic systems versus support for autocracies, like the rule of a strong leader or of the army. It is based on the assumption that people can discriminate between their current regime and conceivable options." I specifically *do not* adopt the position that support for democracy and support for particular forms of nondemocracy are mutually exclusive. In fact, this point is crucial for understanding democratic attitudes in the Middle East. Chapters 5 and 6 demonstrate that, even among democrats, it is often just one potentially acceptable regime among several. Ariely and Davidov recognize this fact empirically (279). The question about "democracy" does not load onto the same factors as the "authoritarian" questions, and they suggest it should be dropped from the scale. Within the Wave I data, these questions also do not demonstrate one latent trait under item response theory (IRT) modeling.

4. The focus on this maximalist definition here poses a challenge to assessing democratic commitment particularly in the Middle East. The question is double-barreled. Survey researchers typically avoid double-barreled questions because they ask about two attitudes at once. The inclusion of multiple items makes it difficult to tell which feature is driving the response. It may also introduce a multiplicative element by indicating that *each* feature, rather than any subset of the features, must be satisfied.

5

Democratic Commitment in Egypt

Bread. Freedom. Social Justice.
—Arab Spring chant

The preceding chapter presented initial evidence that citizens' understandings of *dimuqratiyya* are linked to their political preferences. Middle East/North Africa (MENA) citizens who conceive of *dimuqratiyya* primarily in political-institutional terms (PCD) engage with politics in their countries differently than those who conceive of *dimuqratiyya* primarily in terms of socioeconomic outcomes (SECD). They can also evince different regime-type preferences. This chapter continues this examination of the democracy-*dimuqratiyya* support gap. This chapter and the next engage with the relationship between individuals' understandings of *dimuqratiyya* and their regime-type preferences using recent surveys in Egypt and Morocco. In drawing on these studies, these chapters examine multiple questions related to contemporary democratic attitudes for more specific evaluations of democratic commitment. This chapter focuses on Egypt.

First the chapter provides a brief history of (non)democratization in Egypt. This is the background against which contemporary attitudes can be understood. Next it delineates the questions used to identify citizens' democratic attitudes in these surveys. These surveys were written to avoid the wording threats discussed in Chapter 4.

Multiple metrics have been used in public opinion research on democracy, tapping into different valences of meaning. The inclusion of multiple indicators thus creates a more comprehensive understanding of citizen preferences. Crucially, Egyptians' democratic preferences are not merely

108 *Defining Democracy*

yea or nay. Support for democracy can co-occur with support for autocratic systems. Thus, democracy, where applicable, is just one acceptable choice among several.

This finding exemplifies a central challenge to democratization in any region, including the Middle East. When will citizens stand by democracy? Dozens of photos of ink-stained voter fingers circulated after elections in Egypt and Iraq. These elected regimes did not endure. Democratic commitment—a willingness to stand by the election results—is harder to achieve than setting up a voting booth. This chapter examines relative levels of commitment to democracy and *dimuqratiyya* in Egypt.

Ultimately this chapter demonstrates that researchers have been overestimating popular democratic commitment. While Egyptians are not antidemocracy, they are not only interested in democratic systems. Furthermore, PCD and SECD in Egypt have different regime-type preferences. Namely, the results indicate that PCD Egyptians have more pro-democracy beliefs and are more likely to be committed democrats.

These results emphasize how important it is to understand how people think about these central concepts and institutions. After unpacking the implications of the democracy-*dimuqratiyya* gap for understanding democratization in Egypt, the chapter closes with a discussion of the pro-democracy factors identified in the survey responses. Unfortunately, few of these factors are actionable for would-be democratizers.

Democracy in Egypt

Egypt is an important case for understanding the discord between democracy and *dimuqratiyya* for several reasons. First, Egypt is the largest Arab country, with one hundred million inhabitants, and it plays a tremendous role in Arab culture and media, both within the region and in the Western imaginary. Second, Egypt was at the forefront of the reform-oriented protests of the Arab Spring. Chants from Tahrir Square—"Al-sha'ab yurīd isqāṭ al-niẓām" (The people want the overthrow of the regime)—created defining images of the event. It has a high profile for democratization efforts and for global popular consideration of what a Middle Eastern government can be.

Ultimately, Egypt had a military coup against an elected leadership that was described as a *dimuqratiyya* course of action. Statements both within Egypt and without invoked this point. For instance, a statement from Qatar's foreign ministry described the act as "the will of Egypt and its people." Sheikh Abdullah bin Zayed al-Nahyan, the United Arab

Emirates' foreign minister, stated, "The great Egyptian army was able to prove again that they are the fence of Egypt and that they are the protector and strong shield that guarantee Egypt will remain a state of institutions and law" ("International Reactions" 2013). Governments' responses were often guided by state or political interest rather than a strong sense of political theory. For instance, Tunisia's Islamist Ennahda denounced the act as a "flagrant coup," while the major secular party, Nida Touns, saluted "the victory of the Egyptian people." Saudi officials and Iraqi prime minister Nouri al-Maliki conveyed support for the military-installed president. Al-Maliki's spokesman reported they were "certain that the new president will move on with the new plan in holding elections and safeguarding national reconciliation" ("World Leaders" 2013). Turkey's AKP, which had aligned with Mohamed Morsi, however, struck a different tone, calling the action "unacceptable" ("International Reactions" 2013).

Coups have historically been one of several nondemocratic avenues for democratization, both intentionally and unintentionally (Miller 2021). For further discussion of the democratic legitimacy of military-imposed democratic institutions, see Kirshner (2010). The statements made by other MENA regime figures about this coup bear a greater affinity to expressions of their parties' capacity to work with or against the military-controlled Egyptian government than to strident claims about a philosophy of governance.[1] These regimes seek common cause more than a beacon of popular representation. The nuance captured in this moment linking a military coup to *dimuqratiyya* was a seed that germinated into this book.[2]

A brief history of Egypt's stutter-step democratization process is instructive. Following a military coup in 1952, Egypt spent decades as a functionally single-party state. States of emergency were habitually declared, suspending constitutional rights. In recent decades a single leader, Hosni Mubarak of the National Democratic Party (NDP), controlled the government. For most of his reign, the president was not elected by the public; he was chosen by parliament and affirmed by public referendum. Turnout in the referenda could be as low as 10 percent ("Opposition Claims" 2005). Opposition parties grew in the 1980s, but legal reforms in the 1990s placed limits on free expression and association to curb their involvement: "By the late 1990s not only had parliamentary politics become stagnant and virtually irrelevant to the life of the country, but alternative avenues for political expression were severely hampered as well" (Dunn 2006, 4). The 2000s saw shakeups within the NDP and the strengthening of opposition groups, including

110 Defining Democracy

the Muslim Brotherhood and leftist and Nasserite groups. Despite the repression of the Gamal Abdel Nasser period, the economic improvements of the period can be recalled positively (Beinin 2015). Although reforms were instituted, they were designed to prevent these opposition groups from taking power (Dunn 2006). In 2005, a multicandidate election was held. Mubarak won in a landslide, though voter turnout is estimated at only 30 percent (Williams and Wright 2005). US foreign aid was supposed to promote democracy and human rights, but it did not. Instead, the regime used its strategic importance to the United States to turn aid to economic assistance instead of political liberalization; it was able to ensure that industry privatization and market liberalization favored regime allies (Snider 2022).

The Arab Spring seemed to present a turning point here. Widespread economic challenges led to calls for political and social transformation. Protests spread across the region after initial protests in Tunisia. Informal labor and unemployment, corruption, and poverty were and remain salient challenges in the Middle East. Despite growing gross domestic product in the period before the Arab Spring, unemployment was a "chronic socioeconomic inequity," although rates were decreasing (Hong 2019, 68). The markets were not growing fast enough to sustain the coming of age of the youth-skewed population, especially in countries that relied on the employment-inelastic natural resources sectors (Hong 2019). The Mubarak regime framed itself as the "steward of economic reforms" while sternly policing the public, engaging in corruption, and not saving the economy (El-Ghobashy 2021, 83). Citizens' responses to their economic circumstances and the police responses to their efforts resulted in several deaths, including high-profile suicides, protests, police reprisals, and more protests.

The Arab Spring protests had economic instigations and objectives that naturally intertwined with political goals. Surveys conducted in Egypt in June and July 2011 found that the first and second most important reasons for the protests were demands for economic improvements and reduced corruption (Arab Barometer II). The same pattern was evident in Tunisia (Arab Barometer II). In both cases, civil and political freedoms were only the third most cited motivation at best. In retrospective surveys in 2013, a larger share of respondents identified a desire for political freedoms as a motivator for the Arab Spring protests, though improving the economic conditions and fighting corruption remained prevalent responses (Arab Barometer III). This change could reflect the media narrative of political reform or the political reforms that had occurred in many states—though not all changes favored democratization.

Democratic Commitment in Egypt   111

Retrospective surveys taken in 2018 further demonstrate the protestors' economic considerations. According to Yildirim and McCain (2019, 1), "Improving economic conditions was chosen as the principal goal of the protests in half of the countries in the survey. Respondents in many of these nations also ranked tackling corruption and social justice as important goals, seemingly indicating a perceived relationship between economic woes and corruption." Political freedoms were far less likely to be cited. Yildirim and McCain conclude that their surveys results contradict "the widely held belief that democratization constituted the most important aim of Arab Spring protests" (2). Furthermore, most respondents believed the goals, political or economic, were not attained.

Social movements, such that they challenge the relationship between the state and the citizen, are inherently political in some interpretations, although their motivations may be economic, because they address political relationships: Rachik (2016, 16) writes, "Even if the social movement does not claim to conquer the political power, it is not without reference to politics. The social movement is an indicator that permits, among other things, putting into relief the process of social change and the evolution of the nature of the relationships that connect the State to the citizen, without neglecting its effect on the political public and on politics, in a general manner."[3]

Although the masses may not have assembled initially for politically democratic reasons, they addressed matters of public will and goals for the state. Rachik's interpretation certainly would suggest that governments should take social movements as a political bellwether regardless of expressed focus. The results were, in some of the countries, in favor of democracy, at least for a time (e.g., Tunisia), though in others authoritarian regimes persisted (e.g., Jordan) or the states fell into war (e.g., Libya).

In Egypt, the Arab Spring resulted in the ouster of President Hosni Mubarak. This opened the possibility of fundamental reformation of the state structure. The opposition forces were ultimately not able to accomplish this. They were united enough in what they did *not* want to take down the incumbent without being united enough in what they desired to cooperate in a political vacuum. Horizontal structures formed during the protests, but these were not proto-governing bodies (Stacher 2020).

In order for a shock to the system, such as the unanticipated protests of the Arab Spring, to lead to regime change, there must be potential political actors ready to seize the moment, and there must be a "usable state" "capable of maintaining territorial integrity, holding elections, and establishing a national government" (Miller 2021, 52). In

112 *Defining Democracy*

Egypt, the military and the Muslim Brotherhood were the groups most able to take that opportunity.[4] Neither body was grounded in strong democratic principles.

For democratization, Egypt would then have to navigate what Hassan, Kendall, and Whitefields (2018) dub the Scylla and Charybdis of Egyptian politics: Islamist and military rule. On one hand, the Muslim Brotherhood, which had painted itself as a moral alternative to corrupt governments, was institutionally better prepared for an electoral campaign than other potential parties due to its decades of civil society organization development. The Muslim Brotherhood experienced substantial targeted repression during the old regime. The repression unified the membership, but it also drove a wedge between the Muslim Brotherhood and other opposition groups that made the opposition organizations unable to cooperate in forming a new regime (Nugent 2020).

The military, on the other hand, offered "a symbol of stability and continuity at times of uncertainty" (Hassan, Kendall, and Whitefields 2018, 281). Unlike the security forces, the military has "generally withdrawn from the political realm" (Dunn 2006, 14). It is composed of "citizen-soldiers" and had largely focused on external threats rather than the populace, which garnered it popular goodwill (Hassan, Kendall, and Whitefields 2018, 281). In fact, Feldman (2020) points out that the phraseology of the aforementioned chant willing the overthrow of the regime leaves open that it could be effectuated by any body, including the military, not just the people. In that sense, it may not even be a pro-democracy chant at all. Despite the connection of several nondemocratic leaders in Egypt's history to the military, another Tahrir slogan asserted, "The army and the people are one hand" (Feldman 2020, 16). The idea that the military represents the public voice recalls the argument that the Janissary Corp embodied the public will in the Ottoman Empire (Şiviloğlu's 2018). Subsequent research posits that the military was more complicit in state violence than people, having blamed the police, realized (El-Ghobashy 2021). Ultimately, the military at least cooperated with Mubarak's removal. As such, it presented a potentially compelling source of governance, regardless of its less-than-democratic past.

That Islamism and the military were seen as the sources of stability demonstrates how "the intense fear of democracy's consequences" "drives hybrid authoritarianism" (Stepan and Linz 2013, 23). Seeing democracy as a threat to the social, economic, and cultural well-being of the Arab world makes Arabs less likely to think that it is appropriate for their countries (Benstead 2015). Weak or absent "pacts" between secular and religious forces or civilian and military forces can lead to failure in the face of such fear.

Democratic Commitment in Egypt 113

After Mubarak resigned, a temporary military government, the Supreme Council of the Armed Forces, formed. Following a constitutional referendum in 2011, parliamentary elections were held. The National Democratic Party was banned, leaving an open field for new parties. The elections produced an exclusivist political environment that featured a narrow choice between regime remnants and Islamists and sidelined the Egyptians who wanted to entirely restructure the state (Stacher 2020). The weak civil society, especially combined with the strong military, meant that other groups were ill positioned to oppose the military-Islamist "deal" to keep others out of the elections (Bellin 2018, 459). Civil society development in general has a loose relationship to democratization in the Middle East. While many countries have multitudes of organizations and associations, some affiliate with or support the autocrats, whereas others do not; organizations' ability to promote interpersonal trust, popular mobilization, or interest in participatory government is contingent on their regime (non)affiliation. Before and after the Arab Spring, workers' groups were better positioned to support pro-democracy movements in Tunisia than they were in Egypt because of their position relative to the regimes (Beinin 2015). Similarly, Jamal (2007) shows that civil association groups' clientelistic ties to the Moroccan, Egyptian, Jordanian, and Palestinian regimes promoted or discouraged members' interest in democratization. Ultimately, in Egypt, Islamist parties received large blocs, leading to opposition concerns about their intended policies and the continuation of democracy; the constitutionality of the seat allocations was later challenged. Mohamed Morsi became president in 2012. Shortly after, in July 2013, a coup d'état removed him and put forward a new constitutional referendum.

Field Marshal Abdel Fattah el-Sisi retired from the military after the coup and ran for president in 2014. El-Sisi was somewhat popular with Egyptians, though more so with Coptic Christians and secularists: "In a choice between the authoritarianism of the regime and the Muslim Brotherhood, the liberals will choose the army" (Truex and Tavana 2019, 1023, quoting Steven A. Cook). El-Sisi won an election boycotted by the Muslim Brotherhood and some other parties. In the subsequent election, in 2018, he did not face serious opposition. Post–Arab Spring elections have featured turnout in the 40 to 50 percent range, reflecting these boycotts ("El-Sisi" 2014). Those who challenged him reported "a sweeping effort to kill off their campaigns before they ha[d] begun, with media attacks on candidates, intimidation of supporters and a nomination process stacked in favor of the former general" (Ismail and Abdelaty 2018). Postcoup, Egyptian politics have reverted in many ways. It is against this backdrop that public opinion on Egyptian democracy must be understood.

114 *Defining Democracy*

Measuring Democratic Commitment

Support for democracy is typically measured based on individuals' willingness to identify it as the best form of government and/or their belief that democracy is appropriate for their country (Tessler and Gao 2005). Belief in democracy's superiority is somewhat abstract; it does not indicate that this ideal would or could be realized in a particular context. Addressing only this element risks overestimating democratic commitments, because it does not demonstrate what would happen to support when the rubber met the road (Kiewiet de Jonge 2016). Will respondents support electoral democracy when faced with using it in practice? Those who believe that democracy is both the best form of government and that it is appropriate for their country are referred to as committed democrats.

Fuchs and Roller (2006) propose that consolidation occurs when a majority of the population believes democracy is the best form of government. Linz and Stepan (1996, 15) set a higher standard; a democracy is consolidated when it is "the only game in town." Being the only game implies not only acceptance of democracy but rejection of other systems, like military or expert rule, as acceptable (Mattes and Bratton 2007; Hoffman 2020). Albrecht et al. (2021, 2) specifically call out support for military involvement in particular as "anti-system sentiments" for MENA democracy, whereas support for less overtly political civil society actors (e.g., major unions) is a reflection of "anti-political establishment sentiments" (3). Those who approve only of democracy can be called singular democrats. While such people exist everywhere, they are not the predominant population, even in established democracies (Wike et al. 2017), and nontrivial populations in established democracies express an openness to unelected governments (Wuttke, Gavras, and Schoen 2020). This standard might appear to be a better indicator of consolidation, because it sets a high threshold with the affirmative rejection of alternatives; that even large minorities of residents in what are considered established democracies still accept some alternatives shows that it is not obligatory for stability.

To measure democratic commitment here, I include multiple indicators of regime-type preference. The study draws on standard democratic support questions, but they are rewritten to avoid the *dimuqratiyya/* democracy confusion. They must tap into democratic support without invoking the word *dimuqratiyya*. A brief discussion of these questions is thus in order.

In framing these questions, a minimalist definition of democracy is employed. Chapter 2 demonstrated that when political scientists talk about democracy—and when they measure it empirically—they are most often using a minimalist definition of democracy. Consequently, for these surveys, respondents answered questions not about *dimuqratiyya* but about elected government or choosing the government by election.

In this language, the regime is indicated to be determined by the elections, to have attained power or legitimacy through the electoral process. With this focus, the electoral returns are specified as carrying binding weight for the system. The wording is thus able to combine both reference to the central institutional feature of the democratic system and to encapsulate the idea that it is a choice by the people. It is not the mere act of holding an election.[5]

Attitudes toward electoral democracy were assessed by several questions. The first is a direct-preference question frequently included in cross-national surveys:

> In terms of potential governments, which of these three statements is closest to your opinion?
>
> 1. An elected government is always preferable to any other kind of government.
> 2. There are circumstances when an unelected government can be preferable.
> 3. For someone like me, it doesn't matter what kind of government we have.

A binary variable identifies people who respond that "elected government is always preferable to any other kind of government." They also were asked "To what extent do you think choosing the government by election is appropriate for your country?" on a four-point scale from very inappropriate to very appropriate. A binary indicator for committed democrats identifies those respondents who indicated that choosing the government by election was the best form of government and that it is very or somewhat appropriate for Egypt.

The Egyptian survey takers were also asked to accept or reject several systems of government on a scale from strongly approve to strongly disapprove. Democracy was included in this list as a system with multiple parties competing in elections. The other systems were those in which only one party is allowed to stand for election or hold office; the army governs the country; elections and parliament are abolished, and the president decides everything; and a system governed by Islamic law without elections.[6] Those respondents who disparaged the four alternative options while also approving of the democracy option are the singular democrats.

116 *Defining Democracy*

By these metrics, the surveys here reveal reasonably strong support for democracy among Egyptians: 60.3 percent say that elected government is the best form of government, while only 21 percent believe that there are circumstances in which unelected governments are preferable. This is in line with the support for multiparty elections Hassan, Kendall, and Whitefields (2018) found in 2014. This is less than the 70 percent of Egyptians who reported (strongly) agreeing that *dimuqratiyya* "may have problems" but is "better than other systems" in the 2018 Arab Barometer. This approximately ten-percentage-point disparity is the democracy-*dimuqratiyya* gap.

According to 78.7 percent, choosing the government by election is appropriate for Egypt. A supermajority of respondents, then, are open to instituting elected government in their country as it currently is. This is an indication that acceptance of democracy is stronger than a belief in its superiority as a system: it could work, but something else might be better.

What is best and what is acceptable do not necessarily go hand in hand, however. Of those who said that elections are the best way to choose the government, only 82.3 percent said that this method was very or somewhat appropriate for Egypt. This leaves nearly a fifth of Egyptians who think it is a good idea in theory but that it would not be right in practice. These people are unlikely then to push for democratization, at least right now. In turn, 61.7 percent of those who said it did not matter to them if the government was elected and 76.7 percent of those who said that unelected governments were sometimes best indicated that democracy was very or somewhat appropriate for Egypt. Democracy, then, is something these people would settle for, not idealize. Half (50.6 percent) of respondents are committed democrats, meaning they said democracy is best and that it is appropriate. Egypt clears Fuchs and Roller's (2006) threshold for democratic commitment.

As for the more conservative standard, 36 percent of Egyptians are singular democrats. A large share of Egyptians reported approving multiparty electoral democracy (83.9 percent). However, they accept other systems as well: 25.6 percent approved of one-party systems, 38.6 percent approved of military government, 19.3 percent endorsed strongman governance, and 30.3 percent would approve a system that employed Islamic law without elections. The particularly high acceptance of a military system should be unsurprising given Egypt's history and the argument that the military can represent the voice or will of the people. Recall from Chapter 2 that 20.5 percent of Egyptians stated that a country run by the military would qualify as somewhat or very *dimuqratiyya*. Not only are many Egyptians accepting of military intervention, but some affirm its connection to *dimuqratiyya*. Nontrivial endorsement of a religious regime is consistent with the history as well. The negative experiences under one-party rule by the New Democratic Party would explain the particularly low scores for single-party and strongman systems. Still 16.4 percent considered it *dimuqratiyya* if the elected leader was never challenged; 13.2 percent thought *dimuqratiyya* included banning parties. While low, these levels are higher than have been identified in other states; the 2017 Global Attitudes Survey found that a median 27 percent of MENA respondents supported "representative democracy" and rejected rule by a strongman, experts, and the military (Wike et al. 2017). Thus Egyptians are not overtly and en masse opposed to democracy. Democracy is merely one of several potentially permissible regimes.

Carrión (2008, 21) characterizes those who "choose democracy as their preferred system of government but are also willing to support authoritarian or 'delegative' acts 'when circumstances merit it'" as ambivalents. He proposes that "'democrats' are not willing to sacrifice the [democracy] for [economic development] whereas the 'ambivalents' are" (21). This recalls Habib Bourguiba's characterization of Tunisians who "prioritized bread over loyalty to the party and the nation" as "khobzists," which is to say bread-ists (Beinin 2016, 21). This concern about a willingness to trade away democracy will be discussed further in Chapter 7.

Surveying Egyptians

In order to introduce these modified democracy questions, original surveys were required. Surveys were conducted in both Egypt and Morocco using YouGov's Middle East/North Africa panel. This panel has been used in previous political science studies (Nyhan and Zeitzoff 2018; Blackman and Jackson 2019; Ridge 2022a). YouGov MENA is an online opt-in panel that encompasses multiple Middle East/North African countries; YouGov aims to provide an age- and gender-representative panel. The survey was anonymous. The questionnaire was available both in English and in Arabic. Analyses focus on the 946 Egyptian nationals who completed the Arabic-language survey questionnaire in order to focus on interpretations of *dimuqratiyya*. For more information about conducting surveys in the Middle East, respondent demographics, and the respondents' feelings about participating in a political survey, consult Appendix A.

The crucial variables here are the respondents' conceptions of *dimuqratiyya*. The same measurement is used here as was used in Chapter 3. The respondents are grouped by what they identified as the first and

118 *Defining Democracy*

second most essential features of *dimuqratiyya* and labeled as PCD, Mixed PCD, Mixed SECD, or SECD. This grouping is included in the models as a factor variable with SECD as the reference category. As in Chapter 4, it is anticipated that these groups have different regime-type preferences. This chapter continues the demonstration of the different levels of public support that democracy and *dimuqratiyya* enjoy.

Additional variables are included based on prior studies of democratic opinion. Modernization theory, religion, social integration, and present circumstances are all seen as drivers of public opinion formation. Modernization theory, in its earliest iterations, focused on a broad trend in state development, in which economic development, education, secularization, and democratization are co-occurring phenomena, rather than on individual attitudes (Lerner 1958). Subsequent modifications propose that wealth accumulation leads to increases in "self-expression values," like participation, environmentalism, and tolerance, that would lead to support for democratization (Welzel 2021a). This updated modernization theory is expressly describing an individuated transformation. If modernization theory, in either conception, translates to the individual level, then urban dwellers, the educated, and the wealthy would all be more supportive of electoral democracy. A strong effect of urbanization has not been demonstrated in previous studies of the Arab world (Ciftci 2013; Jamal 2006); while urban dwellers anticipate gains through democratization (Mernissi 1992), they also witness the inefficiencies of democratizing regimes (Jamal 2006). Education and higher incomes are often associated with democratic preferences (Carrión 2008; Rose 2002), though the effects are inconsistent across contexts (Shafiq 2010; Ciftci 2013; Jamal 2006). Liberal values (e.g., gender egalitarianism and outgroup tolerance) have also been linked to democratic attitudes in the Middle East, although not all liberals are democrats (Ciftci 2010; Ridge 2022b). Political engagement has also been linked to democratic interest (Benstead 2015) and rejection of nondemocratic alternatives (Mattes and Bratton 2007).

Religious groups may have different democratic preferences. Although Islam has been treated as antidemocratic, Muslims may support democracy, especially when they are in a majority (Hoffman 2020; Rafiqi 2019), while minorities may fear the loss of rights from democratization (Ridge 2022a). Secularists are also supposedly more likely to support democracy (Ciftci 2010). Those who view democracy as a threat to Islam and Islamic values may oppose it on that basis (Benstead 2015). They might even favor an Islamic regime. Religiosity has been linked inconsistently to regime-type preferences both for democracy and for religious regimes (Breznau et al. 2011; Ciftci 2013).

Democratic Commitment in Egypt **119**

Satisfaction with a nondemocratic regime can also reduce interest in democracy. Individuals who benefit from the regime, including via clientelism and corruption, have less incentive to support change (Jamal 2007). Those who are financially secure might similarly resist transitions, despite the assumed connections between economic development and democratic support. Interpersonal trust is linked to supporting the current regime, undermining democratic interest (Jamal and Nooruddin 2010). Similarly, those who fear losing the stability that nondemocratic governments provide may oppose alternative regime structures (Benstead 2015). That does not mean all nondemocratic alternatives would be equal in their eyes. These citizens may evince instrumental democratic or nondemocratic preferences (Mattes and Bratton 2007); that is different from having an institutional-elements-based or socioeconomic-outcomes-based view of *dimuqratiyya* or democracy, but it could make their regime support more fluid. After all, intrinsic support for democracy, a strongman, or shari'a law would persist despite temporary circumstances and contextual appropriateness; instrumental support would be more context dependent.

Experience with the West is also considered. Mernissi (1992), for instance, linked support for democracy to access to Western culture and knowledge. Certainly not all MENA nationals who live or work in the West have positive experiences with democracy or secularism. The relationship between visiting Europe, the United States, or Canada and regime-type preferences, though, remains to be explored.

Table 5.1 presents the crosstabulations of the four-part understanding categorization and expressed democratic support. In no case is conception of *dimuqratiyya* perfectly predictive of democratic attitudes. The PCD-SECD allotment are indications of how citizens describe *dimuqratiyya*. They are not, themselves, statements of whether or not the respondent supports or opposes democracy or *dimuqratiyya*. They are indications of meaning. There are democrats and skeptics in both camps. Nevertheless, the support is significantly different between the groups for several democratic indicators. This indicates that studies that have casually grouped them to study public opinion on *dimuqratiyya* have misestimated at least some citizens' interest in democracy.

Regression analyses introduces covariates that could make citizens more or less responsive to democratic governance in theory or in practice. Variables include satisfaction with the ruling regime, whether it is "more important to have a government that can get things done, even if we have no influence over what it does," and whether the respondent would subordinate electoral participation because "elections sometimes produce bad results." Several religious covariates are included, especially

Table 5.1 Conception of *Dimuqratiyya* and Democratic Attitudes in Egypt

	Elected Government Is Preferable to Any Other Kind of Government		Extent to Which Electoral Democracy Is Appropriate for Egypt				Committed Democrat		Singular Democrat	
	No	Yes**	Very Inappropriate	Somewhat Inappropriate	Somewhat Appropriate	Very Appropriate*	No	Yes**	No	Yes
SECD	161	181	27	55	179	81	191	151	217	125
Mixed SECD	71	106	11	21	88	57	84	93	118	59
Mixed PCD	100	175	20	48	119	88	134	141	180	95
PCD	42	110	11	24	56	61	64	88	96	56

Notes: ** ANOVA test $p < 0.05$. * ANOVA test $p < 0.10$ ($n = 946$).

Democratic Commitment in Egypt   121

whether the respondent is a Muslim or a member of another religion. While most Egyptians are Muslim, about 10 percent are Christians. Daily engagement with prayer and scripture is included. Secularist orientation is also noted based on favoring religious people holding public office, believing religious leaders should not attempt to influence citizens' vote choices, and believing the government should attempt to enact Islamic law. Another variable indicates agreement that electing the government is compliant with Islamic law. Demographic characteristics, such as gender, urban residence, interpersonal trust, tertiary education, income sufficiency, age, political interest, news viewership, and region of residence, are also addressed. Experiencing living or working in the West recently and holding gender-egalitarian views are included. For more information on the coding of these variables, see Appendix C.

As belief that elected government is the best form of government is measured with binary variables, the effects are tested with binary logistic regression. Whether government by election is appropriate for the country is evaluated using an ordered linear regression model. Being a committed democrat and being a singular democrat are both binary categorizations. Recall that the former refers to individuals who fulfill two criteria; they must state that elected government is the best form of government and that it is appropriate or very appropriate for the country. The latter are those who approved of multiparty democracy while disapproving of all the nondemocratic options. The models also use binary logistic regression.

Predictors of support for these nondemocratic additional regime types are also evaluated. In most research, "scholars of democratic consolidation have largely neglected the political alternatives that citizens are willing to support," but if political science is to understand democratization and democratic durability, the citizens' attitudes toward these alternatives must also be understood (Albrecht et al. 2021, 20). These alternate-structure questions provide a necessary complement to the understanding of citizens' preferences over democracy. They are ordered logistic regression models using the four-point scale of acceptability. All models include the YouGov survey weights. Region-fixed effects are included; Cairo is the reference category.

PCD, SECD, and Democracy

PCD and SECD in Egypt have different regime-type preferences. These results show then that not only do these citizens have different understandings of *dimuqratiyya* as a construct but these conceptions relate

122 *Defining Democracy*

distinctly to their attitudes toward democracy. This measurable difference between the meaning clusters manifests in their attitudes both toward electoral democracy and toward other systems of government.

The results show a significant positive relationship between PCD and support for government by election in Egypt (Table 5.2). The more political the individual's conception of *dimuqratiyya*, the more likely he is to believe that choosing the government by election is the best system. More political understandings of *dimuqratiyya* are also associated

Table 5.2 Democratic Commitment in Egypt

	Model 1	Model 2	Model 3	Model 4
(Intercept)	−0.91*		−1.44***	−1.93***
	(0.50)		(0.49)	(0.55)
Mixed SECD	0.48**	0.44**	0.45**	−0.13
	(0.20)	(0.18)	(0.20)	(0.23)
Mixed PCD	0.47***	0.18	0.31*	−0.12
	(0.18)	(0.16)	(0.17)	(0.19)
PCD	0.88***	0.57***	0.60***	−0.08
	(0.23)	(0.20)	(0.22)	(0.24)
Government	−0.27***	0.49***	0.09	−0.90***
evaluation	(0.09)	(0.09)	(0.09)	(0.11)
Most people	−0.08	−0.29	−0.16	0.46**
can be trusted	(0.21)	(0.18)	(0.20)	(0.23)
News consumption:	0.18	0.15	0.18	0.29
daily	(0.17)	(0.15)	(0.16)	(0.18)
Scripture reading:	0.04	0.39***	0.02	−0.35**
daily	(0.16)	(0.14)	(0.16)	(0.18)
Prayer: daily	0.36**	−0.06	0.12	0.10
	(0.18)	(0.16)	(0.18)	(0.19)
Interested in politics	0.49***	0.36**	0.47***	0.14
	(0.16)	(0.14)	(0.16)	(0.18)
Gender	−0.23**	0.01	−0.17	−0.45***
traditionalism	(0.11)	(0.10)	(0.11)	(0.12)
More important for	−0.14	0.34	0.11	0.38
the government	(0.27)	(0.23)	(0.26)	(0.28)
to be effective				
Elections can	−0.50***	−0.52***	−0.59***	−0.74***
produce bad results	(0.15)	(0.13)	(0.15)	(0.16)
Secularist orientation	−0.45***	−0.10	−0.32***	0.34***
	(0.10)	(0.09)	(0.10)	(0.11)
Elections are	0.68***	0.47***	0.74***	0.15
acceptable in	(0.20)	(0.18)	(0.20)	(0.22)
Islamic law				

continues

Table 5.2 Continued

	Model 1	Model 2	Model 3	Model 4
Male	0.13	−0.21	−0.03	0.24
	(0.17)	(0.15)	(0.16)	(0.19)
Unemployed	0.12	−0.09	−0.04	−0.22
	(0.17)	(0.15)	(0.17)	(0.19)
Religion: Christianity	0.03	−0.49**	−0.31	0.26
	(0.27)	(0.23)	(0.27)	(0.29)
Religion: none	1.10	−0.41	0.44	−14.81
	(0.86)	(0.69)	(0.77)	(473.57)
Income: covers	0.23	−0.01	0.13	0.35**
expenses	(0.16)	(0.14)	(0.15)	(0.17)
College education	−0.06	−0.14	0.04	0.55**
	(0.19)	(0.17)	(0.19)	(0.22)
Urban	−0.01	0.02	0.05	−0.15
	(0.19)	(0.17)	(0.19)	(0.22)
Spend time in	0.38	0.53**	0.30	−0.40
the West	(0.24)	(0.21)	(0.23)	(0.27)
25–29	0.24	0.39*	0.32	0.52*
	(0.24)	(0.21)	(0.23)	(0.27)
30–34	0.12	0.31	0.26	0.62*
	(0.28)	(0.25)	(0.27)	(0.32)
35–39	0.46	0.01	0.31	0.88***
	(0.30)	(0.26)	(0.29)	(0.33)
40+	0.12	0.68***	0.39*	0.86***
	(0.22)	(0.20)	(0.22)	(0.26)
Region: Canal Zone	−0.33	0.63**	−0.04	−0.04
	(0.35)	(0.31)	(0.34)	(0.40)
Region: Upper Egypt	−0.12	0.51***	0.02	−0.44*
	(0.22)	(0.19)	(0.21)	(0.23)
Region: Delta	−0.39**	0.26	−0.20	−0.16
	(0.20)	(0.17)	(0.19)	(0.21)
Region: Alexandria	−0.19	0.19	0.07	−0.05
	(0.22)	(0.19)	(0.21)	(0.23)
Region: Other	0.04	0.15	0.32	−0.49
	(0.50)	(0.42)	(0.48)	(0.58)
1|2		−1.60***		
		(0.44)		
2|3		−0.13		
		(0.43)		
3|4		2.23***		
		(0.44)		
AIC	1,315.82	2,137.95	1,375.48	1,169.10
Log likelihood	−625.91	−1,034.98	−655.74	−552.55
N	946	946	946	946

Notes: ***$p < 0.01$, **$p < 0.05$, *$p < 0.1$. Model 1: Best form of government (binary). Model 2: Appropriate for Egypt (ordered). Model 3: Committed democrat (binary). Model 4: Singular democrat (binary).

124 *Defining Democracy*

with believing that choosing the government by election is appropriate for Egypt. PCD are also significantly more likely to be committed democrats than SECD are.

There is no significant relationship between Egyptians' understanding of *dimuqratiyya* and their propensity to approve only of multiparty democracy as a system of government (Model 4). This could result from the weak relationship between citizens' understanding of *dimuqratiyya* and their (dis)approval of some of the regime types involved (Table 5.3). PCD in Egypt are more likely to approve of multiparty electoral

Table 5.3   Regime-Type Preferences in Egypt

	Model 1	Model 2	Model 3	Model 4	Model 5
Mixed SECD	−0.01	0.09	0.02	−0.03	0.19
	(0.18)	(0.18)	(0.19)	(0.18)	(0.18)
Mixed PCD	−0.41***	−0.02	−0.33**	−0.21	0.38**
	(0.16)	(0.16)	(0.16)	(0.16)	(0.16)
PCD	−0.15	−0.02	−0.45**	−0.53***	0.64***
	(0.19)	(0.20)	(0.21)	(0.20)	(0.20)
Government	1.47***	0.65***	1.17***	0.18**	−0.51***
evaluation	(0.09)	(0.09)	(0.09)	(0.08)	(0.08)
Most people	−0.50***	0.11	−0.00	0.18	0.26
can be trusted	(0.18)	(0.18)	(0.19)	(0.18)	(0.18)
News consumption:	0.01	−0.23	−0.27*	−0.31**	0.64***
daily	(0.14)	(0.15)	(0.15)	(0.15)	(0.15)
Scripture reading:	0.32**	−0.08	0.02	0.25*	−0.01
daily	(0.14)	(0.14)	(0.15)	(0.14)	(0.14)
Prayer: daily	−0.10	−0.14	−0.00	0.20	0.15
	(0.16)	(0.16)	(0.17)	(0.16)	(0.16)
Interested	−0.06	0.13	−0.28*	0.16	0.15
in politics	(0.14)	(0.15)	(0.15)	(0.15)	(0.15)
Gender	0.26***	0.30***	0.54***	0.71***	0.06
traditionalism	(0.10)	(0.10)	(0.10)	(0.10)	(0.10)
More important	−0.27	0.39	0.28	0.04	0.09
for the	(0.24)	(0.24)	(0.26)	(0.24)	(0.24)
government to					
be effective					
Elections	0.65***	1.07***	0.72***	0.51***	−0.30**
can produce	(0.13)	(0.14)	(0.14)	(0.14)	(0.13)
bad results					
Secularist	0.03	−0.55***	−0.27***	−0.83***	−0.04
orientation	(0.09)	(0.09)	(0.09)	(0.09)	(0.09)
Elections are	0.04	0.13	0.13	0.35*	0.22
acceptable in	(0.18)	(0.18)	(0.19)	(0.18)	(0.18)
Islamic law					

continues

Table 5.3 Continued

	Model 1	Model 2	Model 3	Model 4	Model 5
Male	−0.32**	−0.09	−0.20	−0.17	0.38**
	(0.15)	(0.15)	(0.16)	(0.15)	(0.15)
Unemployed	0.34**	0.06	0.26	0.01	−0.17
	(0.15)	(0.15)	(0.16)	(0.15)	(0.15)
Religion:	0.18	0.48**	0.38	−0.88***	−0.09
Christianity	(0.23)	(0.24)	(0.25)	(0.26)	(0.24)
Religion: none	0.39	1.42**	0.62	0.63	−1.60**
	(0.67)	(0.67)	(0.64)	(0.64)	(0.64)
Income: able to	−0.24*	−0.12	−0.24*	−0.03	0.10
meet needs	(0.14)	(0.14)	(0.14)	(0.14)	(0.14)
College education	−0.10	−0.02	−0.21	−0.46***	−0.17
	(0.17)	(0.17)	(0.18)	(0.17)	(0.17)
Urban	−0.03	0.17	−0.28	−0.16	0.15
	(0.17)	(0.17)	(0.18)	(0.18)	(0.17)
Spend time in	0.13	0.36*	0.25	0.06	0.54**
the West	(0.21)	(0.22)	(0.22)	(0.22)	(0.22)
25–29	0.16	0.04	−0.13	−0.28	0.53**
	(0.21)	(0.21)	(0.22)	(0.21)	(0.21)
30–34	0.10	−0.49*	−0.20	−0.22	0.67***
	(0.25)	(0.25)	(0.26)	(0.25)	(0.25)
35–39	0.07	−0.15	0.04	−0.26	0.68**
	(0.26)	(0.27)	(0.27)	(0.27)	(0.27)
40+	0.06	−0.45**	−0.18	−0.48**	0.58***
	(0.20)	(0.20)	(0.21)	(0.20)	(0.20)
Region:	0.01	−0.25	0.18	0.61*	−0.04
Canal Zone	(0.30)	(0.31)	(0.34)	(0.32)	(0.32)
Region:	0.16	0.02	0.14	0.35*	−0.34*
Upper Egypt	(0.19)	(0.19)	(0.19)	(0.19)	(0.19)
Region: Delta	0.17	0.02	0.13	0.34*	−0.44**
	(0.17)	(0.18)	(0.18)	(0.18)	(0.18)
Region:	−0.21	−0.16	−0.19	0.09	−0.30
Alexandria	(0.19)	(0.19)	(0.20)	(0.19)	(0.20)
Region: Other	0.20	0.23	0.15	−0.26	−0.13
	(0.41)	(0.43)	(0.44)	(0.43)	(0.44)
1|2	−1.36***	−0.46	−0.83*	−1.62***	−1.96***
	(0.45)	(0.45)	(0.47)	(0.46)	(0.46)
2|3	0.48	2.23***	1.75***	1.04**	−0.54
	(0.45)	(0.46)	(0.48)	(0.46)	(0.45)
3|4	2.57***	4.26***	3.10***	3.13***	1.92***
	(0.45)	(0.48)	(0.49)	(0.47)	(0.45)
AIC	2,185.92	2,027.59	1,918.25	2,028.25	2,044.99
Log likelihood	−1,058.96	−979.80	−925.13	−980.12	−988.50
N	946	946	946	946	946

Notes: ***p < 0.01, **p < 0.05, *p < 0.1. Model 1: Army runs the government (ordered). Model 2: Only one legal party (ordered). Model 3: Abolish elections and parliament (ordered). Model 4: Government by Islamic law (ordered). Model 5: Multiparty elections (ordered).

126 *Defining Democracy*

democracy. They are also less likely to approve of a system governed by Islamic law without elections or strongman rule. Mixed PCD are less likely than SECD to endorse army and strongman rule. In general, though, the conception of *dimuqratiyya* among Egyptians does not predict support for military regimes or having only one legal party.

Attitudes toward authoritarians and elections themselves are also driving democratic opinion. Egyptians who are pleased with the current authoritarian regime are less likely to think that democracy is the answer. Afterall, nondemocracy is working out. Unsurprisingly, then, they are more likely to endorse the several nondemocratic alternative regimes. These citizens are open to the idea of democracy in Egypt; they are not, however, committed to democracy.

Egyptians who believe elections may need to be replaced because they can produce bad results are, rather unsurprisingly, less likely to think electoral democracy is the best form of government or that it is appropriate for Egypt, and they are less likely to be committed or singular democrats. Egyptians who believe elections are prone to produce bad results are more likely to accept military rule, abolishing parliament, having only one legal party, and a system governed by Islamic law, and they are less likely to endorse multiparty elections. This matches recent Egyptian history. When Egyptian democracy produced "a bad result"— it elected Islamists—it was replaced through military intervention.

Secularists in Egypt are less likely to believe that choosing the government by election is the best form of government or to be committed democrats. This could reflect the relationship between elections and the Muslim Brotherhood in Egypt, which would not generalize to other countries.[7] The Moroccan results in the next chapter, for instance, do not mirror that pattern. The connection between secular government preferences and democracy would depend on the results these secularists anticipate from democracy. Although they are opposed to many nondemocratic alternatives, they privilege secularism over democracy when that democracy can elect Islamists. This includes, in the Egyptian case, having backed a military coup.

On the other hand, Egyptians who believe that electing government is acceptable according to the teachings of Islam are more likely to endorse elected government in theory and for their own country. One thirty-five-to-thirty-nine-year-old, college-educated Muslim Cairene man expressly linked his attitudes on politics to his religion: "I do not support *dimuqratiyya* as an Islamic political system, and I do not support party pluralism or the formation of parties at all."[8] Not all respondents drew such overt links. Even if they were to do so, they did not all oppose *dimuqratiyya* on that basis: 82.1 percent of the Egyptian respondents agreed with the statement "Electing governments is acceptable under the teachings of Islam"; the rate was 85.5 percent among the Muslims.

Christian Egyptians are less likely to think Muslims can endorse democracy—only 48.3 percent of the Christian respondents said they were compatible. The groups did not significantly differ in their belief in the superiority of electoral democracy. However, Christian Egyptians are less likely than Muslim Egyptians to believe that choosing the government by election is appropriate for Egypt; this may reflect their minority status. Reasonably, Christians in Egypt are also less likely than Muslims to support a system based on Islamic law. When religious groups think that elections will work poorly for their group, they are less likely to endorse them (Hoffman 2020). Egyptian Christians are rationally more likely to be liberal than majoritarian because of those consequences (Ridge 2022a).

Conclusion

This data develops the signals from Chapter 4 that the distinctions in citizens' understandings of *dimuqratiyya* are relevant to understanding their attitudes about democracy. First, by asking about *dimuqratiyya* instead of democracy, researchers have artificially inflated the apparent level of support for democracy in Egypt. The democracy-*dimuqratiyya* gap demonstrates this mismeasurement.

These findings thus both emphasize the importance of asking the right questions and indicate how democratic backsliding could occur in the face of so much support. Furthermore, while there is interest in democracy, it is not interest *only* in democracy. For researchers to understand democratization in the Middle East, they must first accurately characterize MENA interest in democracy and the other options on the table.

How does this gap happen? Democratic commitment is higher among PCD citizens. By introducing *dimuqratiyya*, instead of democracy, researchers have expanded the scope to include economic deliverables. Egyptians strongly favor economic equality and a functioning welfare state (Ridge 2022a). Democracy does not guarantee either. These SECD are less likely to approve of a competitive multiparty electoral system, and they are more open to nondemocratic alternatives. As such, concentrations of these SECD are a reservoir of potential threats to binding elections and political rights. Thus, the support for *dimuqratiyya* is higher because it can include SECD.

128 *Defining Democracy*

As shown in Chapter 3, the SECD make up half of the population of Egypt. Decades of Arab Barometer data show no sign that the SECD population of the Middle East is receding. The relatively lower democratic commitment and the relative openness to some of the authoritarian alternatives are then noteworthy.

These results are consistent with some of the prior work on democratic commitment. For instance, citizens who find nondemocracy is working out are less likely to think change is required. Although democracy may be an acceptable option for Egypt, it is far from the only one. Democracy, in their opinion, is certainly not best. These results also are consistent with Benstead's (2015) argument that democratic reticence in the Arab world reflects concerns about the outcomes it will generate. If the outcomes are bad for society, or for the individual for that matter, the respondent becomes skeptical. The results, though, are highly inconsistent with any arguments that Islam is inherently antidemocratic or that secularism is naturally democratic. Rather, this chapter suggests that secularists' democratic credentials are dependent on the likely results of that democracy. In the same vein, although sectarian affiliation is not a predictor of normative attitudes toward democracy, it impacts the sense of its appropriateness. If religious minorities could be assured their rights would not be trampled by democratization, they may be more sanguine toward participatory government in their country (Ridge 2022a). To avoid a redux of minority support for Mubarak and a military coup (Truex and Tavana 2019), would-be democratizers may have to offer guarantees of liberalism as well. Modernization theory finds less support at the individual level in this study than in prior works. This could be an artifact of the use of *dimuqratiyya* in those studies.

In terms of avenues to support democratic attitudes, there are a few available. While conception of *dimuqratiyya* is linked to democratic support in Egypt, it is not evident that this fact can be manipulated in favor of democratization (Chapter 3). Understanding (of *dimuqratiyya*), support (for democracy), and actualization (of democratization) are distinct elements of MENA politics. This chapter has probed the connection between them.

Some of these areas, however, do point to avenues for potential democracy boosting. Fear of the instability or cultural problems that democracy would cause poses a major challenge to popular democratic interest. Rather than framing democracy promotion around lectures on democratic theory and normative exercises, acknowledging the potential outcomes and developing programs to mitigate instability-induced problems would be more attuned to these concerns. The problem is not mass public opposition, so touting the normative good is going to run into ceiling effects. The question is rather how to make democracy good enough in practice to withstand the appeal of the other acceptable options.

Some of this may be done by increasing citizens' interest in politics and their trust in their compatriots. Those who are interested in politics are more likely to think that democracy is the answer. Citizens who report political interest and who are following the news are more skeptical of nondemocratic alternative systems. However, as shown here and in prior research (Jamal 2007; Jamal and Nooruddin 2010), the confluence of trust, participation, and democratic ideation is highly context dependent. Interest in politics aligns with support for and theoretical commitment to an election-based regime. If citizens' interest in their country's politics can be developed, especially if this could co-occur with assuaging concerns about democracy's producing bad results, then citizens will be more likely to support elections. Promoting secularism— or the idea that democracy is naturally secular—is unlikely to be fruitful. Secularists' commitments to secularism, at least in the Egyptian case, can undermine their democratic interests. Developing instead the voices and arguments that democracy is compatible with both religion and culture would be more favorable for popular acceptance and defense.

Whether or not Inglehart and Norris (2003) and Fish (2002) are right that gender attitudes separate the West and the rest, gender traditionalism is opposed to democratic support. Equal citizen participation does not align with the view that women should be kept out of public life. Programs that support gender-egalitarian mind-sets can then ameliorate a potential counterweight to democratic support. Programs targeting these attitudes are not overtly threatening to many nondemocratic regime structures, though they might, depending on their content and framing, be opposed by some Islamist groups. This indirectness makes them more viable. Avenues that pose less threat to the autocratic regimes, at least and maybe especially in the early stages of democratization, are least likely to trigger a backlash from status quo powers. An opportunity to weaken the antidemocratic counterweight could then be a growth opportunity for more stable democratic attitudes or democratic culture.

Programs, however, that appear patronizing can have opposite effects. The perception that gender egalitarianism is an external imposition can undermine support for egalitarianism and for foreign engagement (Rawłuszko 2021). Recent foreign aid is not well reputed in the region. Arab Barometer VI (2021) shows that MENA residents feel that US foreign aid has not been very successful at promoting women's

130 Defining Democracy

rights or civil society development; 41.3 percent report the US foreign aid has been "not at all" successful at advancing women's rights, and 16.9 percent say it has only worked "to a small extent." For strengthening civil society, the results are 38.5 and 17.8 percent respectively. Aid programs are doubly burdened by being seen as foreign and ineffectual.[9] Scholars have also advised that civil society organizations can only breed democratic interest and train citizens for democratic mobilization if they are separated from regime clientelism and corruption. Civil society groups that integrate citizens into the state structure, even indirectly, can turn into vehicles of autocratic persistence (Jamal 2007). That possibility would return to the above points about system satisfaction and authoritarian openness.

Improving economic circumstances is another avenue forward. It would also do good in itself by ameliorating suffering. The Egyptian economy has been in turmoil in recent years (Stacher 2020), and the situation is worsening. The government is appealing for increased International Monetary Fund support. The Egyptian government announced in January 2023 that it would expand the subsidized bread program to address food insecurity and inflation, although the national budget will struggle to accommodate the costs without foreign assistance (El Safty 2023). Food insecurity is a substantial regional concern, and Egypt is particularly struggling (Arab Barometer VII). Economically secure citizens are better proof against populist and antidemocratic appeals. Food and financial aid would be more useful than a lecture—for life and for democracy. The Arab Spring slogan was "Bread, freedom, and social justice." The foundations for durable democracy in the Middle East would seem to rest on those very axes. Providing them, however, poses major regional challenges.

The factor most amenable to foreign intervention is contact with the West. Respondents who had recently lived, worked, or studied in the United States, Canada, or Europe were more favorably disposed to election-based governments. Since educated citizens are also somewhat more likely to endorse electoral democracy or oppose authoritarianism, getting MENA students into Western colleges could be doubly beneficial. It cannot be assured in observational data that there is no selection effect here. In theory, it is possible that democrats or marginals were more willing to spend time in a democratic state; alternatively, refusing to live in a country on that basis would demonstrate a profound allegiance to opposing democracy. Exploration of an experience effect must be left to other research. Such that it might be true, making these kinds of opportunities available to MENA residents could be an avenue to support pro-democratic attitudes. It is also normatively and practically

Democratic Commitment in Egypt 131

under the purview of these democratic governments to determine whom to invite into their countries. As such, it is a more palatable lever for influence if democratic states are interested. Policies that would bar such engagement—such as restrictions on travel or student/worker visas for MENA-country nationals—undermine a pro-democratic opportunity.

There is more to say about the import of these findings for political science and for understanding MENA-based social movements. This volume's conclusion will address the impact on interpreting democratic and *dimuqratiyya* movements and public opinion in the Middle East. First, though, this book will consider another case study—Morocco—and the relationship between *dimuqratiyya* and state-structural preferences.

Notes

1. Western leaders were less inclined to view the military as a feature of or avenue to democratization. British prime minster David Cameron publicly opposed the military's intervention and stated, "What we need to happen now in Egypt is for democracy to flourish, and for a genuine democratic transition to take place," while the foreign secretary pointed out that "if this can happen to one elected president, it can happen to another." France's François Hollande, without mentioning the coup, stated, "The democratic process has stopped and must return." US President Barack Obama waffled: "We are deeply concerned by the decision of the Egyptian armed forces to remove President Morsi and suspend the Egyptian Constitution." A US National Security Council spokeswoman clarified that the United States' position on the "the importance of a quick and responsible return of full authority to a democratically elected civilian government as soon as possible; a transparent political process that is inclusive of all parties and groups; avoiding any arbitrary arrests of President Morsi and his supporters; and the responsibility of all groups and parties to avoid violence" had been relayed behind closed doors ("World Leaders" 2013). These statements generally do not convey a sense that military intervention is *democratic*.

2. During a roundtable discussion at the University of Chicago after the coup, an Egyptian speaker rebutted comments about democratic retrenchment in Egypt by stating that the coup had been democratic. He explained that the army is populist because any Egyptian could join it, whereas the Muslim Brotherhood was inherently undemocratic. Thus, for the military to replace the Muslim Brotherhood–affiliated Morsi and to crack down on the Muslim Brotherhood itself was democratic. That the government had been elected did not signify. In his view of "democracy," which he averred was hardly unique in Egypt, elections were not the defining sources of political—or even democratic—legitimacy, and military coups could correct their results. Chapter 2 showed that he was right in his view of the public sentiment. This view reflects an *of the people* mentality toward the military coup.

3. "Si le mouvement social ne prétend pas à la conquête du pouvoir politique, il n'est pas pour autant sans référence au politique. Le mouvement social est un indicateur qui permet, entre autres, de mettre en relief le processus du changement social et l'évolution de la nature de la relation qui lie l'Etat au citoyen, sans négliger ses effets sur la politique publique et sur la politique, d'une manière générale."

4. The state structure in Egypt may not constitute much of a useable state for these purposes. There was a strong repressive apparatus (see Nugent 2020 for more

132 Defining Democracy

on its origins), and the postcoup government maintained strategic use of violence to build up the regime. The bigger challenge is the political economy of Egypt, which the revolution and coup did not resolve. The new regime continues the old practice of outspending the state revenues, and the military is masking deficit spending by drawing on its own investments; Stacher (2020) proposes that the government is trapped in reliance on foreign aid and on rents to a degree that is not viable in the long term. That much aid is available from nondemocratic backers limits the likelihood that aid will encourage democratization (Bellin 2018). Economic turmoil in 2023 is increasing potential for renewed destabilization.

5. Votes that do not determine who holds power are not without interest; they are just not democracy. Each vote is a "subgame" in which regimes can be moved toward democratic consolidation by honoring the results or autocratization by ignoring the results (Lindberg 2009). Polls under nondemocratic leaders have contributed to autocratic breakdown and the furtherance of democratization, even against the wishes or intentions of the nondemocrats who instituted them (Lust 2009).

6. Whether having only one party constitutes a restriction on democracy or an authoritarian system is a potential area for debate, especially if party membership is open. Sklar (1983, 16) posits that a one-party system in which "political competition is severely restricted" is a "participatory democracy" if the citizenry's participation is uncoerced. However, it is commonly treated in the literature as an "authoritarian alternative" (e.g., Albrecht et al. 2021).

7. Work on belief in negative statements about *dimuqratiyya*—their economies work poorly, they are inefficient, they are disorderly, and they are incompatible with Islam—in an Egyptian and Saudi Arabian sample finds secularists hold more negative beliefs about *dimuqratiyya* (Ridge 2021).

8. Anā lā u'īd al-dīmuqrāṭiyya ka-niẓām siyyāsī islāmī li-ldawla wa lā u'īd [*sic*] al-ta'addudiyya al-ḥizbiyya wa lā takwīn aḥzāb āṣlan.

9. Furthermore, citizens would prefer that foreign aid serve their needs, which they identify differently. When asked where they would prefer foreign assistance to be dedicated, the most common responses were building infrastructure (26.4 percent) and improving education (38.8 percent). Promoting women's rights was only chosen by 10.8 percent of the respondents, and promoting women's freedom was chosen by 3.4 percent. Such focus on domains not preferred by the local population risks appearing patronizing—telling them what help they need rather than addressing ongoing concerns—and, if it is not working, it is not buying progress or goodwill. This note is an argument not against freedom but rather on where money would actually be helpful.

6

Democratic Commitment in Morocco

You can't eat freedom. And a ballot is not to be confused with a dollar bill.

—Ezra Cunningham

This chapter picks up the discussion of the democracy-*dimuqratiyya* gap with a focus on Morocco. Morocco has an active monarchy comingled with the parliamentary system, which was not profoundly altered by the Arab Spring. The examination of the relationship between Moroccans' conception of *dimuqratiyya* and their attitudes to democracy starts with a brief history of the Moroccan parliamentary monarchical regime. Most crucially, the monarchy has a history of dodging scandal and democratization, and it has sought to "depoliticize" Moroccan politics—focusing all political activity on economic policy rather than state institutions. While the mechanisms of state action are up for debate and electoral contestation, the system structure itself is not given the same scrutiny. This history forms the background against which contemporary public opinion and recent democratization pushes can be interpreted.

Recall that democratic preference is about more than electoral governance. To maintain a democratic regime, a community would have to accept the idea of democracy in theory and in practice. It would also have to resist the temptation of nondemocratic alternatives. In Morocco, that requires disempowering the king. This survey probes each of these facets.

The democracy-*dimuqratiyya* gap is starker in Morocco than in Egypt. Support for democracy has been profoundly overestimated in this case. Furthermore, Moroccan citizens who conceive of *dimuqratiyya*

134 *Defining Democracy*

primarily in political-institutional terms (PCD) or in socioeconomic terms (SECD) have different regime-type preferences. Namely, PCD Moroccans are more likely than SECD Moroccans to be democrats. PCD Moroccans, however, are not open only to democracy; they would accept several nondemocratic regimes.

These results underscore the necessity of accounting for citizens' understanding of *dimuqratiyya* in examining public opinion and of distinguishing attitudes toward *dimuqratiyya* from attitudes toward democracy. They also highlight the importance of grasping the PCD and SECD distinction for understanding Middle East/North Africa (MENA) public opinion. The chapter closes with a discussion of the pro-democracy factors identified in the survey responses and considers their practicality from a pro-democratization perspective.

Governance in Morocco

Morocco represents a complementary case to Egypt for several reasons. Morocco has both a different institutional past and a different experience of the Arab Spring. These divides demonstrate that the difference in propensities is not unique to Egypt. Furthermore, Morocco's recent protest pattern was instrumental in forming the reasoning behind this book.

A brief discussion of Morocco's government is instructive. Morocco is a parliamentary monarchy, and the king plays an active role in government. Prior to the establishment of the French and Spanish protectorates, Morocco was a sultanate in the same Alaouite dynasty as rules now; the dynastic line claims descent from the Prophet Muhammad and has claimed leadership since 1631. The title was converted from sultan to king in 1957 with the state's conversion into the Kingdom of Morocco with the removal of the European protectorate powers. The constitutional monarchy featured a Consultative National Assembly that "gather[ed] key figures, handpicked by the monarchy, from political parties, associations, and professional groups to serve as a cabinet of advisors" without "real power" (Jamal 2007, 101).

The constitution, drafted shortly after independence, incorporated the parliament. The first elections were held in 1963. King Hassan II temporarily suspended parliament under a state of emergency; new elections were held in 1970. Some political parties support the king's policies, while other parties formed in opposition to the monarchists. Pro-monarchy parties won the early elections, with the first opposition government

Democratic Commitment in Morocco   135

forming in 1998. Over the decades, the monarchy faced internal and external pressure to grant more power to the opposition. Several constitutional revisions occurred under Hassan II's rule; however, these processes ultimately affirmed "the preeminence of the monarchy" over other institutions (Jamal 2007, 101). To this day parties are often identified as either pro-monarchy/loyalist or not. All parties that wish to compete in elections must recognize the king's role as the religious head of the country, including his title Commander of the Faithful, in order to be in government. The Justice and Development Party (PJD), for instance, recognized this status and has served in parliament; the al-Adl wal-Ihsan Party did not and has been excluded from politics, rendering it ineffectual (Ottaway 2019).

After years of heavy-handed reign, known as the Years of Lead, King Hassan II instituted constitutional reforms and showed more concern for human rights; these included allowing opposition parties to form the government. This transition of power marked the true political reform, while prior reforms were largely economic; it was not true democratization, though, but rather a "pluralization" of power (Hibou 2011, 2). The monarchy retained the real power still, including the loyalty of the Ministries of Sovereignty: Justice, Defense, Foreign Affairs, Religious Affairs, and Interior. Monarchical approval of the prime minister's choices ensures the positions are allotted to friendly figures. The coming of Mohammed VI, Hassan II's son, to power in 1999 was viewed as an opening for liberalization. The regime even marketed itself this way to the West in order to curry favor and support. King Mohammed VI, in fact, retracted some of his father's reforms, including reclaiming the option to select the prime minister without considering the election returns, and he gave patronage to a new monarchist party, the Authenticity and Modernity Party (King 2019). The new king accepted American "democracy" aid that was used to finance infrastructure projects. Rather than fomenting democratization, these benefits, concentrated in the major coastal cities (e.g., Rabat and Casablanca), perpetuated the formation of "two different Moroccos—that of the prosperous coastal cities and the neglected interior cities and villages" (Snider 2022, 139). Uneven development across country regions is not a singularly Moroccan phenomenon; inland regions in Tunisia have similarly experienced unequal development and been sources of mobilization (Beinin 2016).

King Mohammed VI, the current monarch, was in power for Morocco's Arab Spring. A series of protests spread in Morocco from February 20 through the spring; they became the February 20 Movement. Unlike many protests during this period, the protests under the

136 *Defining Democracy*

Jordanian and Moroccan monarchies called not for "the overthrow of the regime," meaning a wholesale rewriting of the rules, but rather for changing "the balance of power between the monarch and the government" (Feldman 2020, 19). The movement called for political reforms and economic development, such as rooting out widespread corruption, improving education and health care, and increasing social justice (Hibou 2011). Short-distance protest marches in the capital, Rabat, were popularized by the late 2000s, but this route from Bab al-Had to the parliament offered little engagement with people who were not already protesting. That meant the protests could not draw new people to the movement. February 20 protest marches were started in popular neighborhoods in several cities from which they would move toward symbolic locations in those cities, which allowed more engagement with nonparticipants over the longer distances (Bishara 2021a). The government has been more tolerant of spontaneous protests populated by the public. The more social movement organizations—"named organizations that organize and sponsor protest events in pursuit of an agenda" —are involved in protests, the greater the likelihood that the Moroccan police will respond violently (Berman 2021, 735). Berman (2021) argues that these groups and their protests are perceived as a greater threat to the incumbent parties.

In response to the demonstrations, a new constitution was approved by referendum. The king agreed to transfer some powers to the prime minister—namely, the power to appoint government officials, such as cabinet members, and to dissolve parliament. The king also agreed that the prime minister would be appointed from the party winning the most seats in the election. Some of these were reforms previously introduced by his father and retracted under his rule. Amazigh was made an official language alongside Arabic. Elections were moved forward to that year. The election would determine the party from which the king would appoint the prime minister and which parties—among those approved by the Ministry of the Interior—would form the governing coalition (King 2019). Although the constitutional referendum passed with more than 98 percent support and voter turnout was over 70 percent (Labott and Alami 2011), subsequent elections had turnout in the 40 to 50 percent range, partially due to party boycotts (Hatim 2020). Ultimately, a government was formed under the Islamist PJD, which won a plurality of seats. The PJD remained in power through the 2021 election, which had an official turnout of 50.35 percent ("Legislative Elections" 2021). Given that the new constitution did not institute dramatic change, activists were often more successful working through secular civil society organizations, like women's rights groups (Ottaway 2019). Reform movements remained constrained by the extent of the monarch's support for their agendas; radical transformation was not in the offing.

The February 20 Movement's underlying concerns, however, were not resolved. Protests recurred the following year. Demonstrators objected to the parliament's failure to resolve unemployment, inflation, and corruption in the *makhzen*, the governing clique close to the monarchy. The *makhzen* is the "extensive network of senior administrative, judiciary, military, and security officials" that facilitate the king's control: "The elected municipal or parliamentary bodies, and the governments that emerged after the 2011 reforms, have been in every meaningful way subservient to the Makhzen" (Maghraoui 2019, 264).[1] Devoting state resources to corruption in the governing clique and to clientelism usually supports regime longevity and dampens democratic interest (Jamal 2007). That system can break down, though, if enough individuals are outside the clientelist network and are not recompensed with state services. These protests would not be the last.

The subsequent protests developed the narrative of thought that would lead to this book. Since the Arab Spring, economic-based protests have been recurrent. Flashpoint events are tied to economic circumstances. In those cases, someone does something illegal and/or dangerous to make money in the face of poverty. In a 2016 case, a man tried to retrieve illegal swordfish the police were destroying and was accidentally crushed; in another, in 2018, men died in cave-ins at a defunct mine. These events become points of organization for protests against economic problems and unfulfilled promises to fix them. The former case, in particular, triggered the Hirak Rif protests in the Rif, a region that revolted in the early independence period and has felt politically and economically marginalized for decades. The tactics used to diffuse these protests included public statements in support of investigating the police and facilitating economic development, coupled with traditional authoritarian tools of control, such as mass arrests, physical intimidation, and harassment of human rights activists. The government's handling of the protests "suggests a new confidence in the classic authoritarian tactics" (Maghraoui 2019, 264). Later protests challenged the lengthy jail sentences received by some organizers of the previous demonstrations. The protests that mimicked the February 20 Movement's longer-distance marches were more likely to receive a security-services response (Bishara 2021a). The government has sought to avert extensions of these protests or further protests by targeting the economic circumstances. For instance, there is intentional lax enforcement of commercial regulations

138 *Defining Democracy*

on small vendors, and popular development is promised. When protestors objected to a state austerity program, the police averted several self-immolations, reminiscent of the public suicides that touched off the Arab Spring. These economic problems and programs are the target of public action, not the structure of the state, though the words *democracy* and *dimuqratiyya* may be used in the signs and statements.[2]

These recurrent protests suggest that the Arab Spring reforms and the subsequent government reaction share an important feature with earlier reform programs. That is that "if these former [reforms] succeeded in defusing the explosive potential of the claims, they did not truly respond to the problems that were raised" (Hibou 2011, 3).[3] The reforms were driven by the king and his advisors and technocrats, rather than by political parties. Having the monarchy govern the process led to a "depoliticization" of the reform process, both in the Arab Spring reforms and in those previous attempts (3). It is an apolitical process that makes reform the subject of the king's decisions rather than public debate or negotiation among political parties or action groups. This is consistent with Maghraoui's (2002) argument that the monarchy has depoliticized the political system in general by centering political activity on economic and technocratic questions while siphoning off questions about legitimacy and institutional structure. To say that Moroccan politics is apolitical or depoliticized is to say that it allows active debate over some domains, including some political domains, but the central political structures of the country—especially the monarchy—are not treated as eligible for debate or reformation. The monarchy's history of ducking crises has made it flexible in the face of new protests (Maghraoui 2015, 2019).

Although the Covid-19 pandemic has placed stresses on the country, especially the large tourism sector of the economy, it has not diminished monarchical authority. In fact, the monarchy was able to centralize decisionmaking during the crisis, retrenching efforts to regionalize power. Morocco's constitution has prescheduled elections, which were held during the pandemic. In the recent elections, pro-monarchy parties were empowered. Upcoming years will thus pose a new challenge to the monarchy. If the parliament is in line with the king and he has his chosen technocrats, it will be harder for him to deflect blame to other elements of the government than it was when the PJD held parliament.

At present, the king appears quite popular. He has even seemingly imbued some sense of *dimuqratiyya* into the monarchy insofar as he seems to be linking the crown with the public. Recall that 40 percent of Moroccan respondents said it was very or somewhat *dimuqratiyya* for an unelected figure to make decisions alongside the elected ones. The king, as an embodiment of tradition predating the protectorate period, has cultivated an image of stability in the state in the face of tumult. Prior to the French protectorate, Sultan Moulay 'Abdal-'Aziz used the Council of Notables as a proxy for the voice of the people, which he could claim to incorporate into his efforts to represent them. During independence, "the sultan fashioned himself the embodied representation of the Moroccan people" (Khanani 2021, 17). The contemporary efforts then have historical precedent. Nowadays, the king can blame his parliament for not enacting his reforms or fulfilling his promises or his advisors for giving him bad advice. He may call for an investigation, replace government officials, or pardon some of the arrested protestors. Some protestors have worried about whether the king's involvement is sufficient: "The king forgot about us. He tours the country helping people, and he never comes to this region. . . . He is our father, and he has forgotten about his children" (Alami 2014). The solution then becomes appeals for monarchical engagement. Protestors urge the king to visit these areas: "The king is probably the only one who can solve this" (Laessing 2018). Questioning him or the monarchy means challenging one of the few seemingly working parts of the state apparatus.

Those who might favor removing the monarchy from a philosophical perspective could focus their reform agenda on changing the king's advisors rather than attacking the monarchy directly. It would be less threatening, and it could still turn politics in their favor through the influence of sympathetic advisors. Criticism of monarchies can also be couched in criticism of advisors. Monarchists level blame at advisors when bad choices are made, so the assertion itself does not betray pro- or antimonarchical sentiment.

Young activists now push to negotiate more directly with the king rather than through intermediaries, who have been blamed for failures and thereby discredited (Maghraoui 2019). Such engagement by the monarch would put greater pressure on him ultimately to deliver, as he would be more intimately linked to any promises and outcomes. If the king's previous success at dodging accountability resulted from significant strategic acumen, then he could recognize this possibility, and either that engagement would be avoided or the potential for blowback would limit any agreements to those the *makhzen* was most confident could be fulfilled, avoiding discrediting the king himself.

This is not to say that the king is untouchable. There are movements to downgrade his authority to something more resembling that of the Spanish or British monarchies. The durability of the monarchy, if it were heavily tried, is questionable despite these appeals to the king and

140 *Defining Democracy*

his role in government: "There is no doubt that many Moroccans identify with the monarchy and love their king. But the ultimate test is whether Moroccans would mobilize to resist another ruler should the monarchy collapse. The passivity of most Moroccans during the 1971–72 military coup attempts and various opposition movements to the monarchy under Hassan II does not gibe with the legitimacy thesis" (Maghraoui 2019, 268–269). Thus, republican sentiments are tolerated, but a movement that hints too strongly at an antimonarchical move would likely trigger a stronger response from the throne. Nevertheless, an effort that actually removed the monarchy, rather than merely questioning it, might be successful. This might be a function of unthought ideas rather than unthinkable ideas. Stable regimes may be brought down when the opening of discourse exposes more citizens to the idea that the regime is replaceable, after which they can adopt an opinion supporting removal (Kuran 1997). Expanded discourse opposed to the monarchy could generate support. This would align with the principle that, were the monarchy interrupted, the public would not be forceful in reinstating it. This is challenging to predict given the difficulties conducting surveys on pro- and antimonarchical sentiment (Hegasy 2007). A ten-year ascension anniversary job-approval poll "showed that 91 percent of Moroccans are very satisfied or satisfied with the king's performance" (Reuters 2009). Publication of the poll was suppressed despite this positive rating to avoid the precedent that the king is subject to public opinion polling.

Immediately after the Arab Spring/February 20 Movement, some scholars argued the stopgap measures the king imposed would eventually lead, whether intentionally or unintentionally on his part, to the disempowerment of the monarchy (Dalmasso 2012; King 2011). In the decade since, however, he has maintained control. The representative of the unelected branch of government can present himself in the public imaginary as standing tall while the elected agents are failing the public. Antimonarchists and pro-democracy advocates must face that version of the king, parliament, and parties when proposing further reforms.

Measuring Democratic Commitment in Morocco

This chapter draws on the questions about regime support that were used in the Egypt chapter. Moroccans expressed lower levels of support for democracy than the Egyptians did. Only about a third of Moroccans indicated that elected government is always preferable to any other kind of government (33.96 percent). This is far less than the 63.7 percent of

Moroccans who reported (strongly) agreeing that *dimuqratiyya* "may have problems" but is "better than other systems" in the 2018 Arab Barometer. Nearly as many (31.34 percent) believed that there are circumstances in which unelected governments are preferable. The democracy-*dimuqratiyya* gap in this case is substantial.

Although democracy is not necessarily superior, it is viewed as acceptable: 75.2 percent say that choosing the government by election is appropriate for Morocco. Thus, these Moroccans are not avowedly antidemocracy. They are not, though, to be looked at as bulwarks of democratic support. Only 30.5 percent of Moroccans are committed democrats. While electing the government may seem appropriate to Moroccans, electoral democracy is far from the only game in town.

The best form of government and an appropriate form of government are no more one and the same in Morocco than they were in Egypt. Of those who said that electing the government is the best way to choose the government, only 89.9 percent said that it was very or somewhat appropriate for Morocco. This leaves one in ten who think it is a good idea in theory but not right in practice. These people are unlikely then to push for democratization, at least in the short term. Why would they, if it is not appropriate in their eyes? In turn, 64.3 percent of those who said it did not matter to them if the government was elected and 71.7 percent of those who said that unelected governments were sometimes best indicated that democracy was very or somewhat appropriate for Morocco. Democracy, then, is something these people would settle for, not idealize. Not even a full third of Moroccans are committed democrats, meaning they said both that democracy is best and that it is appropriate. Morocco falls well short of Fuchs and Roller's (2006) 50 percent threshold for democratic commitment.

One of the respondents viewed elections as inappropriate for Morocco for a very particular reason. The thirty-to-thirty-four-year-old Muslim man in Marrakech with vocational training described unlikely international intervention:

> As for my country, Morocco, it is not the government that governs. If we elected 1,000 governments a year, the situation will remain as it is, such as economic rents. We do not have a government at all. Rather, it is a group of agents of darkness in the service of their personal interests, and they cover up the deep state. . . . There is a lot of talk, but it cannot be mentioned. No one from those who appear before the world and the United Nations governs us. We are at the mercy of the International Monetary Bank [*sic*] . . . and Morocco is a country owned by the Jews. We live in it and rent [it].[4]

142 *Defining Democracy*

He saw elections, under such conditions, as pointless. In fact, when asked about choosing the government by election or authoritarianism, he said that for someone like him, it did not matter, and he said he did not think choosing by election was appropriate for Morocco. While his reasoning likely does not explain many or most other Moroccans' thoughts, conspiratorial beliefs' connection to support for democracy could be a fruitful area for further research. Conspiracists may have lower thresholds for democratization because of antisystem sentiment (Ridge 2021). That does not necessarily mean that they are democrats.

In terms of the more conservative standard, 30.8 percent of the Moroccans are singular democrats. A large share of Moroccans, then, are accepting of democracy (73.7 percent). However, they accept—if to a lesser degree—other systems as well: 28.7 percent (strongly) approved of one-party systems, 10.1 percent approved of military government, 36.6 percent endorsed strongman governance, and 42.3 percent would approve a system in which Islamic law is employed without elections. Nontrivial endorsement of a religious regime and a strongman system are consistent with a monarchy with a religious sheen in a state with an official religion (Maliki Islam). Democracy is merely one of several potentially permissible regime types.

The Moroccan respondents also answered a country-specific regime-type question. So that the results would be comparable across Egypt and Morocco, this question was not included in the metric for singular democrats. This question gestures toward support for monarchical governance. To avoid sensitivity concerns about addressing the king directly, the question asked whether respondents approved of a government system that includes both elected and unelected offices that take an active part in the decisionmaking and policy. This framing is similar to the framing Khanani (2021, 80) identifies among Moroccan Islamists for addressing the monarchy. He interprets statements by his interlocutors about political figures who were not "accountable" as statements about the king. He also notes that some individuals would overtly criticize the monarchical structure while others were indirect.

Of Moroccans surveyed, 68.6 percent approved of a system that included an active unelected body alongside the elected government, as the monarchy does. This is lower than the endorsement for multiparty democracy, which could indicate some nonapproval (if not outright opposition) to the monarchy. Since responses for this differed from those to the question related to multiparty elections without reference to an active unelected segment of the regime, respondents were apparently able to appreciate a distinction. At least one respondent would have preferred a direct question about the king. A college-educated, forty-plus-year-old Muslim woman wrote the following:

> Thank you for the set of questions, but I live in a country with a monarchical system, and I see that the monarchy is more stable than the rest of the systems, at least because we believe it is a permanent system. He is not like an elected president, but he refuses to give up the seat and he forces individuals to accept him permanently. Also, the monarchy contributes greatly to the stability of the country from a security and economic standpoint. The system of government was not touched on in all the questions.[5]

The public can recognize that the king is not democratic (even if he may be *dimuqratiyya*) but that nondemocracy may be tolerable or even laudable if it is useful. Potential instability, for instance, can seem like a greater problem. On the whole, the Moroccan public seems to accept this less-than-democratic option.

Surveying Moroccans

The Moroccan survey employed the questions about democracy used in the Egypt survey. Recall that it was necessary to use question wording that specifies an elected government and choosing governments by election rather than questions using the word *dimuqratiyya*. Nine hundred thirty Moroccan nationals completed the Arabic-language survey questionnaire. The survey data includes weights for gender and age representativeness. For more information about conducting surveys in the Middle East, respondent demographics, and the respondents' feelings about participating in a political survey, see Appendix A.

The classification of respondents by their conception of *dimuqratiyya* is the same in this chapter as in Chapters 3 and 5. The respondents are grouped into four categories—PCD, Mixed PCD, Mixed SECD, SECD—based on their selections for the first and second most essential features of *dimuqratiyya*. This grouping is included in the models as a factor variable with SECD as the reference category. As in Chapter 5, it is anticipated these groups will have different regime-type preferences. Afterall, that democracy and *dimuqratiyya* enjoy different levels of public support has already been demonstrated. *Dimuqratiyya* is liked more, which implies that those whose opinion is based on the socioeconomic outcomes are less supportive of the system itself than of those outcomes. They may accept democracy—it is more acceptable than superior, according to these

144 *Defining Democracy*

surveys—but that support may be instrumental rather than intrinsic. That is to say, they would like it only insofar as it might generate socioeconomic outcomes of which they would approve. This is not to conflate an instrumental interest in democracy with a socioeconomic understanding of *dimuqratiyya*. The latter relates to how a construct is defined. The former is interest in a system of government. This analysis holds them distinct while positing a relationship between conception and commitment.

Table 6.1 presents the crosstabulations of the four-part understanding categorization and expressed democratic support. It shows a relationship between citizens' understanding of *dimuqratiyya* and their attitudes toward democracy. Citizens' conception of democracy is not perfectly predictive of their democratic attitudes. There are democrats and skeptics in both camps. The support is significantly different between the groups for their belief that it is the best form of government and that it is appropriate for Morocco. It is also significantly associated with being a committed democrat, though not with being a singular democrat.

Regression analyses that include covariates for attitudes toward democracy, especially those argued by prior literature to be pertinent to citizens' "democratic" attitudes, are useful. Note, most prior validations were done using surveys on *dimuqratiyya* attitudes. They include variables associated with modernization theory (Lerner 1958), democratic culture theory (Welzel 2021b; Ridge 2022a), religion and religiosity (Hoffman 2020; Rafiqi 2019; Benstead 2015; Breznau et al. 2011; Ciftci 2013), social capital theory (Jamal and Nooruddin 2010; Jamal 2007), and system satisfaction (Benstead 2015). The same covariates and operationalizations of these variables employed in the previous chapter are included here.

As belief that elected government is the best form of government is a binary variable, a logistic regression model is used. Whether government by election is appropriate for Morocco uses an ordered linear regression model. Being a committed democrat and being a singular democrat are both binary categorizations. Recall that committed democrats are those who state both that democracy is the best form of government and that it is appropriate or very appropriate for the country. Singular democrats are those who approve of multiparty democracy while disapproving of a series of nondemocratic options. Binary logistic regressions are used for evaluating these relationships.

The ratings of multiple potential regime types that were used to identify the singular democrats are also considered. As Albrecht et al. (2021, 20) note, "Scholars of democratic consolidation have largely neglected the political alternatives that citizens are willing to support."

Table 6.1 Conception of *Dimuqratiyya* and Democratic Attitudes in Morocco

	Elected Government Is Preferable to Any Other Kind of Government		Extent to Which Electoral Democracy Is Appropriate for Egypt				Committed Democrat		Singular Democrat	
	No	Yes**	Very Inappropriate	Somewhat Inappropriate	Somewhat Appropriate	Very Appropriate*	No	Yes**	No	Yes
SECD	277	114	25	85	190	91	291	100	283	108
Mixed SECD	80	47	9	27	60	31	87	40	81	46
Mixed PCD	197	104	18	41	150	92	203	98	204	97
PCD	68	43	11	16	51	33	73	38	79	32

Notes: ** ANOVA test $p < 0.05$. * ANOVA test $p < 0.1$ ($n = 930$).

146 *Defining Democracy*

For political science to understand democratization and democratic durability, the citizens' attitudes toward these nondemocratic alternatives must be understood as well. For Morocco, the additional regime type—a government in which both elected and unelected officials play an active role in state decisionmaking—was also evaluated. These are ordered models using the four-point scale of acceptability. All the models include YouGov's survey weights. Region fixed effects are also included. In this case, the reference region is Casablanca.

PCD, SECD, and Democracy

As in Egypt, PCD and SECD are found to have different regime-type preferences. The relationship, though, is not as democratic as it was in Egypt. Among the Moroccans, conception of *dimuqratiyya* is not tightly linked to theoretical democratic support, once the covariates are included (Table 6.2). That it is not significantly related to supporting only multiparty democracy as a system of government, however, does not mean is not linked to regime-type preferences (Table 6.3).

Moroccans with different understandings of *dimuqratiyya* express differing propensities toward (dis)approval of several regimes (Table 6.3). Moroccans with a more political-institutional view of *dimuqratiyya* are more likely to approve of multiparty electoral democracy.

At the same time, though, they are also more likely to accept military intervention in the government. They are less likely to accept strongman rule. Thus, while they are more likely to be democrats, they are not *only* democrats.

Other factors influencing democratic attitudes are also noteworthy. Although Morocco is not fully democratic—since the king plays a role as well as the elected government—people who are satisfied with how Morocco is working are more likely to say that electoral democracy is the best form of government and that it is appropriate for Morocco. This could reflect the fact that Morocco's parliament and regional offices are elected. These satisfied individuals, though, are far from staunch democrats. They are also more open to the nondemocratic alternatives, save a system that would abolish elections in favor of Islamic law. At the time of the Morocco survey, an Islamist party was in power in parliament. However, the king has the highest religious position in the country, so any Islamist party is constrained by his dual authorities. It does not seem that satisfaction with the PJD government reflected any popular drift toward Islamism.

147

Table 6.2 Democratic Commitment in Morocco

	Model 1	Model 2	Model 3	Model 4
(Intercept)	−3.05***		−3.27***	−1.81***
	(0.53)		(0.56)	(0.53)
Mixed SECD	0.29	−0.13	0.19	0.43*
	(0.25)	(0.20)	(0.26)	(0.25)
Mixed PCD	0.14	0.37**	0.26	0.28
	(0.19)	(0.15)	(0.19)	(0.19)
PCD	0.27	0.03	0.22	−0.23
	(0.26)	(0.22)	(0.27)	(0.27)
Government	0.39***	0.84***	0.50***	0.03
evaluation	(0.10)	(0.09)	(0.10)	(0.10)
Most people can	0.56**	−0.01	0.56**	0.16
be trusted	(0.25)	(0.22)	(0.26)	(0.28)
News consumption:	0.16	0.37***	0.30*	0.11
daily	(0.17)	(0.14)	(0.17)	(0.17)
Scripture reading:	−0.09	0.35**	−0.20	−0.11
daily	(0.19)	(0.16)	(0.20)	(0.20)
Prayer: daily	0.07	−0.18	0.08	−0.49**
	(0.21)	(0.16)	(0.22)	(0.20)
Interested in politics	0.73***	0.53***	0.84***	0.60***
	(0.17)	(0.14)	(0.18)	(0.18)
Gender traditionalism	−0.42***	−0.20**	−0.34***	−0.43***
	(0.11)	(0.09)	(0.11)	(0.12)
More important for	0.15	0.25	0.23	0.65**
the government	(0.26)	(0.21)	(0.28)	(0.28)
to be effective				
Elections can produce	−0.67***	−0.61***	−0.70***	−0.89***
bad results	(0.18)	(0.15)	(0.18)	(0.18)
Secularist orientation	−0.14	−0.04	−0.09	0.69***
	(0.11)	(0.09)	(0.11)	(0.12)
Elections are acceptable	0.84***	0.68***	0.84***	0.27
in Islamic law	(0.18)	(0.14)	(0.19)	(0.18)
Male	0.59***	0.02	0.50***	0.22
	(0.18)	(0.15)	(0.19)	(0.18)
Unemployed	0.31*	−0.04	0.20	−0.34*
	(0.18)	(0.15)	(0.19)	(0.19)
Religion: none	0.66	0.60	0.66	0.26
	(0.54)	(0.49)	(0.57)	(0.56)
Religion:	−14.12	−0.86	−13.46	−0.33
Christianity	(485.14)	(1.23)	(504.13)	(1.66)
Income:	0.08	−0.05	0.18	0.07
covers expenses	(0.17)	(0.14)	(0.17)	(0.18)
College education	0.14	0.21	0.21	0.47***
	(0.17)	(0.14)	(0.18)	(0.18)
Urban	−0.06	−0.06	−0.05	0.03
	(0.20)	(0.17)	(0.21)	(0.21)

continues

148 Defining Democracy

Table 6.2 Continued

	Model 1	Model 2	Model 3	Model 4
Spend time in the West	0.74***	−0.06	0.31	0.19
	(0.22)	(0.20)	(0.23)	(0.23)
25–29	0.81**	0.09	0.73**	0.16
	(0.32)	(0.24)	(0.34)	(0.33)
30–34	0.89***	0.62**	0.88***	0.23
	(0.32)	(0.24)	(0.33)	(0.32)
35–39	0.92***	−0.10	0.48	0.32
	(0.35)	(0.28)	(0.38)	(0.37)
40+	0.86***	0.17	0.83***	0.48*
	(0.27)	(0.20)	(0.29)	(0.28)
Region: Agadir	0.27	0.20	0.14	−0.08
	(0.34)	(0.29)	(0.35)	(0.35)
Region: Marrakech	−0.06	0.20	−0.08	0.54*
	(0.32)	(0.26)	(0.33)	(0.32)
Region: Rabat	0.17	−0.24	0.12	0.09
	(0.35)	(0.29)	(0.36)	(0.36)
Region: Fès	−0.11	−0.04	−0.15	−0.47
	(0.34)	(0.28)	(0.36)	(0.36)
Region: Salé	−0.17	−0.67*	−0.45	−0.81*
	(0.44)	(0.35)	(0.47)	(0.49)
Region: Tangier	−0.19	−0.99***	−0.47	−1.08**
	(0.39)	(0.32)	(0.41)	(0.47)
Region: Kenitra	0.40	−0.30	0.31	−0.36
	(0.50)	(0.47)	(0.51)	(0.60)
Region: Other	−0.12	−0.13	−0.19	0.02
	(0.23)	(0.19)	(0.24)	(0.24)
1|2		−2.22***		
		(0.42)		
2|3		−0.46		
		(0.40)		
3|4		2.15***		
		(0.41)		
AIC	1,068.10	2,034.01	1,010.33	1,005.95
Log likelihood	−499.05	−980.01	−470.16	−467.97
N	930	930	930	930

Notes: ***$p < 0.01$, **$p < 0.05$, *$p < 0.1$. Model 1: Best form of government (binary). Model 2: Appropriate for Morocco (ordered). Model 3: Committed democrat (binary). Model 4: Singular democrat (binary).

As with Egypt, gender traditionalism is associated with antidemocratic preferences. Gender traditionalists are less likely to believe that democracy is the best form of government or that it is appropriate for Morocco. They are also less likely to be singular or committed democrats.

Table 6.3 Regime-Type Preferences in Morocco

	Model 1	Model 2	Model 3	Model 4	Model 5	Model 6
Mixed SECD	−0.22	−0.18	−0.49**	−0.34*	−0.14	0.40**
	(0.21)	(0.20)	(0.19)	(0.20)	(0.20)	(0.20)
Mixed PCD	0.21	0.21	−0.24*	0.01	−0.16	0.41***
	(0.16)	(0.15)	(0.14)	(0.15)	(0.15)	(0.15)
PCD	0.56**	0.35	−0.09	−0.20	0.01	0.26
	(0.22)	(0.21)	(0.21)	(0.22)	(0.21)	(0.22)
Government	0.33***	0.21**	0.15*	0.24***	−0.26***	0.14*
evaluation	(0.09)	(0.08)	(0.08)	(0.08)	(0.08)	(0.08)
Most people	−0.04	0.00	−0.16	0.02	−0.13	0.34
can be trusted	(0.23)	(0.21)	(0.21)	(0.23)	(0.22)	(0.22)
News	−0.22	−0.15	−0.03	0.67***	−0.02	0.56***
consumption: daily	(0.15)	(0.14)	(0.13)	(0.14)	(0.14)	(0.14)
Scripture	−0.11	0.01	0.04	0.03	0.12	−0.13
reading: daily	(0.16)	(0.15)	(0.15)	(0.16)	(0.15)	(0.16)
Prayer: daily	0.04	0.16	0.07	−0.08	0.37**	−0.23
	(0.17)	(0.16)	(0.16)	(0.17)	(0.16)	(0.16)
Interested	−0.05	−0.30**	−0.42***	0.29**	−0.59***	0.33**
in politics	(0.14)	(0.14)	(0.13)	(0.14)	(0.14)	(0.14)
Gender	0.50***	0.70***	0.46***	0.10	0.36***	−0.23**
traditionalism	(0.10)	(0.09)	(0.09)	(0.09)	(0.09)	(0.09)
More important	−0.25	0.13	0.07	0.85***	−0.14	0.84***
for the government to be effective	(0.22)	(0.21)	(0.20)	(0.21)	(0.21)	(0.21)
Elections	0.36**	0.52***	0.45***	0.69***	0.49***	−0.55***
can produce bad results	(0.16)	(0.15)	(0.15)	(0.15)	(0.15)	(0.15)
Secularist	−0.36***	−0.36***	−0.16*	0.01	−1.21***	0.06
orientation	(0.09)	(0.09)	(0.09)	(0.09)	(0.10)	(0.09)
Elections are	−0.09	−0.11	−0.28**	0.18	−0.14	0.55***
acceptable in Islamic law	(0.15)	(0.14)	(0.14)	(0.14)	(0.14)	(0.14)
Male	−0.68***	−0.50***	−0.32**	0.07	−0.30**	0.12
	(0.16)	(0.15)	(0.14)	(0.15)	(0.14)	(0.15)
Unemployed	−0.06	0.12	−0.01	−0.15	0.04	−0.11
	(0.15)	(0.15)	(0.14)	(0.15)	(0.15)	(0.15)
Religion: none	0.70	0.22	−0.27	0.04	−0.77	0.68
	(0.46)	(0.46)	(0.43)	(0.44)	(0.47)	(0.46)
Religion:	−1.20	−0.59	−13.23***	1.45	−14.61***	−1.43
Christianity	(1.45)	(1.44)	(0.00)	(1.76)	(0.00)	(1.25)
Income: covers	0.13	−0.09	−0.09	−0.07	−0.02	0.02
expenses	(0.14)	(0.14)	(0.13)	(0.14)	(0.14)	(0.14)

continues

Table 6.3 Continued

	Model 1	Model 2	Model 3	Model 4	Model 5	Model 6
College	0.07	−0.34**	−0.20	0.03	0.00	0.34**
education	(0.14)	(0.14)	(0.13)	(0.14)	(0.13)	(0.14)
Urban	−0.26	−0.07	0.13	0.33**	0.26	0.36**
	(0.17)	(0.16)	(0.16)	(0.17)	(0.16)	(0.16)
Spend time in	−0.09	0.16	−0.07	0.04	−0.11	−0.41**
the West	(0.20)	(0.19)	(0.19)	(0.20)	(0.19)	(0.19)
25–29	−0.48*	−0.49**	−0.08	−0.17	0.03	−0.50**
	(0.25)	(0.24)	(0.23)	(0.24)	(0.24)	(0.24)
30–34	−0.47*	−0.02	0.04	−0.34	−0.17	−0.48**
	(0.25)	(0.24)	(0.23)	(0.24)	(0.24)	(0.24)
35–39	−0.70**	−0.34	0.11	−0.03	−0.13	−0.07
	(0.29)	(0.27)	(0.26)	(0.28)	(0.27)	(0.28)
40+	−0.94***	−0.50**	−0.15	−0.02	−0.10	−0.19
	(0.22)	(0.20)	(0.20)	(0.21)	(0.20)	(0.21)
Region: Agadir	0.14	0.18	0.38	−0.17	−0.56**	−0.32
	(0.30)	(0.29)	(0.27)	(0.29)	(0.28)	(0.29)
Region:	−0.04	−0.12	0.27	−0.16	−0.09	0.09
Marrakech	(0.27)	(0.25)	(0.25)	(0.26)	(0.25)	(0.26)
Region: Rabat	−0.23	0.08	0.28	−0.06	−0.34	−0.36
	(0.32)	(0.30)	(0.29)	(0.32)	(0.30)	(0.30)
Region: Fès	0.22	0.17	0.84***	0.06	−0.39	0.06
	(0.29)	(0.28)	(0.26)	(0.28)	(0.27)	(0.28)
Region: Salé	0.09	−0.07	0.54	0.20	0.00	−0.51
	(0.38)	(0.38)	(0.36)	(0.37)	(0.36)	(0.36)
Region: Tangier	0.20	0.03	0.57*	−0.01	0.29	−0.03
	(0.34)	(0.31)	(0.30)	(0.32)	(0.31)	(0.32)
Region: Kenitra	0.36	0.06	0.97**	0.33	−0.23	0.11
	(0.46)	(0.43)	(0.41)	(0.45)	(0.42)	(0.45)
Region: Other	−0.08	0.03	0.31*	0.28	−0.01	0.04
	(0.20)	(0.19)	(0.18)	(0.20)	(0.19)	(0.19)
1|2	−1.48***	−1.63***	−1.32***	−1.00**	−2.22***	−1.45***
	(0.43)	(0.41)	(0.39)	(0.42)	(0.41)	(0.42)
2|3	1.59***	0.81**	0.54	1.11***	0.23	0.21
	(0.43)	(0.40)	(0.39)	(0.41)	(0.40)	(0.41)
3|4	2.88***	2.73***	2.13***	4.13***	2.30***	3.00***
	(0.46)	(0.42)	(0.40)	(0.44)	(0.41)	(0.43)
AIC	1,729.44	2,120.16	2,384.41	1,996.33	2,125.41	2,076.93
Log	−827.72	−1,023.08	−1,155.20	−961.17	−1,025.71	−1,001.46
likelihood						
N	930	930	930	930	930	930

Notes: ***$p < 0.01$, **$p < 0.05$, *$p < 0.1$. Model 1: Army runs the government (ordered). Model 2: Only one legal party (ordered). Model 3: Abolish elections and parliament (ordered). Model 4: Elected and unelected government officials (ordered). Model 5: Government by Islamic law (ordered). Model 6: Multiparty elections (ordered).

Democratic Commitment in Morocco   151

Moroccans who hold more traditional views are more likely to accept military rule, abolishing parliament, having only one legal party, and a system governed by Islamic law. They are less likely, though, to endorse multiparty elections. These illiberal views are fertile soil for antidemocratic activism, especially if they draw on the language of religious or cultural threat.

Concerns about electoral regimes also influence support. Moroccans who believe that elections may need to be replaced because they can produce bad results are, unsurprisingly, less likely to think electoral democracy is the best form of government or that it is appropriate for Morocco, and they are less likely to be committed or singular democrats. Moroccans who believe elections are prone to producing bad results are more likely to accept military rule, abolishing parliament, having only one legal party, having a system in which both elected and unelected agents make decisions, and having a system governed by Islamic law, and they are less likely to endorse multiparty elections. These findings are consistent with Benstead's (2015) argument that concern about the effects of *dimuqratiyya* dampens support for *dimuqratiyya*.

Perspectives on Islam and its connection to government are also pertinent. Individuals who believe that electing the government is acceptable according to the teachings of Islam are more likely to endorse elected government in theory and for Morocco. They are also more likely to be committed democrats. Secularist Moroccans are more likely to be singular democrats. When juxtaposed with the findings from Egypt, this suggests that MENA secularists are not generally more skeptical of democracy. Moroccan secularists are less likely to approve of a military regime, a single-party system, a strongman government, or an Islamic-law-based government.

Conclusion

These findings develop the impression from Chapter 4 that the distinction in citizens' understandings of *dimuqratiyya* are relevant to understanding their attitudes about democracy. The democracy-*dimuqratiyya* gap in Morocco is substantial; researchers have been tremendously overestimating Moroccans democratic commitments by conflating *dimuqratiyya* and democracy.

Among Moroccans, only a minority are committed or singular democrats. Although many would accept democracy in Morocco, there is also substantial support for a series of nondemocratic alternatives. Chief

152 *Defining Democracy*

among these is the ready and apparently widespread acceptance of Morocco's monarchy. There are antimonarchists in Morocco, but the data do not indicate that the institution is in peril.

Democratic commitment is higher among citizens with a more political-institutional conception of *dimuqratiyya*. This finding justifies empirically the necessity of keeping these constructs separate and distinct in political scientists' thinking. PCD Moroccans are more committed to electoral democracy, but they are not uniquely interested in that system. They are also disposed to some nondemocracy alternatives. The Moroccan case then demonstrates that multiple forms of mismeasurement and miscommunication can result from assuming the meaning "democracy" into the word *dimuqratiyya*.

Moroccan politics—including the relationship between *dimuqratiyya* and the variety of potential political systems—is colored by the monarchical agenda, including the "depoliticization" of the public sphere (Maghraoui 2002). This process has refocused politics on technical elements of economic development (a concept that can fit within SECD) rather than questions of legitimacy and distribution of power. Although these topics are inherently political in the worldview of political scientists, in terms of Moroccan politics, they have been functionally siphoned off.

The legitimacy of the monarch is not directly questioned in the survey. However, some patterns are evident when considering Moroccan citizens' support for a government that includes both elected and unelected offices that take an active part in decision-making. Moroccans who are satisfied with the current regime are much more likely to endorse including unelected officers in policymaking. The same is true both for those who think that sometimes it is more important for the government to be effective than it is for government to be participatory (88.2 percent) and for those who think that sometimes democracies produce bad results and need to be replaced (74.2 percent). An unelected figure's role in government is a way around these potential deficits in a democratic system. The elected figures can hear the voice of the people in the regularly scheduled elections. However, the unelected leader, painting himself as the father of the country and representative of stability, tradition, and decisive action during a crisis, can embody the needs and will of the people too. Thus, the monarchy can shape the impression of a government for the people while placing limits on the "of the people" or "by the people" elements of democracy.

Individuals seeking to republicanize Moroccan politics will have to repoliticize it first. Though a majority (59.4 percent) of the Moroccan respondents expressed an interest in politics, that does not mean that they engage habitually with the idea of reshaping the system. Central issues—the economy, public health, and security—can be adjudicated and debated in the current system and draw mass public attention. The king has so far stayed above the fray, holding onto his position. Whether he will continue to do so in the coming years, as crises batter the economy and infrastructure and the elected elements of government are seen as aligned with his will rather than as a threat to his vision, is an open question. This represents a crucible for the monarchy. The apolitical nature of the politics, though, may insulate him even through a period of unpopularity.

The relationships between the other features and citizens' attitudes toward democracy are also noteworthy. Several proposed theories of public sentiment can be evaluated within this sample. In this case, social trust is positively associated with democratic interest. This is not always the case in the Middle East. In Morocco's case, it should not be assumed that it would breed antimonarchist sentiment. Trust is not linked to opposition to antidemocratic options. To really build democratic sentiment through civil society organizations and interpersonal trust, effective civil society organizations that are not arms of the monarchy would be necessary (Jamal 2007).

Theories of security and democratic concern are substantiated here (Benstead 2015). Those who worry about the results of elections are less interested in holding them. Moreover, Moroccans are open to all manner of nondemocratic alternatives. This bespeaks at least some highly instrumental interest in democracy—or government of any stripe. Intriguingly, those who think the government needs to be effective more than it needs to be participatory are endorsing multiparty democracy here; they are also endorsing the monarchy proxy system. This could reflect the king's embeddedness in the parliamentary system. If he continues to project efficacy, then his unelectedness is apparently forgivable. That would seem especially true if he can maintain the sense that he is the father or voice of the people.

Gender traditionalism in Morocco is associated with antidemocratic sentiment. Women's groups have previously worked successfully with the monarchy to advance women's rights in Morocco. In doing so, they have relied on the king's role as Commander of the Faithful. This insulated them somewhat from arguments that their liberal values are a religious or cultural threat. Although gender egalitarians are more likely to support democracy, that has not been the easiest route to achieving women's rights in recent decades. Liberalizers going forward may have to replicate this choice to operate with an unelected agent—potentially

154 *Defining Democracy*

against elected agents or other voters—to promote their interests. This would suggest that the liberal-democratic tension in the Middle East will not be easily resolved. Liberals, though, would do well to remember the (il)liberal backsliding process in Tunisia when evaluating these choices (Ridge 2022b).

Morocco differs from Egypt in the Islam and Islamism patterns. Secularists in Morocco are far less fearful of democracy—even though Morocco elected the PJD. Religious minorities are also not espousing democratic skepticism. In fact, secularists and minorities are less likely to endorse some of the nondemocratic alternatives. Thus, although they may not be more committed to democracy, they are still better proof against authoritarian musings. This suggests again that the role of religion in politics is a matter not of Islamic culture but rather of sociopolitical context. Local democrats might amplify voices promoting these views. The extent to which this could be done, though, would be constrained by the monarchy. There is a constitutional religion in Morocco, and the king is a religious leader. Secularism that opposes theocracy would likely be acceptable, but retracting the king's role as Commander of the Faithful or the official religion would be a heavy lift. As the following chapter will discuss, there does not seem to be great public interest in removing the Islamic patina from the state.

There are levers that activists might pull in order to engender public support for democratic governance. The practicality of these options is constrained. Changing gender attitudes or citizens' views on the role religion should play in government is a slow process. Much ink has already been spilled on whether elections are Islamic-law compliant. That debate can continue, but there is no reason to expect an imminent sea change. As noted in the last chapter, however, foreign interventions to change values risk backfiring if seen as paternalistic or being shut down if perceived as antigovernment. Democrats could attempt to promote popular political engagement generally. Those who are interested in politics and who watch or read the news are more likely to express interest in democracy. They are also better proofed against some antidemocratic systems. As political engagement does not appear to foment antimonarchical sentiment, it could also be a more accessible domain. The lack of relationship on that point could reflect limited opportunities to criticize the *makhzen* in the media. Morocco has faced external criticism for the treatment of critical journalists, including a 2023 EU Parliament resolution. To borrow Jamal's (2007, 107) phrasing, "The kingdom today continues to balance its authority by simultaneously tightening and loosening its political grip. It caters to its base of support

Democratic Commitment in Morocco **155**

and is less tolerant to voices of dissent." Agents seeking to utilize these systems would have to be strategic.

Another avenue is addressing the concerns about "bad results" from electoral systems. Western regimes can, to some extent, model the running of elections without "bad results." More important though would be to assuage fears about potential domestic instability or cultural peril from holding elections. Morocco has successfully run elections, including in 2021. That the elected branch of government takes the blame for the king, however, compromises citizens' ability to perceive accurately whether an election has had good or bad results.

Foreign powers could attempt to manipulate domestic sentiment toward the existing regime. It would be profoundly unethical, though, to destabilize a state in the hopes that the clamor breaks for democracy. More promising would be facilitating options for working or studying in the West, especially to work or attend university. Higher education is linked to democratic support, although the results here are not as strong as in other contexts. Promoting development is useful as an end in itself, and many bodies have tried. The limited efficacy of these options, especially this last, was unpacked in greater detail in Chapter 5. The outside world can be helpful to local democrats, but true democratization must come from within.

This evaluation of the implications of different conceptions of *dimuqratiyya* has considered how citizens engage with politics, including their active political behavior. These chapters have identified discrepancies in regime-type preferences. We now turn to differences in PCD and SECD respondents' preferences for the state writ large.

Notes

1. The *makhzen* is supposed to fulfil the Islamic political principle of *shūrā* (consultation) (Hibou 2011). Consultation as a principle has been treated as an indication that participatory democracy is an Islam-compliant system of government. Moroccan Islamists link *dimuqraityya* and *shūrā*, although *shūrā* is more about sharing opinions and forming consensus than making decisions (Khanani 2021). In practice, the *makhzen* is not a representation of popular will, since it is not a representative group. The religious veneer over the king's court can make it harder to object to the body. However, the practical level of control this religious veneer actually exerts over the public has been questioned (Maghraoui 2019).

2. This usage can be explained by the reverse of the survey methodology problem; protestors take the English translation for *dimuqratiyya* to employ in their demonstrations although it does not necessarily convey all that can be included in their view of *dimuqratiyya*. English signs are more accessible to Western observers, so protestors may use them to draw international attention to pressure the regime.

156 *Defining Democracy*

3. "Si ces dernières ont réussi à désamorcer le potentiel explosif des revendications, elles n'ont pas véritablement répondu aux problèmes soulevés."

4. Bi-l-nisba li-baladī al-maghrab, fa-laysat al-ḥukūma hiyya allatī taḥkum walaw intakhabnā alf ḥukūma fī al-ʿām al-waḍʿ sa-yabqā kamā huwwa ʿalayhi min al-rīʾ al-iqtṣādiyy. Wanaḥnu laysat lidaynā aṣlan ḥukūma innamā hiyya majmūʿa min aʿwān al-ẓulma fī khidma maṣāliḥihim al-shakhṣiyya wa tusattir ʿalā al-dawla al-ʿamīqa . . . al-kalām kathīr lākin lā yasir dhikruh innmā huwwa lā aḥad yaḥkumnā min huʾwalāʾ aldhīn yamthalūn amām al-ʿālim wa al-umum al-mutaḥida fa-naḥnu taḥt raḥma al-bank al-naqd al-dawaliyy . . . wa al-maghrab balad mulk li-lyahūd wa naḥnu naʾīsh fīhi wa iyjār.

5. Shukran ʿalā majmūʿ al-asiʾla lākin anā aʿīsh fī dawla bi-niẓām malakī wa arā an al-niẓām yakūn akthar istiqrār min bāqī al-nuẓum ʿalā al-aqal liʾannanā nuʾmin bi-annahu niẓām dāʾim wa laysa karaʾīs muntakhib lākin yarfuḍ al-insiḥāb min al-kursī wa yajbar al-afrād ʿalā qablūlihi bi-shakl dāʾim kamā an al-niẓām [a]l-malakī yusāhim bi-shakl kabīr fī istiqrār al-balad min al-nāḥiyya al-amaniyya wa al-iqtiṣādiyya . . . lam yatam al-taṭarruq al-ḥukm fī mujmal al-asʾila.

7

Making Choices

Salus populi suprema lex esto.
The welfare of the people shall be the supreme law.

—Cicero

Arab respondents who think of dimuqratiyya in political-institutional terms (PCD) and those who think of it in socioeconomic terms (SECD) engage differently in politics. PCD citizens are more politically active. These differences extend to their expressed preferences for democracy. They are more supportive of democracy, if not singularly so. They should then be potential proponents of viable and stable democratization in their communities.

Asking people what they want is the usual method in the democratic-attitudes literature. This technique alone, however, can only provide a partial impression of citizens' democratic attitudes and propensities. This chapter evaluates what they wish the state were. To do this, it draws on a conjoint experiment embedded in the Egypt and Morocco surveys.

Asking directly about the regime type a citizen would support or oppose has a fundamental limitation. State design is rarely a question of democracy yes/no or military dictatorship yes/no in isolation. Citizens evaluate the states they live in (or could live in) holistically. To understand their preferences accurately, a more complete image of the state is needed.

After all, "values, also value components of one ideology, are often at odds and compete in real-life situations" (Shamir and Shamir 1995, 107). The same is true for components of the state. Direct questions about support for democracy or desire for democracy cannot indicate whether this desire would withstand pressures to forgo democracy in favor of

157

158 *Defining Democracy*

something else. Even if citizens support electoral democracy generally, they may be willing to trade it for economic success or a religious regime. After all, they cannot eat elections. Recall the characterization of Tunisians who "prioritized bread over loyalty to the party and the nation" as "khobzists," which is to say bread-ists (Beinin 2016, 21). This possibility is particularly pertinent in the Middle East, where democracy and Islamism are often framed as oppositional propositions and where economic deprivation could make economic security more valuable. Properly accounting for citizens' preferences and accurately anticipating behavior requires considering several facets of government in conjunction with each other.

This provides a more realistic assessment of the relative valuation of regimes' structural elements. To understand the level and durability of popular support for democracy, it is necessary to examine how democracy fares when packaged with other regime elements. Each component could objectively be valued; the interest lies in how they are valued relative to each other. After all, maintaining a democracy in the real world requires valuing elections and participation in government over some desired outcomes an undemocratic system might promise or more efficiently deliver.

Conjoint analysis allows the identification of the relative valuation of potential regime features. It also addresses concerns about respondents' intentional or unintentional preference concealment and self-deception. This technique, discussed in greater detail shortly, shows participants' descriptions of potential regimes and then asks them to choose which of the two descriptions they would prefer. From the aggregation of multiple preference indications, the features that make a regime favorable to the citizenry can be identified.

Citizens do not engage in a daily plebiscite on their state structure. They live in the state structure they already have, which they may or may not be seeking to change. As such, this choice exercise might seem artificial. Communities in the Middle East region, however, through the Arab Spring and the subsequent reforms, coups, and demonstrations, have recently, even recurrently, faced the question of what they would want a new government to look like, whether or not the country ended up reincarnating. As such, questions about what is most valuable or necessary in a government are far less hypothetical in the Arab world

In the study, potential states were described along three dimensions. The first is the presence of elections and restrictions on political participation. In keeping with regional considerations and the expansive understanding of *dimuqratiyya*, economic and religious dimensions are included. To account for the interest in economic issues and deliver-

Making Choices 159

ables as potential sources of (un)democratic flexibility, public provision of private goods and unemployment levels are employed. Given the concern that latent or active Islamist tendencies are undermining Middle Eastern democratization, the option for an official religion and religious leaders' involvement in government are described.

An initial examination of citizens' average preferences is considered. Subsequent analyses look for structural differences between committed democrats and the less committed citizens and between PCD and SECD. To forecast the results: the public is broadly in favor of electoral democracy and a strong economy. The expressed openness to democracy found in the direct questions is then evident in the demonstrated preferences, even accounting for factors like economic efficacy. Furthermore, committed democrats evince a greater focus on participatory government. This is a good sign for the direct assessments of democratic commitment; they really are finding the people more likely to endorse democracy.

Most pertinently for this analysis of the democracy-*dimuqratiyya* gap, citizens' state-structural preferences diverge with their conception of *dimuqratiyya*. SECD in Egypt and Morocco place greater weight on the economic circumstances and the religious character of the state. PCD citizens give more consideration to the opportunities for political participation. This is consistent with the disparities in democratic commitment identified in Chapters 5 and 6. These differences open the possibility that *dimuqratiyya*, rather than being a shared construct over which citizens have preferences, is the term onto which these citizens are casting their preferences. *Dimuqratiyya* would then most appropriately mean "the state as it should be" rather than "democracy."

State-Structural Preferences

The results are initially presented for the public at large. Given the expressed support for *dimuqratiyya* in multiple surveys and the support for government by election discussed in the previous chapters, elections and unrestricted popular participation should be favored elements. Low levels of unemployment and strong provision of necessities should also be favored because they would indicate a strong economy from which respondents could benefit.

As noted in the preceding chapters, committed democrats are those who state that electoral democracy is the best form of government and that it is appropriate for Egypt or Morocco. Individuals who express great commitment to the idea of choosing a government by election

160 *Defining Democracy*

should place greater weight on having elections and opportunities for citizen participation in a potential government. Since democracy makes no promises about the economy, there is no theoretical reason to expect a particular emphasis on or apathy toward economic success or baseline social welfare policies among committed democrats. While secularism is often linked to democracy, committed democrats need not have a religious preference.

Differences are anticipated between respondents with different conceptions of *dimuqratiyya*. The previous chapters have shown that those who have a political-institutional conception of *dimuqratiyya* are more likely to support electoral democracy and to be committed democrats. In turn, it is expected that they will place greater value on systems with multiparty elections and low barriers to political participation. Recall from Chapter 4 that PCD are more likely to engage in many political behaviors. This is not an argument that SECD respondents are anti-democracy; rather, it is a statement about the comparative likelihood of assigning more weight to these state features. By contrast, respondents who conceive of *dimuqratiyya* as a set of socioeconomic outcomes are expected to place greater weight on reducing unemployment rates and government provision of necessities.

Respondents who conceive of *dimuqratiyya* as a set of socioeconomic outcomes are expected to be more supportive of religion's involvement in government. This relates to the idea that respondents cast *dimuqratiyya* over their preferred state. Researchers have theorized a link between religiosity and support for redistributive policies or baseline social service systems (Arikan 2013; Neustadt 2011).[1] Social justice rhetoric has been taken up by Middle East Islamists who focus on economic programs over political justice in their policy manifestos (Ciftci 2022). Furthermore, if a state is expected to subsidize religion, then the religious poor are more likely to break from the religious rich, with whom they would otherwise join in favoring fiscal conservatism, and unite with the secular poor in supporting parties that promote higher taxes and state investment and services programs (Huber and Stanig 2011). This would further align a focus on government-provision programs with government support for religion. As Khanani (2021, 93) shows, Moroccan Islamists link *dimuqratiyya* both to their religio-moral politics and to the redistributive agenda, tacitly linking, at least in that population, religious states and SECD views: "Indeed, standard linguistic practice among Moroccan *ilsāmiyūn* is to articulate a series of distinct, if connected, referents in one illocutionary act that collectively constitute *dimuqrāṭiyya*. Three moral-economic domains constitute *dimuqrāṭiyya*: (1) the ability for people to find work and, conversely, low rates of unemployment, (2) the absence of poverty, and (3) an equitable, or just, distribution of wealth." Reasonably, then, individuals whose conception of *dimuqratiyya* is tied to such economic insurance policies might conceptually link connecting religion to government with facilitating support for redistribution systems.

One respondent, a thirty-to-thirty-four-year-old Muslim Moroccan with a high school education living in Casablanca, made an explicitly religious appeal for economic equality. He wrote, "I hope that the government will reduce the gap between the rich and the poor, because we will stand in the hands of Allah, and I will take vengeance on the king first and the rest of the ministers."[2] He conceives of *dimuqratiyya* in socioeconomic terms. His response also shows that not all Moroccans are reticent to disapprove overtly of the king. Notably, though, religious affiliation and secularist orientation did not reliably predict *dimuqratiyya* classification (Chapter 3). As the previous chapters have shown, no one group is fully secular, religious, or democratic. The analysis here considers the propensities within these diverse groups.

Conjoint Experiment

This chapter draws on the final section of the Egypt and Morocco surveys discussed in the prior chapters: a conjoint experiment. Conjoint analysis has proliferated in political science in recent years. Researchers have used it to study support for judicial nominees (Sen 2017), voters' candidate preferences (Franchino and Zucchini 2015; Carnes and Lupu 2016; Hainmueller, Hopkins, and Yamamoto 2014; Shockley and Gengler 2020), party leaders' candidate preferences (Doherty, Dowling, and Miller 2019), support for climate-regulation agreements (Bechtel and Schreve 2013), issue importance in hypothetical policy bundles (Horiuchi, Smith, and Yamamoto 2018), support for Brexit strategies (Hobart, Tilley, and Leeper 2020), and immigration preferences (Hainmueller, Hangartner, and Yamamoto 2014; Hainmueller, Hopkins, and Yamamoto 2014). Graham and Svolik (2020) use the technique to look at Americans' democratic commitment by comparing the effect of candidates' ideologies and their antidemocratic policy preferences on voters' choices.

The technique is increasingly used in Middle Eastern countries. Cammett et al. (2022) consider security policy preferences in Lebanon, and Cammett et al. (2021) address the role of ethnicity in attitudes toward clientelism in Lebanon. Shockley and Gengler (2020) conducted

162 Defining Democracy

a phone-based candidate-preference conjoint in Qatar to identify the influence of cosectarianism in vote choice. Researchers have considered attitudes toward women's employment in Qatar (Blaydes, Gengler, and Lari 2021) and Jordan (Barnett, Jamal, and Monroe 2021). Ferwerda and Gest (2021) use a conjoint to demonstrate the pull factors for MENA emigration; liberal democratic governance and economic opportunities make target states more appealing. Shamir and Shamir (1995) studied Israelis' preference during the First Intifada for democracy, a Jewish majority, land claims, and peace. This project contributes to the application of this bourgeoning political science survey technique to the Middle East.

The respondents openly acknowledged that the choice task was harder than merely stating a preference. The conjoint was challenging because it could ask them to choose between imperfect, in their opinion, options. A forty-plus-year-old Cairene Muslim man with an advanced degree wrote, "One must make clear, not misleading, choices. It is difficult for one to choose if one must have elections and have religion be unrelated to politics, but one must designate a specific religion for the state, which is Islam. Also, it should provide a decent living for the citizens and a number of parties."[3] His description overtly demonstrates the challenge MENA residents face. Satisfying all preferences at once may be difficult or impossible, even with a clear vision of the desired state.

Another respondent, a college-educated Muslim man, twenty-five to twenty-nine years old, from a rural area, stated, "In this survey, sometimes it gives you a number of choices but there is no ideal choice that represents your point of view 100% . . . so you accept voting for the choice that represents your views only 80% or only 70%."[4] The reference to voting is apt, since in many ways that is the political process being approximated. In forming a new constitution, drafters are required to choose among potential regimes that could be created. Citizens, when voting on a constitutional referendum, which both Morocco and Egypt did after the Arab Spring, are presented with a restricted set of choices; they must choose among the constrained choice set in practice. These responses suggest that the point of the task, insofar as it requires choice and compromises on ideals, was recognized. They made a choice among less-than-ideal alternatives and appreciated that this can be a political frustration.

Moroccans echoed this sentiment. A forty-plus-year-old, college-educated Muslim man from an urban area said, "There are difficult choices at the end of the questionnaire."[5] A college-educated Muslim man from a Kenitra suburb, over age forty, wrote, "The last questions are constrained, and there is no choice in it. For instance, the government is not elected and the clergy and others."[6] Merely stating their ideals is

Making Choices 163

much easier than choosing among compromises, which is what politics often requires in practice.

The descriptions of the state structures consider many dimensions salient in Middle East politics and the literature on democratization. Opportunities for political participation were described in two domains. In terms of elections, the options are no elections, elections with only one recognized party, and elections with multiple recognized parties. Not all democracies include strong party systems; they may have weak parties, or some or all candidates may run independently of parties. For instance, many Egyptian parliamentarians are independent; independent parliamentarians are less common in Morocco. Egyptians may particularly recall the dominance of the National Democratic Party from Anwar Sadat to Hosni Mubarak; although it was dissolved after the Arab Spring, the history of single-party rule could taint the idea. Party membership is also low in the region. According to the fourth wave of the Arab Barometer, only 4.9 percent of Arabs are members of a political party. The rates are 3.2 percent in Morocco and 0.8 percent in Egypt; 56.9 percent of Arabs do not feel close to any political party. That number is higher in Egypt (61.61 percent) and in Morocco (66.2 percent) (Arab Barometer V). Sometimes social features mean only one party is seen as electorally viable, as previously occurred in the American South. Certain parties are restricted, and their supporters join the ranks of unaffiliated candidates to run as independents, as occurs for some Islamist parties. Nonetheless, assessments of democracy may require "at a minimum" "more than one serious political party" (Diamond and Morlino 2004, 21). In practice, based on the regional patterns, respondents might not greatly distinguish election-inclusive systems by the number of parties.

For participation, respondents also considered the level of barriers instituted by a regime to popular participation in politics. Fewer barriers would be more democratic. As discussed in Chapter 2, democracy metrics habitually characterize regimes by their competitive elections. Nonetheless, other forms of political participation are viable, even in regimes with questionable electoral credentials. Wedeen (2007, 60–61) "demonstrates how everyday practices of political contestation outside of electoral channels" can be part of forming "democratic persons" even in authoritarian contexts. Substantial nonelectoral participation happens in the Middle East (Chapter 4). Thus, it is instructive to incorporate the potential opportunities for nonelectoral political participation in describing the state structure.

The description includes the role religion could play in the regime. The Middle East features a variety of religion-state relationships. In many MENA countries, such as Morocco and Saudi Arabia, Islam is

164 *Defining Democracy*

recognized as an official religion. Others, such as Lebanon, maintain no official religion. A role for religious leaders is a recurrent area of concern and consideration. Scholars and foreign powers certainly focus on whether actors are attempting to install religious leaders in government positions. These can range from the somewhat common role of religious scholars who address state actions' compatibility with Islamic law to the theocratic republic structure. For simplicity, however, respondents here are presented with two dichotomized religious elements. The options were to have or not have an official religion for the state and to have or not have a formal role for religious leaders in the government.

In terms of economic outcomes that the government might generate, descriptions of the welfare subsidy system and the level of unemployment were included. The subsidy system described aligns with the description of a welfare system respondents could select when asked about their understanding of *dimuqratiyya*. Providing a social safety net is common in democracies, and even undemocratic Middle Eastern governments are faced with providing these benefits programs for social stability if not policy interest (Salevurakis and Abdel-Haleim 2008; Verme, El-Massnaoui, and Araar 2014). Threats to those subsidy and price-control programs can cause protests or riots (Rollinde and le Saout 1999). "IMF food riots" were common in the Global South from the 1970s to the 1990s, including the 1977 Bread Intifada in Egypt (Beinin 2015). State subsidies for personal necessities, rather than institutionally intense systems like individualized cash transfers, thus represent a reasonable state welfare system and economic outcomes metric. They would also be legible to respondents. The levels of high and low unemployment—specified at 14 and 7 percent, respectively—may seem high in the United States. However, they are realistic for the Middle East. Prior to the Arab Spring, unemployment in North Africa was slightly above 10 percent, heavily concentrated among the youth (Hong 2019). The rates increased in the immediate aftermath, but they are now in a similar range. The unemployment rate in 2019 was 10.76 percent in Egypt and 9.02 percent in Morocco. The described rates are thus high and low relative to the regional economy.

The three elements of state structure then were each represented by two attributes. Each attribute had either two or three levels, so there are 216 potential profiles.[7] The two profiles shown in the choice task were never identical, though they could share features. For instance, both presented regimes could have low unemployment. Hainmueller, Hangartner, and Yamamoto (2014) find that paired conjoints, presenting two options side by side, are closest to behavioral benchmarks from real-life choices.

Respondents were presented with five pairs of randomly generated profiles on sequential screens. Research suggests conjoint studies are "remarkably robust" to increases in the number of attributes and the number of choice tasks (Bansak et al. 2018, 113). However, as the conjoint was included with the other survey questions, it was decided not to lengthen the survey excessively by including more choices.[8]

Results

In a conjoint analysis, there are two measures of interest. The first causal quantity of interest is the average marginal component effect (AMCE). This number is the effect of that component on the individual's propensity to choose that option; it is the "marginal effect of attribute l averaged over the joint distribution of the remaining attributes" (Hainmueller, Hopkins, and Yamamoto 2013, 10). It averages over both the direction and intensity of the respondents' preferences (Abramson, Koçak, and Magazinnik 2022). Intensely held beliefs are unlikely to update with new information or to be abandoned because of additional considerations (Fatas-Villafranca, Dulce Saura, and Vázquez 2011). Intensity does not necessarily mean holding an extreme position; rather intensity means it will consistently inform an individual's choice. Functionally, the AMCE is the change in the likelihood that a profile is chosen if that characteristic is included in the profile instead of the baseline characteristic. Positive numbers mean the choice is more likely, while negative numbers indicate the descriptor makes choice less likely. There is always a reference level for comparison.

The second quantity of interest is the marginal mean. This number "describes the level of favorability toward profiles that have a particular feature level, ignoring all other features" (Leeper, Hobolt, and Tilley 2020, 6). Marginal means are not in comparison to a reference category like the AMCE is. A marginal mean above 0.5 means that the feature increases the support for a given profile, while a marginal mean below 0.5 means that the feature would decrease favorability for that profile. Because the marginal mean does not have a reference level, it is useful in subgroup analyses in place of examining the differences in AMCE scores. Removing the reference category facilitates subgroup analysis because it ensures that the difference is not caused by between-group differences in the reference level. Thus, using the marginal mean is the more conservative approach. Because the results are averages of the respondents' preferences, the results are described in terms of the "average" Egyptian and "average" Moroccan.

166 *Defining Democracy*

Full Sample

The generalized results from each country can be considered first. As in the prior chapters, analysis concentrates on those who took the surveys in Arabic so responses can also be grouped by meaning of *dimuqratiyya*.[9] These indicate whether citizens hold, on average, more or less favorable attitudes toward states with certain features. The numerical results are included in Appendix E.

Despite the differences in these countries' political experiences, the conjoint analysis reveals remarkably similar state-structural preferences. Elections are influential in their regime-type choices. The average Egyptian is more likely to select a state that includes elections. The positive effect of having elections is significantly stronger for multiparty elections than for single-party elections. Similarly, the average Moroccan is more likely to endorse a state with elections, and the boost from multiparty elections is greater than having only one recognized party in the elections. This pattern is consistent with the openness to electoral democracy expressed in Chapters 5 and 6. The only significant differences between the countries appeared on this dimension. Moroccan respondents, on average, were more tolerant of the absence of elections.

Barriers to political participation also matter in both cases. In the Egypt sample, the introduction of barriers to political participation reduces the likelihood of support relative to having few barriers to participation, but having many barriers does not matter more than having only some. In the Morocco sample, systems with many barriers to citizens' political participation were significantly less likely to be chosen than those with few barriers. Having some barriers, however, is not significantly different in choice propensity than having few barriers. These patterns are also consistent with the support for democracy and the levels of popular political participation identified in the Arab Barometer and these surveys.

Economic issues are also important in both countries. For both Egyptians and Moroccans, a system's producing low rates of unemployment makes it more likely to be chosen relative to one that has high levels of unemployment. Notably, this factor is the second most influential in shaping respondents' state-structural preferences. Voting is an important factor in public choice, but the deliverables will also matter.

A potential government is less likely to be favored if it has inferior systems for ensuring access to personal necessities. The average Egyptian respondent is less interested in a regime that has only some provision of individual necessities than in one that features good government provision and prefers some state provision to little state support. The average Moroccan is also less likely to choose a government with limited provision of personal necessities. While having some provision is not significantly different from having good provision, having little provision significantly undermines support. The AMCEs are smaller, though, for goods provision than for unemployment. The unemployment rate then is more important for the average Egyptian's and average Moroccan's choice than providing personal necessities.

Thus far the results fit well with the expectations outlined earlier. It is not particularly surprising that any population would want a strong economy and possibly even a state safety net. Afterall, state subsidies and price controls for daily-needs items are common in the region. The results also show strong support for elections, including even differentiating between systems with many and few parties, despite the relatively low rates of party membership in the MENA region. Preference is also given to states that do not infringe on opportunities for political participation. Recall from Chapter 4, rates of political participation are currently rather low in the Arab world. In 2018, 80.6 percent of Arab Barometer respondents stated that they had never attended a meeting or signed a petition; the nonparticipation rates were higher in Egypt (82.3 percent) but lower in Morocco (77 percent). In the same survey, 78.9 percent of respondents said they had never participated in a protest, march, or sit-in. The rates again were higher in Egypt (83.5 percent) and lower in Morocco (70.7 percent) (Arab Barometer V). Nevertheless, they want the option to do so.

This frequency of nonparticipation in practice could indicate that present participation is suppressed or that it does not seem necessary at the moment. Respondents want the right to exist in case they need to use it, but they do not currently feel the need to do so. Another survey of Egyptians found that 61 percent believed residents should "be allowed to protest peacefully to bring about social change" (Ridge 2022a). Given that only 23 percent of Arabs think their country is heading in the right direction (37 percent in Egypt and 35.1 percent in Morocco), 72.8 percent think their country's economy is (very) bad (52.3 percent in Egypt and 58.9 percent in Morocco), and 28 percent feel that their and their family's safety is not ensured (21.5 percent in Egypt and 31.7 percent in Morocco) (Arab Barometer V), protests would be justified. Low rates of participation may reflect a sense of impotence or danger. If it will accomplish nothing or the anticipated danger outweighs the anticipated gain, then participation would flag even in the face of desire. Nonetheless, respondents express preference for it being their choice.

168 *Defining Democracy*

Taken together, though, these preference patterns seem to align with both democracy and *dimuqratiyya* in its various understandings.

The position that religion should occupy in the preferred state structure is nuanced. On one hand, having an official religion increases both the average Egyptian's and the average Moroccan's likelihood of choosing that hypothetical state. On the other hand, having no role for religious leaders in the government increases the average Egyptian's and the average Moroccan's inclination toward that system relative to having a role for religious leaders. In both the Egypt and Morocco samples, the AMCE spread is larger, though, for official religion than for participation of religious leaders. This indicates that having an official role for religion has, on average, more influence on the responses. This distinction between official religion and involving religious leaders speaks to a nuanced view of the relationship Islam should have to the state. Citizens can desire formalized recognition for religion without supporting religious leaders' direct involvement.

One interpretation of this is that the public wants a patina of religion for the government but for its involvement to be superficial, which is why they do not want a role for religious leaders. Another way to construe this could be that they really do want a position for religion in the state but are skeptical of involving religious leaders. Such men could exercise independent power in the state, and they might push a conservative agenda. They could be corrupt, rather than true representatives of religion and religious law. One college-educated Cairene Muslim man alluded to this quandary: "Religion is the basis of the country, but there are people who govern the country in the name of religion and offend the religion to which they belong."[10] The citizens can value religion for their country while being circumspect about how it should be included or represented. Making these kinds of distinctions shows a considered response to the potential involvement of religion in government, not knee-jerk Islamism. It also shows that these perspectives can coexist with support for elected government.

This is not to say that incorporating religion into the state is neutral with respect to democratization. Gouda and Hanafy (2020) observe a negative relationship between democracy and the incorporation of Islamic law in state constitutions. In general, though contemporary democracies are less likely to involve themselves in religion, global democracies are not fully separated from it (Fox 2007). Functionally assessing the relationship between religion and governance is necessarily a multidimensional process. Thus, multiple avenues of (dis)engagement need to be considered. However, the incorporation of religious elements should be done

Making Choices 169

carefully—and with the considered perspective shown in these results—in order to ensure that it is not deleterious to democratic governance.

Committed Democrats

The previous chapters examined respondents' democratic commitment. Do they believe that elected government is the best form of government, and do they believe that it is appropriate for their countries? Those who affirmed both of these positions are classed as committed democrats. Researchers consider them to be the basis of democratic stability. The differences between committed democrats and other respondents in regime structural preferences are considered here. Recall that MENA citizens have been accused of disingenuousness in their democratic preferences. The preferences exposed in the conjoint can indicate whether those who express support for democracy are more likely to assign weight to democratic institutions in their state-structural preferences.

In the Egyptian sample, committed democrats are significantly more likely than other Egyptians to choose a regime that has multiparty democracy. They are less likely to choose a regime without elections. These clusters do not weight the other state features significantly differently in their choices. Thus, among the Egyptians, the committed democrats are more democratic in their demonstrated preferences.

Among Moroccans, committed democrats were also more inclined toward a regime that featured multiparty elections (p = 0.061). They were also significantly less tolerant of state-imposed barriers to political participation. These clusters did weigh one other feature differently; the committed democrats assigned less weight to state provision of personal necessities. In both Egypt and Morocco, the results, then, indicate that individuals who aver support for electoral democracy pay more attention in their state-structural preferences to opportunities for participation.

These results should not be interpreted to mean that Egyptians and Moroccans who are not committed democrats—sizeable populations in both states, as discussed in Chapters 5 and 6—are opposed to elected government. In both subgroups, the average respondents would prefer a state with elections, especially multiparty elections, to a state without elections. However, the effect is stronger among the committed democrats than among the other respondents.

These results are a favorable indication for the direct survey questions about support for elections-based government. The demonstrated preferences and avowed preferences align. When a choice is actually

170 *Defining Democracy*

required, the respondents who endorsed electoral democracy in the direct question are also more likely to choose a government that has those elections. It was not merely cheap talk or a face-saving falsification to say that they supported democracy (Kuran 1997). Their support was also not washed away by the other regime features, like economic success or Islamic affiliation. These preferences are a positive indicator for their support for democratization in a more practical sense. If anything, the typical analysis may be overinterpreting the scruples revealed in the direct questions as opposition.

Understanding of *Dimuqratiyya*

Do individuals who conceive of *dimuqratiyya* primarily as a system of political institutions and those who view it as a system of socioeconomic outcomes have different preferred state structures? The previous chapters showed differences in their expressed preferences. Here the focus is on demonstrated preferences. It is shown that those with a political understanding of *dimuqratiyya* place greater value on the democratic features of the state, while the outcome-focused respondents place greater weight on the economic circumstances.

For this analysis, respondents are classed by the element they identified as the most important feature for identifying a country as a *dimuqratiyya*. Those who indicated the opportunity to change the government by elections, the freedom to criticize the government, having equal political rights for all citizens, or separating religion from the government are identified with the political-institutional understanding of *dimuqratiyya* (PCD). The citizens who said the most important characteristic is narrowing the gap between the rich and the poor, providing basic items to every individual, eliminating financial corruption, or ensuring law and order are identified as having a socioeconomic understanding of *dimuqratiyya* (SECD).

Among Egyptians, those with the political understanding of *dimuqratiyya* are, on average, less willing to accept a government that imposes some barriers to citizens' political participation. They are also more willing to accept a government with high unemployment and are less invested in having low levels of unemployment. Citizens who conceive of *dimuqratiyya* in socioeconomic terms are, on average, more supportive of having an official state religion.

Again, this is not to say that the other group feels the opposite way about any of these features. Both populations, on average, are less interested in a state that has no official religion and less interested in a system with high rates of unemployment. However, the average weight given to these elements is stronger in SECD than PCD.

Among Moroccans, those who understand *dimuqratiyya* primarily in political-institutional terms are more favorably inclined than those with a socioeconomic understanding toward a system with few barriers to political participation. In turn, they are comparatively less interested in a regime with many barriers to participation. In terms of the economic issues, those with a primarily socioeconomic conception of *dimuqratiyya* place more weight on the level of provision of necessities. They are comparatively more inclined to favor to a system that would have strong state provision of basic items. As with Egypt, the SECD respondents place significantly more weight on having recognition for religion in the government. Individuals who are connecting *dimuqratiyya* with redistributive economics are also in favor of their government's establishing a religion.

These results are consistent with the outlined expectations for the differences between these groups based on their expressed conception of *dimuqratiyya*. Again, the demonstrated and expressed preferences are similar. All in all, these patterns suggest that citizens with different conceptions of *dimuqratiyya* place different weights on the potential features of their preferred state. PCD are more focused on the political features of the hypothetical state; SECD assign more choice weight to the economic deliverables. Even if the group members do not have opposing visions, their relative commitments to these elements diverge. This suggests that, if push came to shove, they would pursue different agendas.

Discussion and Conclusion

Conjoint analysis can reveal what citizens value. In these cases, the preferred condition for the average Egyptian and Moroccan includes multiparty elections, few barriers to political participation, an official religion but no role for religious leaders, low unemployment, and good baseline public welfare. In fact, of the 216 potential regime types, the option that was most likely to be chosen by Egyptians and Moroccans—the case that was selected 86.1 percent of the time it was shown in Egypt and 85.2 percent of the time it was shown in Morocco—included multiparty elections, some barriers to political participation, an official religion but no role for religious leaders in the government, some provision of individual necessities, and low unemployment. In Egypt, a similar regime that had a good personal-necessity provision was equally likely to be chosen.

172 *Defining Democracy*

That any of the regime options achieves such strong support is amazing. In fact, just over half of the potential regimes achieved at least 50 percent support. It is possible that no combination of attribute levels in a conjoint study would receive majority support as a package, even a case featuring the elements that were positively rated on average (Hobalt, Tilley, and Leeper 2020). This could occur, for instance, in cases of bimodal preferences. Where the combinations fail, the results point to infeasibility in practical politics. Even with free rein, drafters would not be able to create a satisfying structure. In both the Egyptian and Moroccan cases, though, it is evident that regimes could be constructed with respect to these features that could obtain majority—even supermajority—support. Whether this can actually be brought to pass is a separate question.

By contrast, the regime that was least likely to be chosen by Egyptians —selected only 16.7 percent of the time it was shown—had no elections, some barriers to political participation, no official religion or role for religious leaders in government, little provision of necessities, and high unemployment. The least likely to be chosen by Moroccans, chosen 13.2 percent of the time it was shown, had only one recognized political party, many barriers to political participation, no role for religious leaders or official religion, high unemployment, and some public provision of necessities.

That the most and least chosen in practice are not perfect sums of the results of the individual level AMCE results reflects the averaging across both preference and intensity that produces the average marginal component effects (Abramson, Koçak, and Magazinnik 2022). Where some respondents feel very strongly about their preference or weigh that item very strongly, the average can be pulled in that direction by those respondents. This could result in the average appearing different from the modal preference. That is why countries hold actual elections, rather than tallying polls or isolated item preferences. This does not mean that the polls and item preferences are not instructive. In this case, however, the results are quite in line with the averages.

The general pattern is not exactly surprising. Economic success in a participatory regime that recognizes the predominant religion without empowering potentially restrictive clerics would seem to be the sweet spot. It is in fact a system modeled by many European states. Furthermore, the results across the country samples were markedly similar. Despite the substantial differences between the country contexts, the citizens were expressing quite similar ideal states. More interesting is what the analysis reveals in terms of potential trade-offs.

Overall, the most important feature for Egyptians and Moroccans in choosing a government is the nature of the elections. Much more weight is placed on the existence of elections than the relative barriers the government could place in front of citizens' methods of participating in politics. The next most influential items are the unemployment rate and the presence of an official religion. Valuing employment speaks to a particular economic vision. They would rather a system generate job opportunities than provide welfare. This could reflect a desire for work as a means of achieving above-baseline economic conditions and a view that high employment suggests a generally healthy economy. It is also consistent with theories that people value working for noneconomic reasons, such as dignity and life satisfaction (Sayer 2009; Clark, Georgellis, and Sanfrey 2001). This contrasts with current regimes that provide subsidies in multiple domains without resolving the substantial and long-standing unemployment situation.

The results here also show a nuanced view of secularism. Rather than linking an official religion with a regime that incorporates religious leaders, these elements are distinguished. An official religion is valued while an official role for religious leaders is disfavored, though this element plays a lesser role in Egyptians' and Moroccans' preferences. Such a system would not be out of step with other democracies. While several Western democracies, such as France and the United States, renounce national religions, others, like Iceland and the United Kingdom, maintain established churches. Most importantly, the support for an official religion coexists with support for a system of elections. This is consistent with the suggestions in the literature that Muslims may seek a nonsecular democracy. This does not mean, though, that they seek a democracy unlike those present elsewhere in the world, nor does it imply a step toward an Iran-style Islamic republic.

More interesting is that the pattern is so similar across the two country contexts. Despite the very different political histories in these states, the citizens are revealing similar desired state structures, including with respect to religion and the state. This invites the question of the extent to which other Middle Eastern or Muslim-majority country populations would have the same preference structure. Future research can expand this analysis to countries with more religious diversity (e.g., Lebanon or Iraq) or other contexts (e.g., Indonesia or Iran) to probe the generalizability.

These results also validate the results in the previous chapters by demonstrating the extent to which citizens' expressed preferences are consistent with their choice task preferences. Committed democrats understandably have different preferences than those who are not similarly

174 *Defining Democracy*

expressly supportive of electoral democracy. They place significantly more emphasis on the inclusion of elections and, to a lesser extent, the ability of parties to participate in them. Committed democrats and other citizens are largely not distinguished with respect to their preferences over the other features of the states. Those respondents who believe elections are the best way to choose a government and that this method is appropriate for their countries are markedly less willing to sacrifice a participatory regime for their country for economic or religious concerns. They are not differently situated with respect to questions like whether to incorporate religion into the regime. Thus, scholars should be cautious about the assumptions they hang on MENA democrats' additional structural preferences.

Pertinently for this examination of the democracy-*dimuqratiyya* gap, these results also speak to the differences associated with diverging conceptions of *dimuqratiyya*. Egyptians whose conception of *dimuqratiyya* is based in political institutions place less value on formalizing religion's position in the state. They also place less weight on economic concerns, like unemployment, than those whose conception is grounded in socioeconomic outcomes. In total, this suggests that citizens who understand *dimuqratiyya* in political terms are less willing to sacrifice the institutional elements of democracy for superior economic outcomes or Islamism. This is consistent with the results from Chapter 5. Egyptians with this political understanding of *dimuqratiyya* are more likely to think affirmingly of an elections-based government, and they are shown here as less likely to be concerned by other regime elements when making their choices.

Moroccans whose conception of *dimuqratiyya* is based in political institutions were distinguished in some respects from Moroccans whose conception of *dimuqratiyya* is based in socioeconomic outcomes. They are less concerned with the efficiency of the welfare system and have greater objection to substantial barriers to political participation. They also place less weight on establishing a religion. Their attitudes toward elections and unemployment levels, though, are not markedly different. They are less likely to be Islamists, but they are not necessarily more assiduous defenders of elections. These results are consistent with Chapter 6 in that PCD Moroccans were not singularly democratic.

Citizens' avowed attitudes and their latent preferences are quite consistent. This consistency gives credence to Benstead's (2018, 536) argument that "worries that the Arab world is a more challenging survey context—or that citizens answer dishonestly—reflect biases of 'Arab exceptionalism,' more than fair assessments of data quality." Citizens who report valuing democracy do seem to mean that. It simply is not all that they value.

Making Choices **175**

The relative values are also important when considering the differences between PCD and SECD. Egyptians and Moroccans favor, in a broad sense, a similar regime structure. The conjoint reveals that PCD and SECD preferences among these features are different. That is to say that some of the subgroups place greater weight on features like political participation and economic strength. The challenge is less about their support in a generalized or theoretical sense—the overall pattern favors employment and elections. It is about their commitments if they feel they must choose between two goals.

Recall that PCD individuals were more likely to report engaging in protests. Protests are among the most visible forms of political engagement—those which might particularly stand out to observers and to scholars. Following these results, sampling for state-structural preferences in such groups would draw more from people whose attention lies on these political-institutional elements of the state. They certainly do not lie only there. For decades MENA protests have drawn attention to workers' demands and food insecurity as well as to calls for elections and representation (Beinin 2015; El-Ghobashy 2021). However, scholars should be aware of the confluence of participation and philosophy that these patterns imply when they consider whose voices are being amplified by the media and by scholarship and whether those samples are sufficiently varied to represent the range of popular sentiment.

These results further substantiate the finding in the last section that democratic commitment is lower in SECD populations. This is practically pertinent. Those with a socioeconomic view of *dimuqratiyya* make up half of each population. This populace might then serve as a pool of weakened democratic persistence from which those with authoritarian leanings can draw support. Recall that 21 percent in Egypt and 31 percent in Morocco, according to Chapters 5 and 6, believed that unelected governments were preferable in some circumstances. Would-be autocrats can use these populations, as well as the people who feel it does not matter, to form coalitions. SECD are more likely hold those views, and they are more likely to direct their focus to the socioeconomic deliverables that an authoritarian leader might offer. Thus, these would-be authoritarians (or current authoritarians) could deliver on the ancillary regime dimensions to prevent backlash against less-than-democratic actions (Snider 2022). Arguably President Kais Saied has engaged in such tactics in Tunisia (Ridge 2022b). Other regimes, like Iran, have tried to capitalize on the religious patina to forestall popular uprisings; at least in Iran's case, the long-term success of that strategy may finally be failing. The relatively lower democratic commitment and the relatively greater outcome-based preferences make the SECD half of the population more

176 *Defining Democracy*

susceptible to such programming. This opening constitutes a democratization problem. As long as citizens see a dim future and economic turmoil continues, would-be autocrats will be primed to look for those opportunities. Although these results show that democracies can achieve majority support, that is not the only path forward.

Notes

1. This pattern has the caveat that, in cases in which religion becomes a cleavage identity, like in secularizing Europe, religiosity can create an opposition to redistribution. This change can reflect an opposition to redistribution across the religious-secular cleavage, akin to the opposition to redistribution across other social divides, or it can reflect an opposition to a secular state structure: "While not necessarily opposed to the general idea of ameliorating the inequalities and social ills generated by markets, they object to the provision of welfare by the secular state" (Stegmueller et al. 2012, 484). The religious group itself can serve as a vehicle for redistribution and insurance (Iannaccone 1992).

2. Atamannā min al-ḥakūma taqlīṣ [*sic*] al-huwwa bayna al-aghnyā' wa al-fuqarā' li-annanā sanaqif bayna yadayi Allāh wa sa'aqtaṣṣ min al-malak awalan wa baqiyya al-wuzarā'.

3. Lā budd min waḍ' ikhtiyārāt wāḍiḥa ghayr muḍallila ṣa'ba al-ikhtiyārāt annahu lā budd min jadd intikhābāt wa laysa li-ldīn 'alāqa bi-lsiyāsa wa lākin lā budd min qirār dīn khāṣṣ bi-ldawla wa huwwa al-islām wa lā budd an tuwwāfir al-'īsha al-karīma l-lmuwāṭinīn wa ta'addud al-aḥzāb.

4. Fī hādhā al-istiṭlā' aḥyānan yu'ṭīk 'adda ikhtibārāt wa lākin lā yūjid min baynahā al-ikhtiyār al-mithālī al-ādhī yu'abbir 'an ra'īk wa wijhat naẓarak 100% ... fataqbal bal-taṣwīt 'alā ikhtiyār yu'abbir 'an ra'īk faqaṭ binisbat 80% aw 70% faqaṭ.

5. Wujūd ikhtiyārāt ṣa'ba fī akhir al-istibiyān.

6. Al-asi'la al-akhīra mafrūḍa wa lā ikhtiyār fīhā mithla. [*sic*] al-ḥakūma laysat muntakhiba., [*sic*] wa rijāl al-dīn wa ghayrihā.

7. This study follows Franchino and Zucchini (2015, 227) in maintaining the order of the attributes "in order to ease the cognitive burden" on the participants. Six attributes might seem like a lot of information for a respondent to consider; however, compared to regular political choices, it is not a large number. For instance, the Comparative Constitutions Project (comparativeconstitutionsproject.org) identifies more than three hundred potential constitutional provisions a country could have. Conjoint analysis has been found robust to even large numbers of "potentially meaningful attributes," and respondents are not "overwhelmed with meaningful information" (Bansak et al. 2021, 69).

8. Though prior studies suggest that having five choice sets is not excessive and should not induce satisficing, the results were tested to see if they are significantly different across the five sets. They were not significantly different in either country's data ($p > 0.05$).

9. The respondents who did the conjoint in English were less likely to support an official religion but were otherwise not significantly different.

10. Al-dīn asās al-dawla walākin hunāk ashkhāṣ yaḥkumūn al-dawla b-ism al-dīn wa yusī'ūn l-ldīn al-muntamīn lahu.

8

For the People

You keep using that word. I do not think it means what you think it means.

—Inigo Montoya, *The Princess Bride*

Blood and treasure (as well as academic ink) have been poured into the idea of Middle Eastern (non)democracy. Even after the Arab Spring, the region lacks democracies. Dozens of reasons have been put forward, from religion, to gender traditionalism, to war, to oil. These theories really boil down to the question of whether democracy would even be possible.

This book enters that discussion by focusing on the meaning that *dimuqratiyya*—which researchers have taken as a synonym for *democracy* —holds in the Arab world. We cannot understand this region and its politics if we look only at the institutions in place and not at how the people there think and what they will for themselves. Durable democratization requires a public that wants to keep democracy, even when it is hard.

Dimuqratiyya is not democracy. This disparity is both theoretically and empirically relevant for understanding public will, support for democracy, and political participation in the Arab world. Political scientists evaluate the level of democracy in a country by looking at the electoral institutional structures—and occasionally associated liberties—that the state utilizes (Chapter 2). It is in these institutions that the governments of the Middle East and North Africa (MENA) are found lacking. These are not the singular, or even primary, metrics by which Arab publics evaluate the level of *dimuqratiyya* in a country. In several waves of Arab Barometer data, free and fair elections contribute to the identification of

177

178 *Defining Democracy*

a country with *dimuqratiyya*, but the regimes' outcomes are the strongest determinants. In particular, respondents' subjective evaluations of the regime's general performance, state efforts to crack down on corruption, and their physical safety determine the *dimuqratiyya* ratings that the public assigns these countries. *Dimuqratiyya* is a system that is for the people, but it is not necessarily of or by the people. It is the "state that works." There is a denotative gap between *democracy* and *dimuqratiyya*.

Approximately half of the respondents in surveys of the Arab world affirmatively identify socioeconomic outcomes (SECD), rather than political institutions (PCD), as the essential elements of *dimuqratiyya* (Chapter 3). For the other half of the respondents, political structures like elections and civil liberties are cornerstones of *dimuqratiyya*. Prevalent answers also included, however, the absence of corruption or the presence of a strong welfare state. A small gap in income between the rich and the poor and the public provision of basic necessities are not requirements or guarantees of democracy as political scientists tend to use or measure the construct. *Dimuqratiyya* may share some elements with democracy, but these constructs are not mutually interchangeable.

These elements tie *dimuqratiyya* to the Greek word roots *demos* and *kratos*, meaning "people's rule." *Dimuqratiyya* could be a government for the people in its inclusion of economic advantage for the common person. It is not, however, of the people or by the people, especially in the willingness to incorporate military rule in *dimuqratiyya* or give short shrift to electoral institutions (Chapter 3). Only the freely chosen outcomes of the public voice could become a government of and by the people.

There are multiple knock-on effects of citizens' diverging views of *dimuqratiyya*. This distinction manifests in differential engagement with real-world politics. Arabs who think of *dimuqratiyya* in terms of political institutions were much more likely to participate in politics (Chapter 4). This was true of institutional political participation (e.g., joining a party) and noninstitutional forms (e.g., signing a petition or joining a protest). Unfortunately, it means they were also more likely to report engaging in politically motivated violence. These citizens are more engaged with trying to inform their leaders of their opinions and trying to sway politics toward their agenda than citizens who conceive of *dimuqratiyya* in terms of socioeconomic outcomes.

The two groups also have different regime-type preferences. Namely, individuals who understand *dimuqratiyya* primarily in terms of the socioeconomic outcomes that the state produces are less likely to endorse a democratic system of government. They are less invested in choosing their government by election and less likely to believe doing so is

For the People 179

appropriate for their countries. The group differences were identified in early waves of the Arab Barometer (Chapter 4) as well as in novel surveys in Egypt (Chapter 5) and Morocco (Chapter 6).

These studies identify a democracy-*dimuqratiyya* gap in public opinion. *Dimuqratiyya* is much more popular than democracy. In both Egypt and Morocco, there is popular support for democracy. However, that support has been dramatically overestimated in surveys that rely on the word *dimuqratiyya*. Expressed support for *dimuqratiyya* is greater than the support for elected democracy in either country. Indicating what democracy is—a political-institutional structure—reduces support, because some of that supposed support was actually a statement of an economic policy preference (or economic outcome preference) rather than support for democracy. That the public endorsement of *dimuqratiyya* has been misconstrued as support for competitive and binding elections means that public interest in democracy itself has been overstated (by researchers rather than a dissembling public).

Furthermore, this support does not exist in isolation. For many people, democracy is one acceptable potential regime among several. Those who would support only democracy are a minority—less than a third of the sample. A regime that allows for military intervention has nontrivial public support, especially in Egypt. Moroccans also expressed great openness to a system in which an unelected leader shares governing responsibilities with the elected government, as currently occurs in the parliamentary monarchy. These publics are not overtly antidemocratic, but they are not singularly invested in democracy, even when they do support it.

Those who think of *dimuqratiyya* politically and those who think of *dimuqratiyya* economically also differ in their idealized state form (Chapter 7). A conjoint experiment finds that these publics as a whole have very understandable preferences for a state structure. They want a system that has elections, even preferring multiparty elections over single-party elections, and opportunities for political engagement. They want it to generate low rates of unemployment while ensuring basic necessities are available through the welfare system. The survey respondents demonstrate nuanced preferences with respect to religion; namely, they want the state to have an official religion while wanting no official office for religious leaders. By these metrics, they are arguably endorsing a model employed by many western European states.

Within this preferred-state framework, however, citizens who conceive of *dimuqratiyya* primarily as a political institution place greater weight on maintaining opportunities for political participation in the state, and they place less value on officially recognizing religion. Those

180 *Defining Democracy*

who conceive of *dimuqratiyya* in terms of socioeconomic outcomes are more interested in recognizing religion in the state. They are also more focused on whether or not the state generates low unemployment.

This finding demonstrates a confluence between the meaning the individuals attribute to *dimuqratiyya* as a construct and their system preferences. It is possible that *dimuqratiyya* as a construct is taking on the flavor of their most preferred state system. That means that *dimuqratiyya* would be divorced from democracy itself and instead be a marker of the parts of the state to which that individual pays particular attention. It is no wonder, then, that so many respondents would say *dimuqratiyya* is the best form of government. They have made it the government they want.

Overall, these studies demonstrate that *democracy* and *dimuqratiyya* are not understood to have equivalent meanings, at least for half of the population. For the other half, the alignment may be incidental to their preferences rather than grounded in a focus on the meaning of democracy. Superior self-awareness would be necessary for citizens or researchers to trace that point. Pertinently, these studies demonstrate not only that there are discontinuities between democracy and *dimuqratiyya* but that the divergences accord with practical differences in political preferences and behaviors.

Consideration of additional ramifications naturally follows from these conclusions. To unpack these corollaries, think back to the question asked in the epigraph of first chapter. It was posed decades ago in Morocco but is still relevant today: "But why does no one explain this *dimuqratiyya* to us?" (Mernissi 1992, 115). This book presents two answers to that question, and each leads to its own discussion. The first is that—despite the disjointed meaning in the Arab world for *dimuqratiyya*—the individuals using the term believe that their audiences understand it in the same fashion that they do. They do not define the term in their studies, surveys, or statements because they do not recognize that doing so would be necessary.

The second answer is that some speakers may recognize the dissimilarities in the way the word is used within the population and/or between the public and the Western observers, but they decline to clarify their meaning to take advantage of the muddled meaning. Schaffer (2000, 127) proposes, "Both factions of the [Senegalese] political elite seek to set the terms of the debate about [the Wolof term] *demokaraasi* and thereby shape the broader population's perception of what counts as legitimate leadership." Whether the language of *dimuqratiyya* is used so strategically is a topic for future research. The activists and newsmen Fatima Mernissi's aunt were watching may have omitted to define "this *dimuqratiyya*" because the meaning was assumed or because the speakers wanted to maintain the ambiguity about the meaning to account for diverse goals or a nonunified audience.

More on *Dimuqratiyya*

In this book, I have focused on the relationship between *dimuqratiyya*, democratic opinion, and political participation. There are other kinds of politics to consider. For instance, foreign aid was only broached in Chapter 5. These groups may have different attitudes toward foreign aid, what role it should have in their state, and how it should be targeted. They may have different preferences with respect to international relations. Do they want their countries to engage with regimes that view democracy as they view *dimuqratiyya* (e.g., PCD favoring engaging the United States and SECD favoring engaging China)? Do these citizens have different potential for emigration? In 2021, a third of Arab Barometer respondents said they had thought about emigrating from their country. In noting the effects of living, working, or studying in the West on citizens' attitudes, I proposed that nondemocrats were probably not specifically avoiding such opportunities on that basis. Would these two blocs, though, divide on that point? Beyond that, would they favor different regimes to which to emigrate? Substantial domains of politics could be impacted by this difference in viewpoints.

The remainder of this chapter unpacks the significance of these findings for Middle Eastern studies and for political science, especially cross-cultural survey research. It considers four primary contributions in turn. First, it discusses how these results undermine the argument that the Middle East has a democracy paradox. Second, it examines the implications of these results for political science's understanding of social movements in the Middle East. These two points offer insight to foreign supporters of MENA democratization. Next, it discusses how democracy as a construct is discussed and analyzed globally. In particular, it advocates for expanding this analysis to other domains. Finally, it discusses other central constructs to comparative politics that merit similar research.

Democracy Nonparadox

Researchers have been fascinated by the so-called democracy paradox or democracy deficit in the Middle East. Reporting on Arab-world

182 *Defining Democracy*

surveys asserts that these populations love democracy. This identified support for democracy relies on surveys assessing individuals' attitudes toward *dimuqratiyya*. Establishing that *dimuqratiyya* does not mean the same thing as *democracy* goes some way to unraveling this supposed paradox.

Failure to define *dimuqratiyya* adequately in these surveys induces miscommunication between the researchers and their interlocutors. By calling on different constructs, they are inadvertently talking past each other. This miscommunication results in mismeasurement. This mismeasurement ultimately generates the appearance of a paradox that does not actually exist. For citizens to state that they like *dimuqratiyya*, if they believe that *dimuqratiyya* means economic equality, does not mean that they like electing their leaders, being bound by electoral outcomes, or adopting liberal values in their country. Still less does it mean that they would take to the streets and bear substantial personal or social costs in order to bring this democratic structure into existence or to keep it. The myriad protests in recent decades against autocratic regimes, often met with violent reprisals, show just how costly this choice can be. When more precisely specified, support for democracy—an election-based system of government—is lower than the previously indicated support for *dimuqratiyya*. The paradox of absence and high support is an artifact of mismeasurement. Rather, moderate support and institutional absence are observed—a far less confusing turn of events.

The misidentification of a paradox relates to the first part of the answer given to Mernissi's question. Researchers are not defining their terms; they are assuming a mutual understanding with their research subjects. More precise specification of survey questions would likely go a long way to improving researchers' grasp of regional political opinion. This conclusion is not to denigrate the work that has been done investigating historical and practical circumstances that hamper democratization. There is a dearth of democracy in the Middle East. This regional situation, however, is more commensurate with public opinion than the democracy paradox literature has been able to recognize.

(Mis)understanding Social Movements

Another domain to consider is social movements. These are actions citizens take on the ground with multiple audiences: their fellow citizens, their political leaders, and outside observers. Bayat (2010) has argued that MENA residents are restricted from common forms of protest under authoritarian regimes but have used "nonmovements" in effective grass-roots mobilization through behaviors in their daily lives that generate social transformation and create pressure from below on regimes. For instance, individual choices by women to pursue education or work outside the home reshape the social imaginary without centralized coordination. The Middle East has also hosted several overt social movements. These have included formal groups and actions, such as labor unions organizing strikes and feminist nongovernmental organizations (NGOs) and Islamists organizing marches. The region has also seen moment-driven actions, like the Arab uprisings or protests inspired by a specific death or court case. Understanding these movements requires paying attention to the language that their members are using.

At this point, the general narrative is that the Arab Spring failed—specifically, it failed as a democratization campaign (Maghraoui 2019; Nugent 2020; Stepan 2018). Functionally, the Arab uprisings occupy "a *terra nullius* between revolutions and democratic transformations" (El-Ghobashy 2021, 33). Freedom House continues to consider the region, at best, "partly free." Tunisia was an exception, but its democratic credentials were undercut by the president's actions in July 2021. The postrevolutionary period has been described as the Arab Winter, even by those who do not consider it an "unmitigated failure" (Feldman 2020).

Bayat (2017) proposes that it was never meant to succeed in that sense. Rather than seeking to change the region, he argues, "they were 'refolutions'—revolutionary movements that emerged to compel the incumbent states to change themselves, to carry out meaningful reforms on behalf of the revolution" rather than to generate actual political revolutions (18). This is distinct from Stacher's (2020) claim that these uprisings were attempted transformations that failed to revolutionize their regimes because of the circumstances in the movements and the countries, from the lack of cohesive structure, to the role of the military, to the economic conditions.

In surveys in 2013, the people on the ground were certainly not arguing that the Arab Spring had worked (Arab Barometer III). When asked whether the movement had achieved its top three goals, most respondents said no.[1] What were those goals, though? Much of the media coverage and even academic literature evaluating the movements focused on their success (or lack thereof) at democratizing the region. This fits very well with the focus on the slogan "al-shaʿab yurīd isqāṭ al-niẓām" (the people want the downfall of the regime). That only sometimes happened. Was that the goal? To some extent, it was. However, the people wanted other things too.

184 *Defining Democracy*

When asked in 2011 for the "most important reason for the protests between January 25 and February 11, 2011," 54.1 percent of Egyptians said it was "demands for improving the economic situation," while 28.6 percent said it was "combatting corruption." Combined, demanding political freedom and preventing Hosni Mubarak from bequeathing his position to his son only reached 14 percent. Politics made a better showing for the second most important reason, in which case those goals received 23.5 percent of the responses. Combatting corruption and improving the economic position still received most credit for getting people into the streets. Similar responses were given in Tunisia, where 63.1 percent gave first importance to improving the economy, while 16.7 percent identified corruption. Civil liberties got 14 percent, and installing Islamists got 4.1 percent. For second most important, combatting corruption received 45.4 percent of the responses, while the economy got 17.9 percent. Political freedom received only 28.6 percent.

In 2013, these attributes had been revised: 43.1 percent of the Arab Barometer III respondents said the number one reason for the Arab Spring—which by this point had spread well beyond Egypt and Tunisia—was civil and political freedom; the second most commonly stated first reason (38.7 percent) was improving the economic conditions, followed by fighting corruption (12.1 percent). Second most important reasons referenced were fighting corruption (38.4 percent), bettering the economic conditions in the country (23.3 percent), and increasing social justice (13.8 percent). Social and economic justice (27.4 percent), dignity (21.7 percent), and fighting corruption (14.8 percent) were the most common tertiary answers. At this point, after seeing and evaluating the widespread public mobilization, the public saw this as a movement grounded in politics and in socioeconomic issues.

A survey done in 2018 retrospectively identified a very socioeconomic view of the protests (Yildirim and McCain 2019). The most commonly cited primary goals were addressing the economic situation, followed by social justice and dignity. Common secondary attributions were the economic situation, corruption, and social justice. Political freedom was the most common tertiary objective, followed by social justice and the economic situation. Socioeconomic framing was more prevalent in the public than it was in Western discussions.

A less commonly considered, yet equally chantable, demand was "'aysh, ḥurriyya, 'adāla ijtimā'iyya" (bread, freedom, and social justice). While "Bring down the authoritarian regime" is a democracy slogan, this is a *dimuqratiyya* slogan. This distinction has gotten lost in translation, which has muddled interpretation. Construing the move-

For the People **185**

ment as pro-democracy misidentifies the goals of the participants. This is not to say the citizens were opposed to democracy, but it was not the primary—or even secondary—target in most eyes. This slogan is a better encapsulation of the uprisings.

The distinction between a democracy movement and a *dimuqratiyya* movement should be kept in mind when evaluating the success of the Arab Spring and other protests. From a democracy standpoint, things did not go well. Unfortunately, the results, though slightly better, are not great from a *dimuqratiyya* perspective either.

Economic circumstances worsened in the immediate aftermath of the protests (Hong 2019). Political turmoil is famously hard on economies. There were a few years with improved economic circumstances, as demonstrated by unemployment rates and corruption metrics. However, ultimately oil revenue, development aid, and personal remittances "remained important sources of national income in the Maghreb" (Pfeiffer 2019, 101). Economic growth has not kept pace with population growth, which ultimately leads to expanding unemployment. Some of this can be offset by emigration and remittance income, but it is hard to see how the home country should construe that as a success. The recessions of the 2020s only heightened the economic turmoil. This *dimuqratiyya* problem can pose a democratic challenge: "Because the job market has not improved and the economic situation has become less stable under the pluralistic order, the lure back to the statist system that existed before the Arab Spring will become more attractive" (Hong 2019, 76). The poor socioeconomic circumstances have been invoked to justify regional democratic retrenchments, such as the 2021 Tunisian self-coup.

In Egypt and Tunisia, four-fifths of respondents reported disliking the prior regimes, but that did not mean they felt the Arab Spring went well. In 2011, 51.6 percent of Egyptians said they felt a "sense of personal gain" after the uprisings, compared to 23.2 percent who felt more a sense of loss (Arab Barometer II). Egyptians were largely optimistic that the events would lead to a *dimuqratiyya* "political system in Egypt guaranteeing political and civil freedoms and the accountability of all authorities" (92.4 percent) and better economic opportunities (92.2 percent). In contrast, only 41 percent of Tunisians identified a sense of gain; 8.4 percent felt a loss. They were also less sanguine that the Arab Spring would lead to a *dimuqratiyya* system (80.9 percent) and improved economic conditions (85.2 percent). Ironically, they had a more democratic outcome, for longer, than Egyptians had.

By 2013, only some Arab respondents (18.2 percent) indicated that they felt a sense of "personal victory" in the Arab Spring (Arab Barometer

III). Even more felt a loss (19.6 percent), but most reported conflicted or confused feelings. In 2018, just over two-fifths believed their country was better off after the Arab Spring (Yildirim and McCain 2019). Just over a quarter believed the movement had delivered on its goals. The socioeconomic elite were viewed as benefiting most from the revolutions. These modest improvements in *dimuqratiyya*, such as they were, have been further undermined by the events of the 2020s and the associated global economic challenges.

Reasonable assessment of social movements requires true consideration of their objectives and their members in order to understand them, cooperate with them, or evaluate them. The Arab uprisings were not the first, nor will they be the last, social movements to populate the Middle East. These movements, like the several protests in Morocco discussed in Chapter 6, have called for economic development and for justice. In some cases, but not all, they are protesting for democracy. This terminology will likely continue to play an important role in the social and political lexicon of these movements. When the word *dimuqratiyya* is used in future, researchers should not assume that the objectives are so unified.

Interpreting protest movements' objectives is vital both academically and practically. The United States has spent over $2 billion in the last decade engaging in nonmilitary "democracy promotion" globally through "supporting fair elections abroad, strengthening civil society, promoting rule of law and human rights, or other aspects of democracy promotion" (Lawson and Epstein 2019). These are democracy objectives. They can, to an extent, square as well with *dimuqratiyya* objectives. However, the goals are not one and the same. In fact, the US-backed programs were sold to the nondemocratic Egyptian and Moroccan governments as economic development policies; these regimes were able to appropriate some of the funds for civil society development to "fulfill government social welfare functions," which bolstered these nondemocratic regimes (Snider 2022, 8). For a call for democracy to achieve what foreign observers and researchers assume when they hear and study the word *democracy*, it must mean what activists and respondents intend: "If calls for democracy are, first and foremost, calls for improved economic conditions, support for democratic regimes may falter if economic conditions do not improve rapidly enough" (Doherty and Mecellem 2013, 3). As no government can always provide a strong economy for all people, this threat would be ever-present.

It should also be acknowledged that social movements do not comprise a random sample of the population. Only a seventh of Arab Barometer respondents participated in the Arab Spring protests. Protests are made of the people who show up. Those people are more likely to be people who conceive of *dimuqratiyya* in political terms (Chapter 4). On one hand, that means researchers who cast the meaning *democracy* over the protestors' invocations of *dimuqratiyya* have a better likelihood of being right. It does not mean, though, that this meaning should be assumed. To understand what the protestors mean, they should be asked. To understand whether the protestors' goals are shared throughout the country, nonparticipants must be considered as well. Do protesters speak for a silent majority, or are they a loud minority?

This is not to say that any particular movement falls into either category. For instance, the Arab Spring was a minority action that most researchers read as speaking for a silenced majority. All social movements should be considered on this basis. Most pertinently, in a context where there can be dueling protests (e.g., for and against women's rights reforms), it is superlatively necessary to consider this factor.

Furthermore, the diversity of opinion can also be exploited by autocrats. They can take advantage of the multiple meanings that terms used in protest to assert that they are responding to the goals or to claim the protestors are a threat. They can also tacitly buy off would-be protestors. The economic-deliverables aspect of *dimuqratiyya* could be used to avoid democratization or conceal incomplete democratization. Many nondemocratic regimes have achieved and maintained strong economies, if only for a time. Authoritarians could trade those for authoritarian persistence with citizens who are not committed to democratic institutions. They would effectively be buying off the "khobzists" (Beinin 2015, 21). The achievement of economic objectives with a smokescreen of participation would then appear to have satisfied the criteria for *dimuqratiyya* while maintaining a political autocrat. As Malik and Awadallah (2013, 309–310) note, "Offering greater political representation is desirable, but unless coupled with a greater access to economic opportunities, it is unlikely to be a game changer." The economic precarity would soften political-institutional commitments.

Researchers have argued that other elements are also necessary to sustain the electoral institutions. In addition to actual economic development (Przeworski 1991; Przeworski et al. 2000) or "subjective well-being" (Inglehart 2003), scholars have posited that a democratic culture is necessary. That is to say that the public must also have emancipative values, tolerance, interpersonal trust, and a participatory orientation (Inglehart 2003; Welzel 2021a) and civil liberties (Rowley and Smith 2009). Without these, the democratic institutions will crumble in the face of "headwinds" like economic turmoil (Welzel 2021b, 142). These

188 *Defining Democracy*

values are present, to varying degrees, in the Middle East (Ridge 2022a, 2022b). They are not necessarily, however, coupled with support for democracy. Thus, the region faces continual threat of authoritarian reversion via illiberal democracy or liberal nondemocracy.

Calls for *dimuqratiyya* are, for a large swath of the population, calls for economic equality and removing corruption. These are features often associated with democracy, though democracy does not guarantee them. Meeting protestors' demands, which would contribute as well to the stability of an electoral regime if one were instituted, would require addressing the SECD citizens' concerns as well as meeting the PCD citizens' expectations for democracy. Achieving democratization may require obtaining *dimuqratization* as well. Western governments, NGOs, and democrats would do well to mark that.

At present, Western engagement in the region is not targeting this principle. Recall President Barack Obama's speech cited in Chapter 1. The stress is laid on self-determination and liberal values. These are valuable and important. Aid is targeted in the same direction. However, as noted in Chapter 5, donor countries do a poor job at structuring that aid (or at least at explaining themselves). Programs aimed at building women's rights and civil society are seen as ineffective. The top two categories MENA residents would target with foreign aid are improving education/vocational training and building infrastructure, not promoting freedom. Freedom is good, but they cannot eat it. Furthermore, it could be self-defeating if it raises the hackles of the regime as an overt threat or does not square with a strategic or desired trade-off.[0] Donor states and MENA residents may also have different views of what these "freedoms" entail, making "promoting freedom" potentially patronizing or self-defeating. The difference appears at a macro-level too. According to Arab Barometer VI respondents, the top two Arab states in need of international aid are Lebanon and Palestine. American attention is elsewhere. As noted in Chapters 5 and 6, promoting development—in addition to satisfying demand for *dimuqratiyya*—can promote democratic attitudes and maybe even democratization. It also addresses public opinion as it exists, not just as we might wish it were or as it may later be. Until then, democratization and *dimuqratization* ought not to be seen as contradictory.

Global Democracy

This examination of *dimuqratiyya* and, by the by, democracy necessarily invokes questions of the global understanding of democracy in the

For the People **189**

myriad forms in which that word is rendered in different languages. Are the evoked constructs truly mutually intelligible and mutually interchangeable? Are there other instances of "false friends"? How can we identify regimes that are of, by, and for the people?

Previous scholarship has suggested that political-institutional understandings of democracy prevail. Is this still the case? Was this ever truly the case? Schaffer (2000), for instance, argued that it was not. Are these many words the same as *democracy* as political scientists understand it? Where there are different understandings of whatever word is invoked in place of *democracy*, citizens' interest in elections-based governance should be studied. For instance, Canache (2012) indicates that most LAPOP respondents understand *democracia* as liberty. That Canache (2012) and Kiewiet de Jonge (2016) find different results for the relationship between understanding of *democracia* and democratic preferences could reflect differences of interpretation. The citizens who espoused different conceptions may also espouse different regime-type or policy preferences. This possibility can be examined in other linguistic regions.

Other Middle Eastern states would seem a prime place to start such analysis. There is extensive shared history and culture with non-Arab MENA states, like Iran and Turkey. Scholars can examine how *demūkrāsiyy* and *demokrasi*, respectively, are conceived of by these publics. Socioeconomic conceptions may be similarly common in these states. That would align with Ciftci's (2022) work on political and socioeconomic conceptions of *adalet* (justice) in Turkey. If that is the case, the deviation from the supposed global norm of a procedural understanding of democracy would be a Middle Eastern phenomenon, not just a feature of the Arabic *dimuqratiyya*.

Country contexts like China and Russia are also ripe for this form of analysis. These governments claim to be representing the public will (establishing governments for the people) even if that requires consolidating power (removing the people from the government). The Chinese word that replaces *democracy* in translation is 民主, meaning "the people are master." Do the citizens understand this term in the way researchers assume they do when the researchers invoke democracy? What about the Russian *демократия*? It sounds like democracy. Does it mean, as Przeworski puts it, a government in which incumbents lose elections and leave office? Sklar (1983, 14) casts the democratic label on nondemocracies in Africa that are "guardians of the public weal." These regimes apply the same reasoning. It is certainly easier for scholars to conduct comparative and large-n research if they can assume the

190 *Defining Democracy*

mutual interpretability of interviews and answers. Reliance on this point, however, is undercutting cross-cultural understanding.

Furthermore, identifying unequal levels of democratic commitment across the interpretations of the word construct *dimuqratiyya* necessarily calls research built on the premise that this word represents one construct, democracy, into question. Future research may then be required to retread old ground to verify what scholars think they know. For instance, it could require reconsidering the inherited wisdom about the democratic tendencies of segments of the population, such as Islamists, the military, the young, or the college educated, all of whom have been recurrent subjects of MENA-focused and protest-focused scholarship. Once the meaning of a key word in the underlying questions has been complicated, researchers must consider whether the relationships being revealed in these empirical studies are the ones that they thought they were. What does it mean to have a positive or negative relationship with *dimuqratiyya* or support for *dimuqratiyya*? That is what the models underlying those studies are evaluating. The extent to which we can generalize to democracy from studies on *dimuqratiyya* opinion merits future study.

Cross-regional studies may also need to drop Arabic-language surveys from their analyses and verify whether the results still hold. For instance, the aforementioned work on Islam and democratization that compares surveys of the Arab world to other regions could be affected. Scholars must consider whether differences in the meaning of key terms across regions are driving their effects.

This is not merely the old saw that the more words like *democracy* and *republic* appear in a country's name, the less democratic that country is likely to be. It is an appeal for honest consideration of what people are talking about—the people in the streets and the people at the podium. As researchers are increasingly concerned with the potential for global democratic backsliding (Bermeo 2016; Meyerrose 2021), scholars cannot be too certain in understanding what people mean when they talk about their (non)democracies. In the meantime, avoiding the word *democracy* altogether may be the only way to mean what we say and say what we mean. In advocating for avoiding the word *democracy*, this conclusion is taking a more conservative approach than most other researchers. For instance, Khanani (2021, 72) regards the vast array of usages and meanings that Moroccan *ilsāmiyūn* find for *dimuqratiyya* and concludes that it "is still comparable to democracy." That is only true for very maximalist views of democracy. Scholars will have to make their own choices. However, for key questions and central constructs, clarity is preferable to ambiguity.

Words and Meanings

In addition to considering the meaning that researchers, politicos, and the public attribute to the word *democracy*, there is strong reason to believe that additional constructs merit serious scrutiny. Central constructs can have loose meanings that can be multiply construed by audiences foreign and domestic. During the 2022–2023 protests in Iran, demonstrators chanted, "Women, life, freedom." Audiences could ascribe different meanings to women's rights or freedom. Khanani (2021) notes that Islamists often think of group rights rather than individual rights. Some important political words defy translation, making cross-cultural discussion and evaluation challenging. *Secularism*, for example, has many meanings, often building on country-specific cultural histories (e.g., Turkish *laiklik*). Others readily translate but are not mutually understood between researchers and the audience. Technical terms like *ideology* or *Communist* may be diversely interpreted. Assuming—overtly or inadvertently—that these words are readily and widely comprehended could lead to a host of miscommunications and misinterpretations. Each case requires a different response.

Researchers have started unpacking words. These may be words that have multiple meanings within one language—for instance, *violence* (Kalmoe and Mason 2022; Westwood et al. 2022), *foreign aid* (Williamson 2019), or *laïcité* (Cohu et al. 2021). Other constructs have been probed cross-culturally, such as civil disobedience (Behr et al. 2014). Still more constructs are ripe for such analysis. Terrorism, happiness, and human rights are just a few examples. In the meantime, comparativists and survey scholars must be on the lookout for disparate meanings and their consequences. Thompson and Dooley (2019) propose that researchers focus on "adaptation" rather than translation, even to the point of decentering a specific language in research design, in order to make multilingual projects more comparable across sociolinguistic contexts. That would be an excellent approach. The purpose of this book is not to say that it is turtles all the way down and that communication is impossible. The purpose is to acknowledge that the Tower of Babel has cast a long shadow over political discourse.

Moving Forward

This work as an invitation rather than a resolution. The world is not on an inevitable and unidimensional march to democracy in the Arab states

192 *Defining Democracy*

or anywhere else. Democratization and democracy are ongoing projects. For democrats in the Middle East, it is an uphill climb. Myriad forces suppress democratization there, from current autocrats to social values to a tempestuous past. Nondemocrats in the general public make for shaky alliances and unstable foundations for democratic institutions.

This research has found that there are democrats in the Arab world. They are, however, not so numerous as has been assumed. Scholars have played no small part in creating their own unrealistic "reality" on that score. These results should be considered an invitation to listen. Understanding what the public is saying, calling for, or demanding is a necessary first step to embodying the public will. That is what democracy is meant to achieve, after all.

Notes

1. The rates ranged from 58.6 to 63.2 percent depending on whether they were rating the first, second, or third goal.

2. American foreign aid programs in the region have had to tread carefully with respect to threats to the current regimes in order to get in the door at all. Although USAID characterized the "four dimensions of democracy" as "rule of law, good governance, competition, and citizen inclusion," substantial aid has been targeted at economic development in the hopes that it would encourage democratic sentiment and because it is what those regimes would allow (Snider 2022, 95–96). It has not resulted in democratization.

Appendix A
Conducting Surveys in the Middle East

In this study, I rely heavily on existing and original survey data gathered in the Middle East/North Africa (MENA). These include the World Values Survey, the Arab Barometer, and two original surveys in Egypt and Morocco. The surveys were approved by the Duke University Institutional Review Board (IRB 2019-0612). The respondents were recruited through YouGov's Middle East/North Africa panel. This has been used in previous political science studies (Nyhan and Zeitzoff 2018; Blackman and Jackson 2019). Information on the World Values Survey and Arab Barometer is available on their websites.

Constraining the studies to one ethnolinguistic region can remove some concerns about multinational survey studies. The first, of course, is the target concern of this literature: translation bias. Additional concerns relate to patterns of bias in responding. Respondents from different regions can show "cultural differences in acquiescence, extreme, and middle category response styles across different cultural groups" that inhibit multicultural analyses (Lyberg et al. 2021, 53). Additionally, multilingual respondents might experience "language dependent recall" (Lyberg et al. 2021, 53). Focusing within the Middle East/North Africa reduces these concerns.

A perennial concern with survey research is that respondents may lie or omit. Strategic and intentional misrepresentation of attitudes, opinions, and preferences is known as *preference falsification* (Kuran 1997). The concern about this is enhanced in nondemocratic settings where respondents are considered to potentially fear the regime when addressing sensitive topics. Researchers must seek to counteract this effect. Middle East/North Africa residents are sometimes considered to be less willing to engage with surveys. They are suspected of being secretive, not having

194 Appendix A

real opinions, or being generally uninformed. To the contrary, researchers have found that Arab publics are positively disposed toward surveys (Gengler et al. 2019). Survey experiments in Lebanon show respondents are more likely to answer surveys sponsored by universities as opposed to governments. University-sponsored surveys also do not show systematic bias in (non)response, while foreign-government sponsorship discouraged participation by those who disliked that country (Corstange 2014). A survey in Qatar found no significant difference in Arabs' response willingness for hypothetical university- or government-sponsored surveys. However, distrust toward the intentions of a survey sponsor could reduce participation due to worry that the data will be manipulated (Gengler et al. 2019). Arab Barometer partners with in-country survey teams to conduct computer-assisted personal interviews of randomly selected homes; the interviewers identified the firm and stated the surveys were conducted for the Arab Barometer, which they identified with Arab and US university researchers. For the Egypt and Morocco studies, YouGov did not identify the survey sponsor of these surveys. Respondents were told the survey would be about public opinion. A recognized survey company and its panelists are less susceptible to suspicion. Because panel members opted in to the panel and have taken part in previous surveys with the company, there is already a relationship of trust.

Nevertheless, conducting a survey in the Middle East poses several challenges. It is logistically challenging due to cost, distance, and language barriers. While many international surveys engage interviewers to conduct in-person meetings to acquire the data, which allows for longer surveys, the presence of an enumerator can alter respondents' responses in key areas. Studies in the Middle East have demonstrated effects on questions pertaining to religion and gender traditionalism (Blaydes and Gillium 2013; Benstead 2014). Respondents may also distrust these enumerators and the anonymity of a survey they take through a person, hand to a person, or are witnessed taking. For instance, a survey of residents of Qatar reported that people would rather take a survey on the phone than face-to-face (Gengler et al. 2019). Self-administered surveys can get around these effects. Online and anonymous surveys also increase response honesty, reduce potential sensitivity response biases, and reduce desire to skip questions (Lupu and Michelitch 2018).

There are downsides to written surveys. The first is length. Since survey takers will only devote so much time and attention to the survey, written surveys must be shorter than in-person surveys. The second is reading. Using a written method of communication excludes potential responders who are illiterate. For the Middle East, literacy has an additional feature: diglossia. Written Arabic is typically a rendering of Modern Standard Ara-

Appendix A   195

bic, though people often speak a regional dialect in daily life. The media (e.g., newscasters) and religious leaders (e.g., imams) use standard Arabic, and religious and political words are typically the same in the dialects as they are in Modern Standard Arabic. In order to use the same survey questions across countries, standardized Arabic was used for the survey rather than the diverging dialects. One respondent commented that YouGov's surveys should be available in Amazigh (Berber), the third most common language in Morocco. Amazigh was omitted for logistical reasons; I do not speak Amazigh, YouGov MENA uses Arabic, Arabic is the near-universal language of communication in Egypt and Morocco, and it could not address *dimuqratiyya* specifically. Lower levels of literacy and numeracy, compared to the rates in developed countries, and the prevalence of multiple languages are challenges for all surveys in the developing world; these must be balanced against concerns about enumerator effects or enumerator shirking (Lupu and Michelitch 2018). The online format was deemed preferable for survey cost and for providing respondent anonymity.

This does not mean, however, that none of the respondents had opinions about the survey or the desire to conduct it. YouGov includes its own open-ended questions after each survey to gather feedback on the experience; this is for the company, but the responses were provided to me on request. Open-ended questions had not been used in the survey because they are more cognitively taxing and less likely to be answered. Though the majority of the survey takers chose not to answer these questions and some addressed comments to YouGov, a few provided substantive comments on the survey.

Several expressed thanks for or interest in the survey. Some respondents in each country expressed pleasure at receiving questions about politics and about religion. For instance, an eighteen-to-twenty-four-year-old Muslim Moroccan woman said, "This questionnaire pleased me a lot, because it is good to know the people's opinions about politics and the government system in their country."[1] Another Muslim Moroccan woman, over age forty, wrote, "This type of survey is very useful to know the citizens' opinions and also to advance the country to the highest of positions."[2]

Others weighed in with more discursive opinions. Some wrote that they did not care about politics or that they did not want to answer political questions or to talk about or debate politics. Maybe they hoped YouGov would send fewer politics-themed surveys. Maybe they do not *actually* object to discussing politics, since they filled out the survey to the end. One forty-plus-year-old Muslim woman in Casablanca, who rated the government's performance quite badly, expressed the view that "the survey is primarily political, and it is not possible for the public to answer it

196 *Appendix A*

objectively."[3] Given her completing the survey and her willingness to rate the government poorly, this statement could also mean that the answers are not "facts" about the government but rather her opinion. Since obtaining the respondents' perspectives is the intention of these questions, that would not pose a problem. That a respondent would lie in a survey, however, is always a risk. This is why choices are made to maximize anonymity. One respondent, a college-educated thirty-five-to-thirty-nine-year-old Cairene Muslim man, would have surveys of politics banned: "I do not agree with this poll. There is no discussion or speaking about the country's politics. Most of the questions are not understood. I wish you could not ask this type of question." He still took the survey. The response was written in a very Egyptian style rather than in Modern Standard Arabic. This could have influenced his comprehension; however, the respondent was highly educated and reported daily engagement with the news and scripture, both of which use formal Arabic, so it is likely that he understood the language. His disapproval of the type of question might have motivated his statement, and his use of the passive participle could have meant he thought poorly of this line of questioning or of other Egyptians' understanding, rather than that he personally did not understand the questions.

Not finishing the survey was actually uncommon. Of the 1,132 residents of Egypt who started the survey, only 75 did not complete it (~6.6 percent). In Morocco, where the survey was a bit longer, of the 1,221 who started the survey, 167 did not complete it (~13.7 percent). The reason for their not completing is unknowable; it could be content related, technology related, or personal. For an internet survey, a 10 to 16 percent dropout rate is common, though other estimates are as high as 34 percent, and the drop-off rate increases as the number of questions increases and in areas where technological problems are more common (Hoerger 2010; Vicente and Reis 2010; Peytchev 2009). These rates suggest that potential respondents were not inordinately likely to quit the study on encountering the survey questions.

Some survey takers felt that these kinds of questions were not at all appropriate. A college-educated thirty-five-to-thirty-nine-year-old Muslim woman from the Delta region wrote, "I am sure the purpose of this poll is not proper."[4] A forty-plus-year-old Muslim woman from Casablanca with an advanced degree was also skeptical: "A suspicious survey that arouses suspicion, almost as if we are in front of a spy network."[5] One respondent in Egypt even thought that the survey was a prelude to an attempt to overthrow the government or that the responses, if made public, could be destabilizing for the regime. A forty-plus-year-old Cairene Muslim man with an advanced degree wrote, "[This is] a political poll that is intended to shake citizens' confidence in the political leadership and to spread the

Appendix A **197**

spirit of rebellion against the current regime in order to destroy the country."[6] These individuals completed the survey. They were concerned, though, about what it might reveal.

The concern about being spied on seems to be rare. One Moroccan respondent, a forty-plus-year-old suburban Muslim woman with an advanced degree used the open space to write, "The worst governments in the world are Arab governments and Islamic governments."[7] This does not betray a great fear of observation or identification, though it might indicate openness to regime change. Heightened levels of concern among researchers that ideology and regime type could lead to systematic misrepresentation may reflect researchers' own biases rather than the realities of regional survey studies. Benstead (2018, 536) argues "that worries that the Arab world is a more challenging survey context—or that citizens answer dishonestly—reflect biases of 'Arab exceptionalism,' more than fair assessments of data quality." It is necessary to consider the choices in survey construction that can influence respondents' behavior, but the Middle East can be treated as functionally similar to other regions of the world in survey studies.

Demographic Characteristics for the Original Surveys in Egypt and Morocco

The Egyptian survey was fielded in August 2019 by YouGov MENA; it includes 1,000 Egyptians. As noted above, 75 of the 1,132 residents of Egypt who started the survey did not complete it. YouGov removed respondents who failed YouGov's built-in attention check (correctly identify an animal or electronic item on a multiple-choice question). This produced a sample of 1,028 residents of Egypt. The Morocco survey was fielded in January 2020 by YouGov MENA. Of the 1,221 residents of Morocco who started it, 167 did not complete the questionnaire for unknown reasons; additional respondents were culled by YouGov's check question before the data was delivered. The final sample included 991 Moroccans. YouGov MENA is an online survey panel that aims to create an age- and gender-representative panel for several countries in the Middle East.

Twenty-eight non-Egyptians of unspecified nationality and eighteen non-Moroccans of unspecified nationality were removed for two reasons. First, as their nationality was unknown, it is hard to say what regimes may influence their views and background. Second, a survey experiment in Qatar suggests that non-nationals are less engaged with politics and less likely to participate in a survey about politics (relative

198 *Appendix A*

to a survey about economics). This could make their responses less precise (Gengler et al. 2019).

Respondents were able to take the survey in Arabic or English; 95.1 percent of Egyptians and 93.8 percent of Moroccans took the survey in Arabic. The survey questions in English and Arabic are presented in Appendix B. Regression analyses use YouGov MENA's weights for representativeness with respect to age and gender.

In the Egyptian survey, 51.3 percent of respondents were men; 40.6 percent were under thirty years of age, while 38.3 percent were forty or older; 80.4 percent of respondents had completed college; 89.9 percent of respondents were Muslim, 9.2 percent were Christian, and 0.86 percent indicated no religious affiliation. The religious demographics line up well with national figures. The sample is slightly more educated than the general population (Arab Barometer V); Egypt has a literacy rate of 80.8 percent and a school life expectancy of thirteen years (World Factbook 2019). Literacy may be achieved separately from formal education in the Middle East; for instance, mosques and other groups offer literacy classes separate from schooling.

In the Moroccan survey, 47.3 percent of respondents were men; 30.4 percent were under thirty years of age, while 46.4 percent were forty or older; 60 percent of respondents had completed college; 97 percent of respondents were Muslim, 0.4 percent were Christian, 0.1 percent indicated another religion, and 2.5 percent indicated no religious affiliation. The religious demographics line up well with national figures. The sample is slightly more educated than the general population (Arab Barometer V); Morocco has a literacy rate of 73.8 percent and a school life expectancy of thirteen years (World Factbook 2020). Note, the above percentages include the demographic weights.

Notes

1. A'jabnī al-istibyān kathīran li'annhu min al-jayyid ma'rifa arā' al-nās ḥawla al-siyāsa wa niẓām al-ḥukm fī baladihim.

2. Hādhā al-naw' min al-istiṭlā'āt mufīd jiddan li-ma'ifa arā' al-muwaṭinīn wa kadhālk li-l-nuhūḍ bil-dawla ilā a'lā al-markākiz.

3. Istiṭlā'āt siyāsa bil-daraja al-ūlā wa lā yumkin l-l'āma al-ijāba 'alayhi bimawḍū'iyya.

4. Akīd gharaḍukum min al-istiṭlā' dā ghayr sawiy.

5. Istiṭlā' murīb wa muthīr l-Ishukūk wa ka'annanā imam qanāa tajassusiyya.

6. Istiṭlā' siyāsa al-gharaḍ minhu za'za'a thiqa al-muwaṭinīn fī al-qiyāda al-siyāsiyya wa bathth rūḥ al-tamarrud 'alā al-niẓām al-ḥālī li-tadmīr al-dawla.

7. Aswa' al-ḥukūmāt fī al-'ālim hiyya al-ḥukūmāt al-'arabiyya wa al-ḥukūmāt al-islāmiyya.

Appendix B
Survey Questions for Egypt and Morocco

Question in English	Question in Arabic (Transliterated)
In which country do you currently live?	Fī ayy balad tuqīm ḫālliyyān?
What is the highest level of education have you completed?	Mā hiyya a'lā shuhāda 'ilmiyya ḥaṣalta 'alayhā?
1) Elementary school	*1) Al-shuhāda al-ibtidā'iyya*
2) Secondary school	*2) Al-shuhāda al-thanawiyya*
3) Vocational college education (e.g., to qualify as an electrician, nurse)	*3) Ta'līm fannī min al-jāmi'a (mithla: an takun ma'uhlān li-tuṣbiḥ mummariḍān aw kahrabā'iyyān*
4) University first degree (e.g., BA, BS)	*4) Shuhāda jāmi'a awaliyya (mithla: al-baklūrīūs aw bal-baklūrīūs fī al-'ulūm)*
5) University higher degree (master's, MBA, PhD)	*5) Shuhāda jāmi'a 'aliyyān (al-mājistīr aw mājistīr idāra al-a'māl aw al-duktūrāa)*
6) Professional higher education (e.g., to qualify as a lawyer, accountant)	*6) Ta'līm mihnī 'āliyy (mithla: Al-ta'hhul li-tuṣbiḥ muḥāmiyyān aw muḥāsibān.*
7) None of these	*7) Lā shay' mimmā sabq*
Would you say the area you live in is . . .?	Kayf taṣif al-minṭaqa allatī ta'īsh fīhā?
1) Urban	*1) Ḥaḍariyya*
2) Suburban	*2) Min al-ḍawāḥiyy*
3) Rural	*3) Rīfiyya*
4) Other	*4) Ukhrā*
Which of these applies to you?	Ayy mimā yalī yanṭabiq 'aliyak
1) Working full-time (30 or more hours per week)	*1) Al-a'māl bidawām kāmil (30 sā'a fī al-usbū')*
2) Working part-time (8–29 hours per week)	*2) Al-a'māl bidawām juz'iy (8–29 sā'a fī al-usbū')*
3) Working part-time (less than 8 hours per week)	*3) Al-a'māl bidawām juz'iy (Aql min 8 sā'āt fī al-usbū')*

continues

200 *Appendix B*

Question in English	Question in Arabic (Transliterated)
4) Full-time student	*4) Ṭālib mutaffarigh*
5) Retired	*5) Mutaqāʿid*
6) Full-time homemaker or housewife	*6) Rubb usra mutaffarigh/rubba usra mutaffarigha*
7) Unemployed	*7) ʿāṭil ʿan al-ʿamal*
8) Other	*8) Ijāba ukhra*
Which of these statements comes closest to describing your household income in the last year?	Ayy min bayna mā yalī yaʿtabir aqrab waṣf l-ldakhl al-shahriyy al-khāṣṣ bi-manzilak khilāl al-ʿām al-māḍī?
1) Our household income covers our expenses well, and we are able to save.	*1) Yughṭī al-dakhl al-shahriyy nafaqātnā bi-shakl jayyid wa yumkinunā al-idkhār minhu.*
2) Our household income covers our expenses without notable difficulties.	*2) Yughṭī al-dakhl al-shahriyy nafaqātnā dūn al-taʿarruḍ l-ṣaʿūbāt al-māddiyya malḥūẓa*
3) Our household income does not cover our expenses, and we face some difficulties in meeting our needs.	*3) Lā yughṭī al-dakhl al-shahriyy nafaqātnā wa nuwājih baʿḍ al-ṣaʿūbāt al-māddiyya fī talbiya iḥtiājātinā*
4) Our household income does not cover our expenses, and we face significant difficulties in meeting our needs.	*4) Lā yughṭī al-dakhl al-shahriyy nafaqātnā wa nuwājih ṣaʿūbāt kabīra fī talbiya iḥtiājātinā*
5) Our household income does not cover our expenses, and we are never able to meet our needs.	*5) Lā yughṭī al-dakhl al-shahriyy nafaqātnā wa lan nastaṭiʿ talbiya iḥtiājātinā ʿalā al-aṭlāq*
In the past five years, have you visited, studied in, or lived in Europe, the United States, or Canada?	Hal zurti aw darasti aw ʿishti fī dawla urūbiyya aw fī al-wilāyāt al-mutaḥida al-amrīkiyya aw kanadā khilāl al-khamsa aʿwām al-māḍiyya?
1) Yes 2) No	*1) Naʿam 2) Lā*
Do you belong to a religion or religious denomination? If yes, which one?	Hal tantamī ilā dīn aw madhhab dīniyy mā? Law ijāba "naʿam" yarjī al-taḥdīd?
1) No	*1) Lā*
2) Yes—Muslim	*2) Naʿam—Al-islām*
3) Yes—Christian	*3) Naʿam—Al-masīḥiiyya*
4) Yes—something else	*4) Naʿam—Madhhabān akhar*
Would you say that the country is going in the wrong direction or going in the right direction?	Hal tarā an al-dawla tasīr fī al-itajāh al-ṣaḥīḥ am al-khāṭiʾ?
1) Right direction	*1) Al-itajāh al-ṣaḥīḥ*
2) Wrong direction	*2) Al-itajāh al-khāṭiʾ*
To what extent are you satisfied with the government's performance?	Mā maddā riḍāʾak ʿan adāʾ al-ḥakūma?
1) Completely satisfied	*1) Rāḍ tamāmān*
2) Somewhat satisfied	*2) Rāḍ nawʿān mā*

continues

Question in English	Question in Arabic (Transliterated)
3) Somewhat unsatisfied	*3) Ghayr rāḍ naw 'ān mā*
4) Completely unsatisfied	*4) Ghayr rāḍ 'ālā aṭlāq*
In general, how would you describe the present condition in this country in terms of	Bi-shakl 'ām, kayf taṣif al-waḍ' al-ḥāliyy l-hādhihi al-dawla min ḥaythu
• Unemployment	• Al-baṭāla
• Keeping prices down	• Inkhifāḍ
• Safety	• Al-amān
1) Very good	*1) Jayyid jiddān*
2) Good	*2) Jayyid*
3) Bad	*3) Sayyi'*
4) Very bad	*4) Sayyi' jiddān*
Generally speaking, would you say that most people can be trusted or that you need to be very careful in dealing with people?	Bi-shakl 'ām, hal ta'taqid annahu yumkinuka al-wuthūq bi-aghlab al-nās am annuka yajib an taḥtarris ma'ahum?
1) Most people can be trusted	*1) Yumkinunī al-wuthūq bi-aghlab al-nās*
2) Need to be careful	*2) Yajib an aḥtarris*
How often, if at all, do you	Kamm marra taqūm bimā yalī:
• Read or watch the news	• Qirā'a aw mushāhida al-akhbār
• Read or listen to the Qur'an/Bible	• Qirā'a aw istimā' ilā al-qir'ān/al-injīl
• Pray	• Al-ṣalāa
1) Every day	*1) Yawmiyyān*
2) Most of the time	*2) Aghlab al-waqt*
3) Sometimes	*3) Aḥyānān*
4) Rarely	*4) Nādirān*
5) Never	*5) Abadān*
How interested, if at all, would you say you are in politics and government?	Mā maddā ihtimāmuka b-alsiyāsa wa adā' al- ḥakūma?
1) Very interested	*1) Muhtamm jiddān*
2) Somewhat interested	*2) Muhtamm naw 'ān mā*
3) Not very interested	*3) Ghayr muhtamm naw 'ān mā*
4) Not at all interested	*4) Ghayr muhtamm 'alā al-aṭlāq*
Below are some statements that relate to the status of women in our society. How much do you agree with the following statements?	Fīma yalī majmū'a min al-'ibārāt al-muta'aliqqa bi-makāna al-mira'a fī al-mujtami'. Mā maddā muwāfiqatak 'alā kull minha?
• Men make better national political leaders (i.e., members of parliament) than women.	• Al-rijāl afḍal min al-nisā' ka-qiyādāt siyāiyya waṭaniyya (mithla: a'ḍā' majlis al-sha'ab)
• University education for men is more important than for women.	• Al-ta'līm al-jāmi'iyy l-lrijāl ahamm min al- ta'līm al-jāmi'iyy li-l-nisā'
• Working mothers can establish just as secure a relationship with	• Yumkin l-l-umahāt al-'āmilāt binā' 'alāqāt usriyya mustaqirra ma'a

continues

202 Appendix B

Question in English	Question in Arabic (Transliterated)

their children as mothers who do not work.
1) Strongly agree
2) Agree
3) Disagree
4) Strongly disagree

In terms of potential governments, which of these three statements is closest to your opinion?
1) An elected government is always preferable to any other kind of government.
2) There are circumstances when an unelected government can be preferable.
3) For someone like me, it doesn't matter what kind of government we have.

How much do you agree with the following statements?
• It is more important to have a government that can get things done, even if we have no influence over what it does.
• Electing governments is acceptable under the teachings of Islam.
• Our country is better off if religious people hold public positions in the state.
• Since elections sometimes produce bad results, we should adopt other methods for choosing this country's leaders.
• Religious leaders like imams and priests should not interfere in voters' decisions in elections.
• The government should enact laws in accordance with Islamic law.

1) Strongly agree
2) Agree
3) Disagree
4) Strongly disagree

There are many ways to govern a country. Would you disapprove or approve of the following alternatives?

abnā'ihin mithlahun kamithla rubbāt al-manzil
1) Uwāfiq bishadda
2) Uwāfiq
3) Lā uwāfiq
4) Lā uwāfiq bishadda

Fīmā yakhuṣṣ al-ḥakūma al-muḥtamilla, ayy min al-'ibārāt al-tāliyya hiyya al-aqrāb li-wijha naẓarak?
1) Al-ḥakūma al-muntakhiba hiyya al-mufaḍḍil dā'mān 'an ayy ḥakūmāt ukhrā
2) Fī ẓurūf mu'ayyina, takūn al-ḥakūma ghayr al-muntakhiba afḍal
3) Lā yahamm nū' al-ḥakūma al-ḥāliyya ashkhāṣ mithliyy

Mā maddā muwāfiqatak 'alā al-'ibārāt al-tāliyya?
• Min al-ḍarūriyy an takūn al-ḥakūma qādira 'alā al-qiyām bi-dūriha ḥatā wa in lam yakun li-nā ta'thīr 'alā adā'ihā
• Al-ḥakūmā al-muntakhiba niẓām mutawāfiq ma'a ta'alīm al-islām
• Satuṣbiḥ al-dawla afḍal law taqallid al-mutadayyinūn al-munāṣib al-'ama fīhā
• Bimā an al-intikhābāt ta'tī aḥyānān bi-nitā'ij sayy' fa-yajib an natabbanā ṭarqān ukhrā fī ikhtiyār qāda al-dawla
• Yajib 'alā rijāl al-dīn mithla al-a'ima wa al-kahna 'adm al-ta'thīr 'alā qirārāt al-muṣawwitīn fī al-intikhābāt
• Yajib an taqūm al-ḥakūma bisann al-qawānīn ṭabqān l-mubādī' al-sharī'a al-islāmiyya

1) Uwāfiq bishadda
2) Uwāfiq
3) Lā uwāfiq
4) Lā uwāfiq bishadda

Hunāk al-'adīd min al-ṭuruq al-mukhtalifa allatī tuḥkam bihā al-duwal, fahal tuwāfiq aw lā tuwāfiq 'alā al-bidā'il al-tāliyya?

continues

Question in English	Question in Arabic (Transliterated)
• Only one political party is allowed to stand for election and hold office	• Yusmaḥ l-ḥizb siyāsiyy wāḥid al-tarashshuḥ l-lintikhābāt wa tuwallī al-manṣub
• The army governs the country	• Al-dawla yaḥkumhā al-jaysh
• Elections and parliament are abolished so that the president can decide everything	• Yatamm il-ghā' al-intikhābāt wa al-barlimān bihaythu yakūn al-qirār al-awal wa al-akhīr li-ra'īs al-dawla
• A system governed by Islamic law without elections	• Niẓām taḥkumuhu al-qawānīn al-islāmiyya dūn intikhābāt
• Multiple political parties compete in elections to hold office	• Aḥzāb muta'addida tatanāqis fī al-intikhābāt min ajl tuwallī manṣub
• The government includes both elected and unelected offices that take an active part in the decision-making and policy	• An tashmal al-ḥakūma 'alā manāṣib muntakhiba wa ghayr muntakhiba li-dayhā dawr fa'āl fī al-siyāsāt wa itikhādh al-qirār
1) Strongly approve	*1) Uwāfiq bishadda*
2) Approve	*2) Uwāfiq*
3) Disapprove	*3) Lā uwāfiq*
4) Strongly disapprove	*4) Lā uwāfiq bishadda*
To what extent do you think choosing the government by election is appropriate for your country?	Fī ra'iyak ilā ayy maddā ya'tabir ikhtiyār al-ḥakūma min khilāl al-intikhābāt munāsib l-dawlatak?
1) Very appropriate	*1) Munāsib jiddān*
2) Somewhat appropriate	*2) Munāsib naw'ān mā*
3) Somewhat inappropriate	*3) Ghayr munāsib naw'ān mā*
4) Very inappropriate	*4) Ghayr munāsib jiddān*
People associate democracy with many different meanings such as the ones below. How important are each of the following for a society to be a democracy?	Yarbiṭ al-nāss al-dīmūqrāṭiyya bi-mafāhīm mukhtalifa min baynihā al-mafāhīm al-tālliyya. Mā ahmiyya kull minhum bal-nisba l-lmujtami' likayy yusbiḥ dīmūqrāṭiyān?
• The opportunity to change the government through elections	• Imkāniya taghyīr al-ḥakūma min khilāl al-intikhābāt
• Freedom to criticize the government	• Al-ḥurriya fī intiqād adā' al- ḥakūma
• Narrowing the gap between rich and poor	• Taqlīl al-fajwa bayn al-aghniya' wa al-fuqra'
• Providing basic items (such as food and housing) to every individual	• Tawfīr al-'anāṣir al-ḥayātiyya (mithla: al-ma'kal wa al-maskan) l-jamī' afrād al-mujtami'
• Equality of political rights between citizens	• Al-musāwāa fī al-ḥuqūq al-siyāsiyya bayna al-muwāṭinīn
• Eliminating financial and administrative corruption	• Al-ḥadd min al-fisād al-māliyy wa al-idāriyy
• Separation of religion and the government	• Al-fasl bayna al-dīn wa al-dawla

continues

204 *Appendix B*

Question in English	Question in Arabic (Transliterated)
• Government ensures law and order	• An takafful al-ḥakūma al-niẓām wa al-qānūn
1) Very important	*1) Muhimm jiddān*
2) Somewhat important	*2) Muhimm naw 'ān mā*
3) Slightly important	*3) Ghayr muhimm naw 'ān mā*
4) Not at all important	*4) Ghayr muhimm jiddān*
Which of the traits is most important for a society to be a democracy? Please rank the top two traits.	Ayy min al-mumayyizāt al-tāliyya hiyya al-ahamm b-alnisba li-l-mujtami' likayy yusbiḥ dīmūqrāṭiyān? Yarjā taḥdīd ahamm mīzatayn.
1) The opportunity to change the government through elections	*1) Imkāniya taghyīr al-ḥakūma min khilāl alintikhābāt*
2) Freedom to criticize the government	*2) Al-ḥurriya fī intiqād adā' al- ḥakūma*
3) Narrowing the gap between rich and poor	*3) Taqlīl al-fajwa bayn al-ghniya' wa al-fuqra'*
4) Providing basic items (such as food and housing) to every individual	*4) Tawfīr al- 'anāṣir al-ḥayātiyya (mithla: al-ma'kal wa al-maskan) l-jamī' afrād al-mujtami'*
5) Equality of political rights between citizens	*5) Al-musāwāa fī al-ḥuqūq al-siyāsiyya bayna al-muwāṭinīn*
6) Eliminating financial and administrative corruption	*6) Al-ḥadd min al-fisād al-māliyy wa al-idāriyy*
7) Separation of religion and the government	*7) Al-fasl bayna al-dīn wa al-dawla*
8) Government ensures law and order	*8) An takafful al-ḥakūma al-niẓām wa al-qānūn*
How democratic is a country if . . .	Kayf takūn al-dawla dīmuqrāṭiyy law . . .
• The elected leader retains power for many decades?	• Taqallud al-ra'īs al-muntakhib al-sulṭa li-'aqūd ṭawīla
• The military is in charge of the government?	• Taḥammul al-jaysh masu'wiliyya al-ḥukūma
• The government is elected but there are high levels of poverty?	• Tamm intikhāb al-ḥukūma lakin yūjid mustawiyāt 'āliyya min al-faqr
• The elected leader must be approved by religious leaders?	• Lam yatarashshuḥ aḥad min ajl al-munaṣib fī muwājiha ma'a al-ra'īs al-muntakhib
• The elected leader is never challenged by another candidate for office?	• Tamm ḥirmān ba'ḍ al-aḥzāb al-siyāsiyya min al-mushārika fī al-intikhābāt
• Some parties are banned from participating in the elections?	
• The government includes both elected and unelected offices that take an active part in the decision-making and policy?	• An tashmal al-ḥukūma 'alā makātib muntakhiba wa ghayr muntakhiba lidayhā dūr fa'āl fī al-siyāsāt watakhād al-qirār

continues

Appendix B 205

Attribute	Levels (English)	Levels (Arabic)
Elections	There are elections with multiple recognized political parties	Ijrā' al-intikhābāt li-ḥuzb siyāsiyy wāḥid mu'tarif bihi
	There are elections with one recognized political party	Ijrā' al-intikhābāt li-ḥuzb siyāsiyy muta'ddida mu'tarif bihā
	There are no elections	Lā yūjid intikhābāt
Citizen participation	Few barriers to citizen political participation	Wujūd al-qalīl min al-'awā' q fīmā yakhuṣṣ mushārika al-muwāṭinīn fī al-ḥayyāa al-siyāsiyya
	Some barriers to citizen political participation	Wujūd ba'ḍ al-'awā'q allatī takhuṣṣ mushārika al-muwāṭinīn fī al-ḥayyāa al-siyāsiyya
	Many barriers to citizen political participation	Wujūd al-'adīd min al-'awā'q allatī takhuṣṣ mushārika al-muwāṭinīn fī al-ḥayyāa al-siyāsiyya
Official religion	There is an official state religion	Al-qirār dīn rasmiyy li-ldawla
	There is no official state religion	Lā yūjid dīn rasmiyy li-ldawla
Role for religious leaders	No formal role for religious leaders in government	Lā yal'ab rijāl al-dīn dawrān rasmiyyān fī al-ḥakūma
	Formal role for religious leaders in government	An yakūn liday rijāl al-dīn dawrān rasmiyyān fī al-ḥakūma
Provision of public services	Little government provision of basic items (i.e., housing and food) to individuals	Tawfīr al-ḥakūma al-qalīl mim al-khidmāt al-asāsiyya (mithla: al-ma'kal wa al-maskan) li-l-afrād
	Some government provision of basic items (i.e., housing and food) to individuals	Tawfīr al-ḥakūma ba'ḍ al-khidmāt al-asāsiyya (mithla: al-ma'kal wa al-maskan) li-l-afrād
	Good government provision of basic items (i.e., housing and food) to individuals	Tawfīr al-ḥakūma li-l-khidmāt al-asāsiyya (mithla: al-ṭa'ām wa al-maskan) bi-shakl jayyid li-l-afrād
	Low unemployment (7%)	Mu'addal biṭāla munkhafiḍ (7%)
	High unemployment (14%)	Mu'addal biṭāla murtafi' (14%)

Appendix C
Variable Operationalization

Arab Barometer Variables

Demographic Variables

Name	Wave	Coding
SECD-PCD	Wave 1 (q702)	People often differ in their views on the characteristics that are essential to democracy. If you had to choose only one thing, what would you choose as the most important characteristic, and what would be the second most important? The opportunity to change the government through elections/freedom to criticize the government/those in power = PCD A small income gap between rich and poor/basic necessities like food, clothing, shelter for everyone = SECD
	Wave 2 (q5151/q5152) Wave 3 (q515)	There is a difference in opinion among people regarding the most important features of democracy. If you had to choose one, which of the following features would you say is the most important? The second most important? The opportunity to change the government through elections/freedom to criticize the government/equality of political rights between citizens = PCD

continues

207

208 *Appendix C*

Name	Wave	Coding
SECD-PCD continued	Wave 2 (q5151/q5152) Wave 3 (q515)	Narrowing the gap between rich and poor/providing basic items (such as food, housing, and clothing) to every individual/eliminating financial and administrative corruption = SECD
	Wave 5 (q515a2)	If you had to choose only one of the statements below, which one would you choose as the most essential characteristics of a democracy? Government ensures law and order/ government ensures job opportunities for all = SECD Media is free to criticize the things government does/multiple parties compete fairly in the election = PCD
Male	Wave 1 (q702) Wave 2 (q1002) Wave 3 (q1002) Wave 4 (q1002) Wave 5 (q1002)	Male = 1 Female = 0
Age	Wave 1 (q701) Wave 2 (q1001) Wave 3 (q1001) Wave 4 (q1001) Wave 5 (q1001)	Age in years
Time in West	Wave 1 (q224) Wave 2 (q702) Wave 3 (q702)	During the last five years, how much time, if any, have you spent in either Europe, the United States, or other Western countries? *Any amount of time = 1* *None = 0*
College education[1]	Wave 1 (q703) Wave 2 (q1003/t1003) Wave 3 (q1003/q1003t/ q1003yem) Wave 4 (q1003/t1003) Wave 5 (q1003)	College diploma—two years/mid-level diploma/professional or technical/BA/MA or higher = 1 Illiterate/elementary/primary/preparatory /secondary/pre–high school diploma = 0
Unemployed	Wave 5 (q1005)	Are you . . . *Unemployed or looking for work = 1* *Employed/self-employed/retired/a housewife/a student/other = 0*
Sufficient income	Wave 5 (q1016)	Which of these statements comes closest to describing your net household income? *Our net household income covers our expenses and we are able to save/our*

continues

Appendix C 209

Name	Wave	Coding
Sufficient income continued	Wave 5 (q1016)	*net household income covers our expenses without notable difficulties= 1* *Our net household income does not cover our expenses; we face some difficulties /our net household income does not cover our expenses; we face significant difficulties= 0*
Political interest	Wave 1 (q215)	Generally speaking, how interested would you say you are in politics? *Very interested/interested = 1* *Little interested/not interested = 0*
	Wave 2 (q404) Wave 3 (q404)	In general, to what extent are you interested in politics? *Very interested/interested = 1* *Slightly interested/not interested = 0*
	Wave 5 (q404)	In general, to what extent are you interested in politics? *Very interested/interested = 1* *Uninterested/very uninterested = 0*
Follows political news	Wave 1 (q216)	How often do you follow news about politics and government in [country]? *Very often/often = 1* *Sometimes/never = 0*
	Wave 2 (q405) Wave 3 (q405)	To what extent do you follow political news in your country? *To a great extent/to a medium extent= 1* *To a limited extent/I don't follow political news = 0*
Religion	Wave 1 (q711) Wave 2 (q1012/sa1012) Wave 3 (q1012) Wave 4 (q1012) Wave 5 (q1012)	Muslim/Sunni/Shi'ite/Hanbali/Shafi'i/ Jaafari = Muslim (reference category) Christian = Christian Jewish/other/Khaki/Druze (Lebanon) = Other Not provided/not usable/not clear/declined to answer/don't know = No answer None = None
Religious	Wave 1 (q714a) Wave 2 (q609) Wave 3 (q609) Wave 4 (q609) Wave 5 (q609)	In general, would you describe yourself as: *Not religious (reference category)* *In between/somewhat religious* *Religious*
Prayer[2]	Wave 1 (q713)	Do you pray? *Yes = 1 No = 0*
	Wave 2 (q610/t610) Wave 3 (q610)	Do you pray daily? *Always/most of the time = 1* *Sometimes/rarely/never = 0*

continues

210 *Appendix C*

Name	Wave	Coding
Prayer[2] continued	Wave 5 (q609a)	How often do you pray? *Once a day/five times a day = 1* *Never/at least once a month/once a week/several times a week = 0* The following questions are your personal opinions about the principles that should determine the behavior and situation of women in our society. For each of the statements listed below, please indicate whether you agree strongly, agree, disagree, or disagree strongly with it.
Gender traditionalist	Wave 1 (q5054) Wave 2 (q6014) Wave 3 (q6014) Wave 5 (q601_4)	"University education for males is more important than university education for females." *I strongly agree/I agree = 1* *I disagree/I strongly disagree = 0*
Secularist orientation	Wave 1 (q401)	"Men of religion should have influence over the decisions of government." *Strongly disagree/disagree = 1* *Strongly agree/agree = 0*
	Wave 2 (q606) Wave 3 (q606)	"Religious leaders (imams, preachers, priests) should have influence over government decisions." *Strongly disagree/disagree = 1* *Strongly agree/agree = 0*
	Wave 5	Partial-credit IRT model based on the following: • "Religious leaders should not interfere in voters' decisions in elections." (q 606_1, reverse coded) • "Your country is better off if religious people hold public positions in the state." (q 606_2) • "Religious clerics should have influence over the decisions of government." (q 606_3) *I strongly agree = 1* *I agree = 2* *I disagree = 3* *I strongly disagree = 4*
Institutional trust	Wave 1	Partial-credit IRT model based on "I'm going to name a number of institutions. For each one, please tell me how much trust you have in them. Is it a great deal of trust, quite a lot of trust, not very much trust, or none at all?" • Prime minister (q2011) • The courts (q2012)

continues

Name	Wave	Coding
Institutional trust continued	Wave 1	• Parliament (q2013) • The police (q2014) • Political parties (q2015) For more information on IRTs, see Appendix D.
	Wave 2	Partial-credit IRT model based on "I will name a number of institutions, and I would like you to tell me to what extent you trust each of them," from I absolutely do not trust it to I trust it to a great extent: • The government (the cabinet) (q2011) • The judiciary (the courts) (q2012) • The elected council of representatives (the parliament) (q2013) • Public security (the police) (q2014) • Political parties (q2015)
	Wave 3	Partial-credit IRT model based on "I will name a number of institutions, and I would like you to tell me to what extent you trust each of them," from I absolutely do not trust it to I trust it to a great extent: • The government (the cabinet) (q2011) • The elected council of representatives (the parliament) (q2013) • Public security (the police) (q2014)
	Wave 4	Partial-credit IRT model based on "I will name a number of institutions, and I would like you to tell me to what extent you trust each of them," from no trust at all to a great deal of trust: • Government (Council of Ministers) (q2011) • Courts and legal system (q2012) • The elected council of representatives (the parliament) (q2013) • Police (q2014) • Political parties (q20120)
	Wave 5	Partial-credit IRT model based on "I'm going to name a number of institutions. For each one, please tell me how much trust you have in them," from no trust at all to a great deal of trust: • Government (Council of Ministers) (q201a_1) • Courts and legal system (q201a_2) • The elected council of representatives (the parliament) (q201a_3) • Police (q201a_42)

continues

212 *Appendix C*

Name	Wave	Coding
Interpersonal trust	Wave 1 (q204) Wave 2 (q103) Wave 3 (q103) Wave 4 (q103) Wave 5 (q103)	Generally speaking, do you think most people are trustworthy or not? *Most people can be trusted = 1 You/I must be very careful in dealing with people = 0 Most people are trustworthy = 1 Most people are not trustworthy = 0*
Civil society member	Wave 1 (q202) Wave 5 (q501)	Are you a member of any organization or formal group (political parties, living cooperatives or local societies, religious organizations, sport and entertainment clubs, cultural organizations, associations or workers' unions, farmer unions, professional unions or associations, economic organizations or associations, entrepreneurial organizations, parent-teacher associations, or other voluntary organizations)? Are you a member of any organization or formal groups (living cooperatives or local societies, religious organizations, sport and entertainment clubs, cultural organizations, associations or workers' unions, farmer unions, professional associations, entrepreneurial organizations, parent-teacher associations, or other voluntary organizations)? *Yes = 1 No = 0*
	Wave 2	Are you a member of . . .? • A political party (q5011) • A charitable society (q5012) • A professional association/trade union (q5013) • A youth/cultural/sports organization (q5014) • A family/tribal association (q5015) • A local development association (q5016) *Yes to any of the above = 1 No to all = 0*
	Wave 3 Wave 4	Are you a member of . . . ? • A political party (q501b) • A charitable society (q5012) • A professional association/trade union (q5013) • A youth/cultural/sports organization (q5014)

continues

Appendix C   213

Name	Wave	Coding
Civil society member continued	Wave 3 Wave 4	• A family/tribal association (q5015) • A local development association (q5016) *Yes to any of the above = 1* *No to all = 0*
Public employee	Wave 1	Employment sector (q708) Employment status (q704) *Public = 1* *Private/other = 0* *Unemployed = 0*
	Wave 2	Employment sector (q1008) Employment status (q1004) *Public = 1* *Private/other = 0* *Unemployed = 0*
	Wave 3 Wave 4	Employment sector (q1006a) Employment status (q1004) *Public = 1* *Private/other = 0* *Unemployed = 0*
	Wave 5	Employment sector (q1006a) Employment status (q1005) *Public = 1* *Private/other = 0* *Unemployed = 0*

Political Variables

Name	Wave	Coding
Dimuqratiyya is a good system	Wave 1(q245) Wave 2 (q517) Wave 3 (q517)	I'm going to describe various types of political systems and ask what you think about each as a way of governing [respondent's country]. For each one, would you say it is a very good, fairly good, fairly bad, or very bad way of governing [country]? *Dimuqratiyya* political system (public freedom, equal political and civil rights, balance of power, accountability and transparency) *Very good/good = 1* *Very bad/bad = 0*

continues

214   *Appendix C*

Name	Wave	Coding
Dimuqratiyya- Autocracy Preference (DAP)	Wave 1(q245)	Binary indicator for viewing *dimuqratiyya* as very good/good and viewing the alternative systems as very bad/bad: • *Dimuqratiyya* political system (public freedom, equal political and civil rights, balance of power, accountability and transparency) • A strong nondemocratic leader that does not bother with parliaments and elections • Having experts rather than government make decisions according to what is best for the country • A system that is a mixture of the above three under one rule
	Wave 2 (q517)	Binary indicator for viewing *dimuqratiyya* as very good/good and viewing the alternative systems as very bad/bad: • A *dimuqratiyya* political system (public freedoms, guarantees equality in political and civil rights, alternation of power, and accountability and transparency of the executive authority). • A political system with an authoritarian president (nondemocratic) who is indifferent to parliament and elections • A political system controlled by experts who make decisions that they think are most appropriate for the country
	Wave 3 (q517)	Binary indicator for viewing *dimuqratiyya* as very good/good and viewing the alternative system as very bad/bad: • A *dimuqratiyya* political system (public freedoms, guarantees equality in political and civil rights, alternation of power, and accountability and transparency of the executive authority). • A political system with an authoritarian president (nondemocratic) who is indifferent to parliament and elections
Regime type suitability	Wave 1 (q2461–2464)	Binary indicator for viewing the regime described as very suitable/suitable and somewhat suitable/not at all suitable: I'm going to describe various types of political systems that exist in the Middle

continues

Appendix C **215**

Name	Wave	Coding
Regime type suitability continued	Wave 1 (q2461–2464)	East and ask what you think about each as a way of governing [your country]. For each one, would you say it is a very good, fairly good, fairly bad, or very bad way of governing [country]? • Parliamentary system in which nationalist, left-wing, and Islamic political parties all compete in elections • A parliamentary system in which only Islamic political parties and factions compete in elections • A system with a strong president and military in which elections and competition among political parties is not important • A system of government by Islamic law in which there are no political parties or elections
	Wave 2 (q5181–5185)	Binary indicator for viewing the regime described as very appropriate/appropriate and somewhat appropriate/absolutely inappropriate: I will mention some of the political systems currently in place in various Middle Eastern and North African countries. I would like to know to what extent you think these systems would be appropriate for your country. • A parliamentary system in which nationalist, left-wing, right-wing, and Islamist parties compete in parliamentary elections • A parliamentary system in which only Islamist parties compete in parliamentary elections • A political system governed by a strong authority which makes decisions without considering electoral results or the opinions of the opposition • A system of government by Islamic law without elections or political parties • A parliamentary system in which only nonreligious parties compete in parliamentary elections

continues

216 *Appendix C*

Name	Wave	Coding
Regime type suitability continued	Wave 3 (q5181–5185)	Binary indicator for viewing the regime described as very appropriate/appropriate and somewhat appropriate/absolutely inappropriate: I will mention some of the political systems currently in place in various Middle Eastern and North African countries. I would like to know to what extent you think these systems would be appropriate for your country. • A parliamentary system in which nationalist, left-wing, right-wing, and Islamist parties compete in parliamentary elections • A parliamentary system in which only Islamist parties compete in parliamentary elections/a parliamentary system based on Islamic law (shari'a) in which only Islamist parties compete in parliamentary elections • A political system governed by a strong authority which makes decisions without considering electoral results or the opinions of the opposition • A system of government by Islamic law without elections or political parties • A parliamentary system in which only nonreligious parties compete in parliamentary elections
Free elections	Wave 1 (q211) Wave 2 (q303) Wave 3 (q303) Wave 4 (q303) Wave 1 (q702)	On the whole, how would you rate the freeness and fairness of the last national election, held on [date]? Was it … *Completely free and fair/free and fair, with minor problems = 1* *Free and fair, with major problems/not free or fair = 0*
	Wave 5 (q303a)	In general, how would you evaluate the last parliamentary elections? Was it . . . *Free and fair = 1* *Free and fair, with major problems/ not free or fair = 0*
Care about needs	Wave 1 (q5072) Wave 2 (q2182) Wave 4 (q2182) Wave 5 (Q218_2)	"Our political leaders care about ordinary citizens." "Political leaders are concerned with the needs of ordinary citizens." *(I) strongly agree/(I) agree = 1* *(I) strongly disagree/(I) disagree = 0*

continues

Appendix C 217

Name	Wave	Coding
Criticize the government	Wave 1 (q2513)	"People are free to criticize government without fear." *(I) strongly agree/(I) agree = 1* *(I) strongly disagree/(I) disagree = 0*
	Wave 2 (q217) Wave 3 (q217) Wave 4 (q217)	In your opinion, are people nowadays able to criticize the government without fear? *Yes = 1 No = 0*
Colony	N/A	Former British colony/protectorate/ mandate (reference category) Former French colony/protectorate/ mandate Former Italian colony/protectorate/ mandate
Government satisfaction	Wave 5	Partial-credit IRT model based on the following questions: • In general, do you think that things in [country] are going in the right or wrong direction? (q100) *Going in the right direction = 3* *In between = 2* *Going in the wrong direction = 1* • To what extent do you feel that your own personal as well as your family's safety and security are currently ensured? (q105) *Fully ensured = 4* *Ensured = 3* *Not ensured = 2* *Not at all ensured = 1* • On a scale from 0–10 measuring the extent of your satisfaction with the current government's performance, in which 0 means that you are completely dissatisfied with its performance and 10 means you are completely satisfied, to what extent are you satisfied with the current government's performance? (q513) *0–10 scale from completely unsatisfied to completely satisfied* • How would you evaluate the current economic situation in your country? (q101) *Very good = 4 Good = 3* *Bad = 2 Very bad = 1*

continues

218 *Appendix C*

Socioeconomic Variables

Name	Wave	Coding
Government performance	Wave 1 (q244)	Using a similar 10-point scale, where 1 means very unsatisfied and 10 means very satisfied, indicate how satisfied you are with the performance of the current [respondent's country] government.
	Wave 2 (q513)	*1–10 from very unsatisfied to very satisfied*
	Wave 3 (q513)	*0–10 on scale from absolutely/very/*
	Wave 4 (q513)	*completely unsatisfied to very/*
	Wave 5 (q513)	*completely satisfied*
Crack down on corruption	Wave 1 (q254)	In your opinion, to what extent is the government working to crackdown on corruption and root out bribes? *To a large extent/to a medium extent = 1* *To a small extent/not at all = 0*
	Wave 2 (q211) Wave 3 (q211)	In your opinion, to what extent is the government working to eliminate corruption in your country? *To a great extent/to a medium extent = 1* *To a limited extent/not at all = 0*
	Wave 4 (q211) Wave 5 (q211)	In your opinion, to what extent is the government working to crackdown on corruption and root out bribes? In your opinion, to what extent is the national government working to crackdown on corruption? *To a large extent/to a medium extent = 1* *To a small extent/not at all = 0* *If q210, coded "not at all" = 0*
Corruption	Wave 1 (q253)	Here are some statements that describe how widespread corruption and bribe taking are in all sectors in [respondent's country]. Which of the following statements reflects your own opinion the best? *Most officials are corrupt/almost everyone is corrupt = 1* *Not a lot of officials are corrupt/hardly anyone is involved in corruption and bribery = 0*
	Wave 2 (q210) Wave 3 (q210)	Do you think that there is corruption within the state's institutions and agencies? *Yes = 1 No = 0*
	Wave 4 (q210) Wave 5 (q210)	To what extent do you think that there is corruption within the national state agencies and institutions in your country?

continues

Appendix C 219

Name	Wave	Coding
Corruption continued	Wave 4 (q210) Wave 5 (q210)	*To a large extent/to a medium extent = 1* *To a small extent/not at all = 0*
Service difficulties	Wave 1	Partial-credit IRT model based on "Based on your experience, how easy or difficult is it to obtain the following administrative or social services from the government?" from easy to very difficult (item not included in IRT where respondent did not attempt that service). • An identity document (such as birth certificate, driver's license, or passport) (q2131) • Registering a child in primary school in the public system (q2132) • Help from the police when you need it (q2134) • Access to individuals or institutions to file a complaint when your rights are violated (q2135) For more information on IRTs, see Appendix D.
	Wave 2	Partial-credit IRT model based on "Based on your actual experience, how difficult or easy is it to obtain . . . ?" from very easy to very difficult (item not included in IRT where respondent did not attempt that service). • Help from the police when you need it (q2054/12054) • Access to individuals or institutions to file a complaint when your rights are violated (q2055/12055)
	Wave 3	Partial-credit IRT model based on "Based on your actual experience, how difficult or easy is it to obtain . . . ?" from very easy to very difficult (item not included in IRT where respondent did not attempt that service). • Help from the police when you need it (q2054) • Access to individuals or institutions to file a complaint when your rights are violated (q2055)
	Wave 5	Partial-credit IRT model based on "Based on your experience, how easy or difficult is it to obtain the following services?" from very easy to very difficult (item not

continues

220 Appendix C

Name	Wave	Coding
Service difficulties continued	Wave 5 continued	included in IRT where respondent did not attempt that service). • Receive an identity document (q2051) • Help from the police when you need it (q2054/q2054leb) • Registering a business (q2056) • Getting a building permit (q2057)
Safe area	Wave 1 (q205)	Generally speaking, how safe is living in this (city/town/village)? *Very safe/safe = 1* *Very unsafe/unsafe = 0*
	Wave 2 (q105) Wave 3 (q105) Wave 4 (q105)	Do you currently feel that your own personal as well as your family's safety and security are ensured or not? *Fully ensured/ensured = 1* *Not ensured/absolutely not ensured = 0*
	Wave 5 (q105)	To what extent do you feel that your own personal as well as your family's safety and security are currently ensured? *Fully ensured/ensured = 1* *Not ensured/absolutely not ensured = 0*
National economy	Wave 1 (q101)	How would you rate the current overall economic condition of [respondent's country] today? *Very good/good = 1* *Very bad/bad = 0*
	Wave 2 (q101) Wave 3 (q101) Wave 4 (q101) Wave 5 (q101)	How would you evaluate the current economic situation in your country? *Very good/good = 1* *Very bad/bad = 0*
Vote	Wave 5 (q301a/q301b)	Did you vote in the last parliamentary elections that were held on [insert date of last local election]? *Yes = 1 No = 0* During the last national parliamentary election held on [insert date of last parliamentary election] many people could not or did not want to cast a ballot for many reasons. What about you? Which of the following statements best apply to you? *I am sure that I voted on [insert date of parliamentary election]/I cast my vote by mail = 1* *I did not vote in the national parliamentary election on [insert date of*

continues

Appendix C 221

Name	Wave	Coding
Vote continued	Wave 5 (q301a/q301b)	*parliamentary election]/I considered voting, but did not this time/usually I vote, but this time I did not = 0*
Close to a party	Wave 5 (q503a)	Which party, if any, do you feel closest to? *Any party = 1 No party = 0*
Protest	Wave 5 (q502_1)	Here is a set of activities that citizens may take part in. During the past three years, did you . . .
Petition	Wave 5 (q502_2)	• Attend a meeting to discuss a subject or sign a petition
Use violence	Wave 5 (q502_4)	• Participate in a protest, march, or sit-in • Used force or violence for a political cause *Once/more than once = 1 I have never participated = 0*

Egypt/Morocco Survey Variables

Variable Name	Coding
SECD-PCD	Which of the traits is most important for a society to be a *dimuqratiyya*? Please rank the top two traits. The opportunity to change the government through elections/freedom to criticize the government/equality of political rights between citizens/separation of religion and the government = PCD Narrowing the gap between rich and poor/providing basic items (such as food and housing) to every individual/eliminating financial and administrative corruption/government ensures law and order = SECD
Elected government is best	In terms of potential governments, which of these three statements is closest to your opinion? An elected government is always preferable to any other kind of government = 1 There are circumstances when an unelected government can be preferable/for someone like me, it doesn't matter what kind of government we have = 0
Elected government is appropriate	To what extent do you think choosing the government by election is appropriate for your country? *Very appropriate=4 Somewhat appropriate=3 Somewhat inappropriate=2 Very inappropriate=1*

continues

222 *Appendix C*

Variable Name	Coding
Acceptable regime types	There are many ways to govern a country. Would you disapprove or approve of the following alternatives? • Only one political party is allowed to stand for election and hold office • The army governs the country • Elections and parliament are abolished so that the president can decide everything • A system governed by Islamic law without elections • Multiple political parties compete in elections to hold office • The government includes both elected and unelected offices that take an active part in decisionmaking and policy *Strongly approve=4*　　*Approve=3* *Disapprove=2*　　*Strongly disapprove=1*
Government evaluation	Partial-credit IRT model based on • Would you say that the country is going in the wrong direction or going in the right direction? *Right direction = 1*　　*Wrong direction = 0* • To what extent are you satisfied with the government's performance? *Completely satisfied =4*　　*Somewhat satisfied = 3* *Somewhat unsatisfied =2*　　*Completely unsatisfied = 1* • In general, how would you describe the present condition in this country in terms of 　○ Unemployment 　○ Keeping prices down 　○ Safety *Very good = 4*　　*Good = 3* *Bad = 2*　　*Very Bad = 1* For more information on IRTs, see Appendix D.
Most people can be trusted	Generally speaking, would you say that most people can be trusted or that you need to be very careful in dealing with people? *Most people can be trusted = 1* *Need to be careful = 0*
News consumption	How often, if at all, do you • Read or watch the news
Scripture reading	• Read or listen to the Qur'an/Bible
Prayer	• Pray *Every day = 1* *Most of the time/sometimes/rarely/never = 0*
Interested in politics	How interested, if at all, would you say you are in politics and government? *Very interested/somewhat interested = 1* *Not very interested/not at all interested = 0*

continues

Appendix C **223**

Variable Name	Coding
Gender traditionalism	Partial-credit IRT model based on agreement with the following statements: • Men make better national political leaders (i.e., members of parliament) than women • University education for men is more important than for women *Strongly agree = 4* *Agree = 3* *Disagree = 2* *Strongly disagree = 1* and disagreement with the following statement: • Working mothers can establish just as secure a relationship with their children as mothers who do not work. *Strongly agree = 1* *Agree = 2* *Disagree = 3* *Strongly disagree = 4* For more information on IRTs, see Appendix D.
Secularist orientation	Partial-credit IRT model based on disagreement with the following statements: • Our country is better off if religious people hold public positions in the state • The government should enact laws in accordance with Islamic law *Strongly agree = 1* *Agree = 2* *Disagree = 3* *Strongly disagree = 4* and agreement with the following statement: • Religious leaders like imams and priests should not interfere in voters' decisions in elections *Strongly agree = 4* *Agree = 3* *Disagree = 2* *Strongly disagree = 1* For more information on IRTs, see Appendix D. • Religious leaders like imams and priests should not interfere in voters' decisions in elections *Strongly agree = 4* *Agree = 3* *Disagree = 2* *Strongly disagree = 1* For more information on IRTs, see Appendix D.
More important for government to be effective Elections can produce bad results Elections are acceptable in Islamic law	How much do you agree with the following statements? • It is more important to have a government that can get things done, even if we have no influence over what it does. • Since elections sometimes produce bad results, we should adopt other methods for choosing this country's leaders. • Electing governments is acceptable under the teachings of Islam. *Strongly agree/agree = 1* *Strongly disagree/disagree = 0*

continues

224 *Appendix C*

Variable Name	Coding
Male	YouGov supplied data: *Male = 1* *Female = 0*
Unemployed	YouGov supplied response as "working" or "not working": *Not working = 1* *Working = 0*
Religion	Do you belong to a religion or religious denomination? If yes, which one? *1) No* *2) Yes—Muslim* *3) Yes—Christian* *4) Yes—Something else* Factor variable (reference category = Muslim)
Income	Which of these statements comes closest to describing your household income in the last year? Our household income covers our expenses well, and we are able to save/our household income covers our expenses without notable difficulties = 1 Our household income does not cover our expenses, and we face some difficulties in meeting our needs/our household income does not cover our expenses, and we face significant difficulties in meeting our needs/our household income does not cover our expenses, and we are never able to meet our needs = 0
College education	What is the highest level of education have you completed? Elementary school/secondary school/vocational college education (e.g., to qualify as an electrician, nurse)/none of these = 0 University first degree (e.g., BA, BS)/university higher degree (master's, MBA, PhD)/professional higher education (e.g., to qualify as a lawyer, accountant) = 1
Urban residence	Would you say the area you live in is . . .? *Urban = 0* *Suburban/rural/other = 0*
Spend time in the West	In the past five years, have you visited, studied in, or lived in Europe, the United States, or Canada? *Yes = 1* *No = 0*
Age	YouGov supplied age brackets: 18–24/25–29/30–24/40+ Factor variable (reference category: 18–24)
Region	YouGov supplied region of residence: Casablanca/Agadir/Marrakech/Rabat/Fes/Sale/Tangier/Kentira/other Cairo/Canal Zone/Upper Egypt/Delta/Alexandria/other Factor variable (reference categories: Casablanca and Cairo)

Notes

1. College education binaries have been used in other MENA protest and democratization survey studies (Hoffman and Jamal 2012, 2014). While many studies use the education scale as a continuous variable, the scale is not linear, so the meaning of the result is obscured. Dummies for each level are possible, but they are less interpretable than the college binary. Moreover, narratives on support for democratization or antiauthoritarianism in the Middle East often reference (un)employed college graduates and their views as central to democratic movements (Campante and Chor 2012; Hoffman and Jamal 2012; Bishara 2021b).

2. These variables for religiosity were favored over the common metric—religious service attendance—because some Muslim communities do not expect women to attend religious services weekly, a regular expectation for Muslim men. Where it would require gender mixing, women's attendance can even be discouraged. As such, service-based measures of religiosity can underreport women's religiosity. Attendance at public services could also reflect an interest in being observed to be religious by proximal individuals rather than piety. Prayer and engagement with religious texts, however, can be done at home and to individualized levels of piety.

Appendix D
Partial-Credit IRT Models

Item response theory (IRT) models are used to identify the latent "ability" of a respondent with respect to a certain trait that is assumed to underly the response to the questions asked (Baker 2001). The technique is based on scoring tests with fact-based answers. The premise is that individuals who have higher ability in a domain, such as math, will get more questions right, and they will get the harder questions correct. Thus, from these correct answers, it is possible to identify individuals' latent capacity to do the task or embody the characteristic.

The questions included in the IRT are evaluated by their difficulty and their discrimination. Difficulty relates to the amount of ability it would take to be correct; the parameter identifies the likelihood that a low-ability individual would get the question correct. The discrimination parameter indicates how well this question distinguishes high-ability respondents from low-ability respondents. In each case, higher scores indicate greater ability.

For questions to be included in one IRT and estimate a respondent's level of the target trait, all the estimated discrimination parameters should be either positive or negative. Questions that move in a different direction measure a different trait or have been substantially and/or systematically misunderstood by (some of) the respondents. Due to the potential misunderstanding of the question and/or measurement of an alternative dimension, those questions are then not informative of the latent ability of the target measure and should be omitted. The discrimination parameters of the questions included in the IRTs used in this project are below.

In this case, the questions used to assess the IRT are respondents' agreement and disagreement statements. Rather than simply code the

228 *Appendix D*

answers as "right" or "wrong"—based on what they would indicate with respect to the key trait—the responses could get "partial credit." For instance, they could disagree, rather than strongly disagree, with a gender-egalitarian statement, which would indicate less gender traditionalism. As such, graded response models are used for these IRT estimations.

Service Difficulty

Variable	Model 1	Model 2	Model 3	Model 4	Model 5
Help from the police	1.026	1.383	4.240		−1.309
Acquire ID	1.668				−1.309
Register child in school	1.552				−2.214
File a complaint	0.941	3.813	1.716		
Acquire a permit					−1.899

Institutional Trust

Variable	Wave 1	Wave 2	Wave 3	Wave 4	Wave 5
Prime minister	−2.315	−3.601	1.760	3.295	−3.121
Court	−2.831	−2.635		2.604	−1.797
Parliament	−2.084	−2.699	2.628	2.580	−1.831
Police	−1.691	−2.180	1.570	1.309	−1.245
Political parties	−1.019	−1.233		1.145	

Government Performance

Variable	Arab Barometer V	Egypt	Morocco
Country is moving in the right direction	0.856	4.898	3.568
Satisfaction with the government's performance	1.502	3.986	3.537
Current economic situation in the country	1.522		
Respondent's and family's safety is assured	0.972		
Government performance (unemployment)		2.233	1.842
Government performance (inflation)		2.262	1.666
Government performance (safety)		2.152	1.485

Gender Traditionalism

Variable	Egypt	Morocco
Men make better political leaders than women	2.043	1.313
University education is more important for men than for women	1.497	3.786
Working mothers can establish just as secure a relationship with their children as women who do not work (Reverse Coded)	0.301	0.350

Secularist Orientation

Variable	Arab Barometer V	Egypt	Morocco
The government should enact laws in accordance with Islamic law (Reverse Coded)		1.084	1.028
Religious leaders, like imams and priests, should not interfere in voters' decisions in elections	−0.630	0.451	0.444
Our country is better off if religious people hold public positions in the state (Reverse Coded)	−1.614	4.102	4.102
Religious clerics should have influence over the decisions of government. (Reverse Coded)	−2.724		

Appendix E
Conjoint Experiment Results

Egyptian Sample Average Marginal Component Effects (Full Sample)

Level	Average Marginal Component Effect	Standard Error	p-value
There are elections with multiple recognized political parties	0.221	0.013	0.00
There are elections with one recognized political party	0.096	0.013	0.00
There are no elections	0	—	—
Few barriers to citizen political participation	0	—	—
Many barriers to citizen political participation	−0.054	0.012	0.00
Some barriers to citizen political participation	−0.039	0.012	0.00
There is an official state religion	0	—	—
There is no official state religion	−0.112	0.012	0.00
Formal role for religious leaders in government	0	—	—
No formal role for religious leaders in government	0.049	0.011	0.00
Good government provision of basic items (i.e., housing and food) to individuals	0	—	—

continues

232 *Appendix E*

Level	Average Marginal Component Effect	Standard Error	p-value
Some government provision of basic items (i.e., housing and food) to individuals	−0.035	0.013	0.00
Little government provision of basic items (i.e., housing and food) to individuals	−0.064	0.013	0.00
High unemployment (14%)	0	—	—
Low unemployment (7%)	0.115	0.011	0.00

Moroccan Sample Average Marginal Component Effects (Full Sample)

Level	Average Marginal Component Effect	Standard Error	p-value
There are elections with multiple recognized political parties	0.175	0.013	0.00
There are elections with one recognized political party	0.048	0.013	0.00
There are no elections	0	—	—
Few barriers to citizen political participation	0	—	—
Some barriers to citizen political participation	−0.022	0.013	0.07
Many barriers to citizen political participation	−0.055	0.012	0.00
There is an official state religion	0	—	—
There is no official state religion	−0.114	0.011	0.00
Formal role for religious leaders in government	0	—	—
No formal role for religious leaders in government	0.046	0.011	0.00
Good government provision of basic items (i.e., housing and food) to individuals	0	—	—

continues

Level	Average Marginal Component Effect	Standard Error	p-value
Some government provision of basic items (i.e., housing and food) to individuals	−0.019	0.013	0.143
Little government provision of basic items (i.e., housing and food) to individuals	−0.065	0.013	0.00
High unemployment (14%)	0	—	—
Low unemployment (7%)	0.143	0.012	0.00

Differences in Marginal Means for Committed Democrats and Other Egyptians

Level	Marginal Mean	Standard Error	p-value
There are elections with multiple recognized political parties	0.049	0.016	0.002
There are elections with one recognized political party	−0.002	0.015	0.912
There are no elections	−0.046	0.015	0.003
Few barriers to citizen political participation	0.021	0.015	0.147
Many barriers to citizen political participation	−0.020	0.015	0.180
Some barriers to citizen political participation	−0.006	0.015	0.704
There is an official state religion	−0.011	0.012	0.378
There is no official state religion	0.006	0.012	0.612
Formal role for religious leaders in government	−0.001	0.011	0.934
No formal role for religious leaders in government	0.002	0.012	0.888
Good government provision of basic items (i.e., housing and food) to individuals	−0.009	0.015	0.573
Some government provision of basic items (i.e., housing and food) to individuals	0.004	0.015	0.805

continues

Level	Marginal Mean	Standard Error	p-value
Little government provision of basic items (i.e., housing and food) to individuals	0.002	0.015	0.901
High unemployment (14%)	0.020	0.012	0.083
Low unemployment (7%)	−0.018	0.011	0.114

Differences in Marginal Means for Committed Democrats and Other Moroccans

Level	Marginal Mean	Standard Error	p-value
There are elections with multiple recognized political parties	0.032	0.017	0.061
There are elections with one recognized political party	−0.015	0.017	0.385
There are no elections	−0.008	0.016	0.625
Few barriers to citizen political participation	0.025	0.016	0.107
Some barriers to citizen political participation	0.006	0.016	0.697
Many barriers to citizen political participation	−0.032	0.016	0.042
There is an official state religion	0.017	0.013	0.176
There is no official state religion	−0.020	0.013	0.113
Formal role for religious leaders in government	0.009	0.013	0.477
No formal role for religious leaders in government	−0.010	0.012	0.412
Good government provision of basic items (i.e., housing and food) to individuals	0.028	0.016	0.092
Some government provision of basic items (i.e., housing and food) to individuals	0.009	0.017	0.585
Little government provision of basic items (i.e., housing and food) to individuals	−0.036	0.016	0.025
High unemployment (14%)	0.011	0.013	0.375
Low unemployment (7%)	−0.004	0.012	0.728

Appendix E **235**

Differences in Marginal Means (PCD–SECD) in Egypt

Level	Marginal Mean	Standard Error	p-value
There are elections with multiple recognized political parties	0.024	0.016	0.121
There are elections with one recognized political party	−0.020	0.015	0.176
There are no elections	−0.008	0.015	0.607
Few barriers to citizen political participation	0.017	0.015	0.229
Many barriers to citizen political participation	0.012	0.015	0.423
Some barriers to citizen political participation	−0.031	0.015	0.037
There is an official state religion	−0.030	0.012	0.012
There is no official state religion	0.027	0.012	0.022
Formal role for religious leaders in government	0.012	0.011	0.268
No formal role for religious leaders in government	−0.012	0.012	0.283
Good government provision of basic items (i.e., housing and food) to individuals	−0.008	0.015	0.614
Some government provision of basic items (i.e., housing and food) to individuals	−0.013	0.015	0.380
Little government provision of basic items (i.e., housing and food) to individuals	0.020	0.015	0.177
High unemployment (14%)	0.027	0.012	0.023
Low unemployment (7%)	−0.025	0.012	0.027

Differences in Marginal Means (PCD–SECD) in Morocco

Level	Marginal Mean	Standard Error	p-value
There are elections with multiple recognized political parties	0.019	0.015	0.208
There are elections with one recognized political party	−0.007	0.015	0.634
There are no elections	−0.002	0.015	0.871

continues

236 Appendix E

Level	Marginal Mean	Standard Error	p-value
Few barriers to citizen political participation	0.035	0.015	0.017
Some barriers to citizen political participation	−0.002	0.015	0.883
Many barriers to citizen political participation	−0.031	0.015	0.039
There is an official state religion	−0.038	0.012	0.001
There is no official state religion	0.036	0.012	0.002
Formal role for religious leaders in government	−0.005	0.011	0.643
No formal role for religious leaders in government	0.004	0.011	0.721
Good government provision of basic items (i.e., housing and food) to individuals	−0.036	0.015	0.018
Some government provision of basic items (i.e., housing and food) to individuals	0.025	0.016	0.116
Little government provision of basic items (i.e., housing and food) to individuals	0.013	0.015	0.368
High unemployment (14%)	0.010	0.012	0.423
Low unemployment (7%)	−0.009	0.011	0.427

Appendix F
Conception of *Dimuqratiyya* (Arab Barometer V) by Country

	Algeria	Egypt	Iraq	Jordan	Lebanon
Intercept	−0.67***	−0.36*	−1.45***	−1.46***	−1.11***
	(0.23)	(0.20)	(0.21)	(0.19)	(0.18)
Government	−0.11	0.34***	0.03	−0.24***	0.11
evaluation	(0.09)	(0.06)	(0.07)	(0.07)	(0.08)
Political	0.68***	0.56***	0.24**	0.34***	0.54***
interest	(0.12)	(0.12)	(0.11)	(0.11)	(0.10)
Gender	0.29**	−0.33***	−0.14	0.06	0.68***
traditionalism	(0.12)	(0.12)	(0.12)	(0.14)	(0.14)
Secularist	−0.09	0.31***	−0.03	0.10	0.22***
orientation	(0.08)	(0.07)	(0.05)	(0.07)	(0.06)
Unemployed	0.15	−0.37**	−0.14	−0.11	−0.11
	(0.14)	(0.16)	(0.17)	(0.14)	(0.18)
Sufficient	−0.10	0.17	0.29***	0.19	0.13
income	(0.10)	(0.11)	(0.10)	(0.12)	(0.09)
Male	−0.13	0.02	0.19*	0.54***	0.11
	(0.10)	(0.10)	(0.11)	(0.11)	(0.09)
College	−0.34***	0.49***	0.04	0.27**	0.23**
education	(0.12)	(0.11)	(0.11)	(0.11)	(0.10)
Christian	−14.60	0.21	0.77	1.40***	−0.21**
	(329.66)	(0.18)	(0.80)	(0.41)	(0.11)
No response	−0.99				
	(1.67)				
No religion	−1.82	−11.48	−11.69		
	(1.25)	(258.50)	(267.64)		
Other					0.04
					(0.19)
Daily prayer	−0.25**	0.14	0.05	−0.07	0.18*
	(0.12)	(0.13)	(0.15)	(0.13)	(0.10)
Age	0.00	−0.02***	−0.00	−0.01	0.00
	(0.00)	(0.00)	(0.00)	(0.00)	(0.00)

continues

238 Appendix F

	Algeria	Egypt	Iraq	Jordan	Lebanon
Civil society	0.40***	0.30**	0.18	0.17	−0.17
member	(0.13)	(0.13)	(0.18)	(0.18)	(0.17)
AIC	2,158.90	2,397.90	2,602.69	2,452.18	2,914.15
Log likelihood	−1,064.45	−1,184.95	−1,287.34	−1,213.09	−1,443.07
N	1,875	2,229	2,319	2,271	2,285

Notes: ***$p < 0.01$; **$p < 0.05$; *$p < 0.1$.

	Libya	Morocco	Palestine	Sudan	Tunisia	Yemen
Intercept	−0.77**	−1.00***	−0.94***	0.49*	−1.83***	−0.35*
	(0.32)	(0.21)	(0.17)	(0.26)	(0.21)	(0.18)
Government	0.18**	−0.06	−0.09	−0.23***	−0.07	0.11**
evaluation	(0.09)	(0.07)	(0.07)	(0.09)	(0.09)	(0.05)
Political	−0.01	0.25**	0.20**	0.07	0.05	−0.01
interest	(0.14)	(0.13)	(0.10)	(0.12)	(0.13)	(0.10)
Gender	−0.24	0.42***	0.30**	0.01	0.33**	−0.42***
traditionalism	(0.18)	(0.15)	(0.12)	(0.13)	(0.13)	(0.10)
Secularist	0.14	−0.16**	0.27***	−0.32***	−0.05	−0.09*
orientation	(0.10)	(0.08)	(0.06)	(0.08)	(0.08)	(0.05)
Unemployed	0.03	−0.44***	−0.30*	−0.01	−0.05	−0.22*
	(0.19)	(0.15)	(0.15)	(0.16)	(0.17)	(0.13)
Sufficient	−0.24*	0.35***	0.33***	0.11	0.07	−0.01
income	(0.12)	(0.12)	(0.09)	(0.11)	(0.12)	(0.11)
Male	0.01	0.16	−0.05	0.08	0.51***	0.24**
	(0.13)	(0.11)	(0.09)	(0.11)	(0.13)	(0.10)
College	0.12	−0.04	−0.15	−0.29**	−0.25*	0.31***
education	(0.13)	(0.12)	(0.10)	(0.12)	(0.15)	(0.12)
Christian			−0.03	−0.46		
			(0.48)	(0.75)		
No response		−0.84			1.18	
		(1.73)			(1.56)	
No religion				0.38	−0.08	
				(0.89)	(0.97)	
Other				12.61	0.90	
				(323.84)	(1.01)	
Daily prayer	−0.18	−0.44***	−0.09	−0.56***	−0.30**	−0.07
	(0.24)	(0.12)	(0.13)	(0.19)	(0.14)	(0.14)
Age	−0.01**	−0.00	0.00	−0.00	0.01	−0.00
	(0.00)	(0.00)	(0.00)	(0.00)	(0.00)	(0.00)
Civil society	0.31*	0.29**	0.11	0.47***	−0.19	0.24**
member	(0.17)	(0.13)	(0.13)	(0.12)	(0.25)	(0.11)
AIC	1,979.49	1,972.10	2,873.02	2,068.31	2,495.27	3,046.21
Log likelihood	−977.75	−973.05	−1,423.51	−1,019.15	−1,232.64	−1,511.10
N	1,711	1,850	2,306	1,497	2,178	2,195

Notes: ***$p < 0.01$; **$p < 0.05$; *$p < 0.1$.

Appendix G
(Non)democratic Regime Country Suitability

Wave I

	Model 1	Model 2	Model 3	Model 4
Intercept	14.70***	18.16***	15.73***	18.33***
	(1.32)	(1.27)	(0.89)	(1.46)
Mixed SECD	−0.17*	−0.09	−0.19	−0.26
	(0.10)	(0.17)	(0.25)	(0.22)
Mixed PCD	0.05	0.01	−0.25*	−0.21**
	(0.18)	(0.07)	(0.15)	(0.10)
PCD	0.20	−0.24***	−0.64***	−0.38***
	(0.18)	(0.08)	(0.22)	(0.12)
Government	−0.01	0.04***	−0.02	0.04*
performance	(0.02)	(0.01)	(0.05)	(0.02)
National economy	0.06	0.15	0.38***	−0.09
	(0.06)	(0.14)	(0.14)	(0.12)
Time in West	0.31**	−0.47**	0.08	−0.47**
	(0.14)	(0.21)	(0.18)	(0.23)
Christian	−0.21***	−1.57***	0.10***	−1.83***
	(0.03)	(0.04)	(0.04)	(0.02)
Not clear	−11.63***	−11.49***	−11.27***	−11.02***
	(1.02)	(0.97)	(0.77)	(1.02)
Other	−1.51***	−0.77***	−0.06	−0.59***
	(0.08)	(0.04)	(0.08)	(0.05)
Pray daily	−0.11	0.23	0.24	0.37***
	(0.20)	(0.21)	(0.23)	(0.10)
Interpersonal trust	0.10	−0.05	0.03	0.03
	(0.13)	(0.13)	(0.10)	(0.10)
Feel safe	0.02	−0.04	−0.20	0.12
	(0.12)	(0.13)	(0.17)	(0.07)

continues

240 *Appendix G*

	Model 1	Model 2	Model 3	Model 4
Age in years	0.01***	0.00	0.01**	−0.01***
	(0.00)	(0.01)	(0.00)	(0.00)
Male	0.39***	−0.16**	−0.26***	0.01
	(0.15)	(0.07)	(0.07)	(0.07)
College education	−0.01	−0.37***	−0.26**	−0.19
	(0.07)	(0.13)	(0.10)	(0.12)
Civil society member	0.57***	−0.19*	0.17	−0.13
	(0.11)	(0.10)	(0.10)	(0.14)
Follows news	0.18***	−0.21***	−0.40***	−0.04
	(0.06)	(0.06)	(0.08)	(0.05)
Political interest	0.06	−0.05	0.09	−0.13
	(0.06)	(0.10)	(0.24)	(0.10)
Gender traditionalist	0.09	0.53***	0.63**	0.39***
	(0.15)	(0.07)	(0.26)	(0.05)
Secularist orientation	−0.06	−0.91***	−0.28	−0.81***
	(0.15)	(0.09)	(0.18)	(0.04)
Colonial: France	31.42***	37.35***	34.50***	36.62***
	(2.81)	(2.85)	(2.21)	(2.89)
GDP per capita	−8.78***	−11.14***	−10.16***	−10.97***
	(0.77)	(0.80)	(0.62)	(0.83)
Bahrain	169.70***	214.99***	195.40***	211.34***
	(14.83)	(15.45)	(11.97)	(15.99)
Jordan	9.09***	11.81***	10.76***	11.94***
	(0.79)	(0.88)	(0.66)	(0.90)

Notes: ***$p < 0.01$; **$p < 0.05$; *$p < 0.1$. Model 1: Multiparty system. Model 2: Parliament with only Islamist parties. Model 3: Strong man leader. Model 4: Islamic law system.

Wave II

	Model 1	Model 2	Model 3	Model 4	Model 5
Intercept	−2.18***	0.77***	0.77***	2.77***	−0.81**
	(0.35)	(0.28)	(0.28)	(0.65)	(0.32)
Mixed SECD	−0.32***	0.03	0.03	0.01	−0.24***
	(0.11)	(0.16)	(0.16)	(0.18)	(0.06)
Mixed PCD	−0.14	0.23	0.23	0.16	−0.46***
	(0.15)	(0.22)	(0.22)	(0.27)	(0.11)
PCD	0.02	0.02	0.02	0.16	−0.47***
	(0.11)	(0.15)	(0.15)	(0.15)	(0.16)
Government	−0.02	0.06***	0.06***	0.05	0.04
performance	(0.03)	(0.02)	(0.02)	(0.04)	(0.03)
National economy	−0.11	0.14	0.14	0.23*	0.04
	(0.17)	(0.11)	(0.11)	(0.12)	(0.22)

continues

Appendix G 241

	Model 1	Model 2	Model 3	Model 4	Model 5
Time in West	0.12	0.40	0.40	0.28	0.68**
	(0.16)	(0.28)	(0.28)	(0.23)	(0.29)
Christian	−0.10	−0.60**	−0.60**	−1.21***	0.80***
	(0.08)	(0.29)	(0.29)	(0.43)	(0.05)
No answer	0.16	−0.02	−0.02	−0.29	−0.90
	(0.24)	(0.53)	(0.53)	(0.26)	(0.71)
Other	0.40	1.01	1.01	0.98*	0.30
	(1.04)	(0.75)	(0.75)	(0.58)	(1.11)
Pray daily	0.17	0.44***	0.44***	0.38***	−0.13
	(0.15)	(0.11)	(0.11)	(0.15)	(0.11)
Interpersonal	0.10*	0.12***	0.12***	0.03	−0.25
trust	(0.05)	(0.04)	(0.04)	(0.06)	(0.19)
Feel safe	0.00	−0.08	−0.08	0.03	−0.15
	(0.09)	(0.13)	(0.13)	(0.12)	(0.15)
Age in years	0.01***	−0.01**	−0.01**	−0.00	0.00
	(0.00)	(0.00)	(0.00)	(0.00)	(0.00)
Male	0.06	−0.18	−0.18	−0.08	−0.08
	(0.09)	(0.14)	(0.14)	(0.13)	(0.18)
College	−0.04	−0.20***	−0.20***	−0.10	−0.33***
education	(0.09)	(0.07)	(0.07)	(0.08)	(0.11)
Civil society	0.05	−0.02	−0.02	0.10*	−0.09
member	(0.09)	(0.12)	(0.12)	(0.06)	(0.12)
Follows news	−0.05	0.04	0.04	−0.01	−0.10
	(0.11)	(0.11)	(0.11)	(0.11)	(0.25)
Political interest	0.17	0.12	0.12	−0.25**	0.24*
	(0.12)	(0.16)	(0.16)	(0.11)	(0.14)
Gender	0.08	0.50***	0.50***	0.35***	0.43**
traditionalist	(0.08)	(0.08)	(0.08)	(0.11)	(0.21)
Secularist	0.13**	−0.84***	−0.84***	−0.91***	0.01
orientation	(0.06)	(0.08)	(0.08)	(0.12)	(0.22)
Colonial: France	−1.37***	−0.52***	−0.52***	−0.25***	0.09
	(0.04)	(0.10)	(0.10)	(0.08)	(0.08)
GDP per capita	0.62***	−0.52***	−0.52***	−0.83***	−0.10**
	(0.03)	(0.04)	(0.04)	(0.04)	(0.04)
Lebanon	−0.91***	1.05***	1.05***	1.22***	0.99***
	(0.07)	(0.09)	(0.09)	(0.09)	(0.09)
Palestine	0.45***	−0.56***	−0.56***	−1.23***	−0.85***
	(0.06)	(0.11)	(0.11)	(0.10)	(0.10)
Saudi Arabia	−13.34***	11.04***	11.04***	16.99***	1.56*
	(0.55)	(0.79)	(0.79)	(0.91)	(0.82)
Sudan	1.57***	−0.84***	−0.84***	−1.75***	−0.47***
	(0.10)	(0.21)	(0.21)	(0.15)	(0.16)
Tunisia	2.07***	0.39***	0.39***	−1.00***	−0.82***
	(0.06)	(0.13)	(0.13)	(0.09)	(0.09)

continues

242 Appendix G

	Model 1	Model 2	Model 3	Model 4	Model 5
Yemen	1.49***	−1.42**	−1.42**	−2.11***	0.38
	(0.28)	(0.61)	(0.61)	(0.30)	(0.74)
Egypt	0.46***	−0.89***	−0.89***	−1.86***	−0.28**
	(0.09)	(0.11)	(0.11)	(0.14)	(0.13)

Notes: ***$p < 0.01$; **$p < 0.05$; *$p < 0.1$. Model 1: Multiparty system. Model 2: Parliament with only Islamist parties. Model 3: Strong man leader. Model 4: Islamic law system. Model 5: Parliament without Islamist parties.

Wave III

	Model 1	Model 2	Model 3	Model 4	Model 5
Intercept	1.20***	−0.60***	0.53*	−1.34***	−0.46**
	(0.24)	(0.21)	(0.29)	(0.25)	(0.21)
Mixed SECD	0.08	−0.04	−0.02	−0.03	−0.08
	(0.09)	(0.10)	(0.10)	(0.07)	(0.12)
Mixed PCD	0.14	0.16	0.02	0.05	0.11
	(0.15)	(0.13)	(0.16)	(0.11)	(0.14)
PCD	0.20	−0.01	0.11	0.07	0.25
	(0.19)	(0.22)	(0.19)	(0.16)	(0.24)
Government	−0.00	0.06**	−0.00	0.03	0.01
performance	(0.02)	(0.03)	(0.03)	(0.03)	(0.03)
National economy	0.08	0.21**	0.02	0.19**	0.13
	(0.10)	(0.11)	(0.12)	(0.08)	(0.16)
Time in West	0.12	0.26***	0.02	0.11	0.17*
	(0.17)	(0.08)	(0.13)	(0.08)	(0.10)
Christian	−0.14	−1.08**	−0.00	−2.18***	0.96***
	(0.11)	(0.50)	(0.12)	(0.24)	(0.15)
Pray daily	0.15*	0.41***	0.09	0.30	−0.55***
	(0.09)	(0.09)	(0.09)	(0.19)	(0.10)
Interpersonal trust	−0.13	0.05	0.04	0.05	0.00
	(0.14)	(0.08)	(0.10)	(0.14)	(0.12)
Feel safe	0.28*	−0.03	0.35**	0.09	−0.31**
	(0.16)	(0.15)	(0.16)	(0.08)	(0.13)
Age in years	0.00	0.00	0.00**	−0.00	−0.00
	(0.00)	(0.00)	(0.00)	(0.00)	(0.00)
Male	0.08	−0.08	0.07	0.03	0.01
	(0.07)	(0.05)	(0.09)	(0.08)	(0.08)
College education	0.04	−0.28***	−0.01	−0.27***	−0.14**
	(0.10)	(0.09)	(0.08)	(0.09)	(0.07)
Civil society	0.05	0.15	−0.04	0.13	0.10
member	(0.11)	(0.10)	(0.18)	(0.11)	(0.09)

continues

	Model 1	Model 2	Model 3	Model 4	Model 5
Follows news	−0.09	−0.07	−0.10	0.07	−0.04
	(0.09)	(0.10)	(0.13)	(0.09)	(0.07)
Political interest	0.24**	0.06	0.23*	0.12	−0.04
	(0.12)	(0.09)	(0.13)	(0.11)	(0.09)
Gender −0.06 traditionalist	0.47***	−0.19**	0.45***	0.55***	
	(0.12)	(0.07)	(0.10)	(0.11)	(0.16)
Secularist orientation	0.22	−0.82***	0.29	−0.88***	−0.21
	(0.17)	(0.13)	(0.24)	(0.13)	(0.17)
Colonial: France	1.58***	1.31***	1.21***	−0.41*	1.25***
	(0.34)	(0.27)	(0.40)	(0.22)	(0.39)
Colonial: Italy	3.86***	4.40***	2.75**	0.23	4.76***
	(0.99)	(0.76)	(1.16)	(0.63)	(1.05)
GDP per capita	−0.62***	−0.51***	−0.48***	0.03	−0.50***
	(0.11)	(0.08)	(0.13)	(0.07)	(0.11)
Egypt	1.53***	0.43**	1.44***	−0.35**	0.82***
	(0.29)	(0.19)	(0.34)	(0.15)	(0.31)
Iraq	3.70***	1.88***	2.98***	−1.23***	1.82***
	(0.57)	(0.45)	(0.66)	(0.36)	(0.62)
Jordan	1.51***	1.38***	1.16***	0.47***	1.82***
	(0.22)	(0.21)	(0.27)	(0.16)	(0.27)
Kuwait	29.59***	23.63***	22.71***	−1.67	23.92***
	(4.97)	(3.80)	(5.89)	(3.20)	(5.34)
Lebanon	2.20***	0.42	1.94***	−0.66**	3.37***
	(0.48)	(0.34)	(0.54)	(0.30)	(0.46)
Morocco	−0.31*	−0.27*	−0.10	0.72***	−1.29***
	(0.19)	(0.15)	(0.21)	(0.13)	(0.21)
Palestine	1.04***	1.13***	0.57**	0.34**	0.67***
	(0.20)	(0.17)	(0.22)	(0.14)	(0.22)
Sudan	−0.20***	0.40***	0.04	0.48***	−0.66***
	(0.04)	(0.06)	(0.05)	(0.03)	(0.05)

Notes: ***$p < 0.01$; **$p < 0.05$; *$p < 0.1$. Model 1: Multiparty system. Model 2: Parliament with only Islamist parties. Model 3: Strong man leader. Model 4: Islamic law system. Model 5: Parliament without Islamist parties.

Works Cited

Abdo-Katsipis, Carla B. 2017. "Women, Political Participation, and the Arab Spring: Political Awareness and Participation in Democratizing Tunisia." *Journal of Women, Politics & Policy* 38, no. 4: 413–429.

Abramson, Scott F., Korhan Koçak, and Asya Magazinnik. 2022. "What Do We Learn About Voter Preferences from Conjoint Experiments?" *American Journal of Political Science*: 1–12

Adcock, Robert, and David Collier. 2001. "Measurement Validity: A Shared Standard for Qualitative and Quantitative Research." *American Political Science Review* 95, no. 3: 529–546.

Alami, Aida. 2014. "On Moroccan Hill, Villagers Make Stand Against a Mine." *New York Times*. January 23.

AlAzzawi, Shireen, and Moamen Gouda. 2017. "How Muslims Understand Democracy: An Empirical Investigation." In "Topics in Middle Eastern and African Economies." *Proceedings of Middle East Economic Association* 19, no. 2 (September).

Albrecht, Holger, Dina Bishara, Michael Bufano, and Kevin Koehler. 2021. "Popular Support for Military Intervention and Anti-establishment Alternatives in Tunisia: Appraising Outsider Eclecticism." *Mediterranean Politics*: 1–25.

Alkadry, Mohamad G. 2002. "Reciting Colonial Scripts: Colonialism, Globalization and Democracy in the Decolonized Middle East." *Administrative Theory & Praxis* 24, no. 4: 739–762.

Almond, Gabriel A., and Sidney Verba. 1963. *An Approach to Political Culture.* Princeton, NJ: Princeton University Press.

Alvarez, Mike, José Antonio Cheibub, Fernando Limongi, and Adam Przeworski. 1996. "Classifying Political Regimes." *Studies in Comparative International Development* 31, no. 2: 3–36.

Alvarez, Alejandro Moreno, and Christian Welzel. 2017. "How Values Shape People's Views on Democracy: A Global Comparison." https://www.democracy.uci.edu/files/docs/conferences/2011/Moreno%20Welzel_Chapter.pdf

An-Na'im, Abdullahi Ahmed. 2008. *Islam and the Secular State: Negotiating the Future of Shari'a.* Cambridge, MA: Harvard University Press.

Arab Barometer Data, Wave I, 2007, available at www.arabbarometer.org.

246 *Works Cited*

Arab Barometer Data, Wave II, 2011, available at www.arabbarometer.org.
Arab Barometer Data, Wave III, 2013, available at www.arabbarometer.org.
Arab Barometer Data, Wave IV, 2016, available at www.arabbarometer.org.
Arab Barometer Data, Wave V, 2018, available at www.arabbarometer.org.
Arab Barometer Data, Wave VI, 2021, available at www.arabbarometer.org.
Arab Barometer Data, Wave VII, 2022, available at www.arabbarometer.org.
Ariely, Gal. 2015. "Democracy-Assessment in Cross-National Surveys: A Critical Examination of How People Evaluate Their Regime." *Social Indicators Research* 121, no. 3: 621–635.
Ariely, Gal, and Eldad Davidov. 2011. "Can We Rate Public Support for Democracy in a Comparable Way? Cross-National Equivalence of Democratic Attitudes in the World Value Survey." *Social Indicators Research* 104, no. 2: 271–286.
Arikan, Gizem. 2013. "Values, Religiosity and Support for Redistribution and Social Policy in Turkey." *Turkish Studies* 14, no. 1: 34–52.
Arikan, Gizem, and Pazit Ben-Nun Bloom. 2019. "Religion and Political Protest: A Cross-Country Analysis." *Comparative Political Studies* 52, no. 2: 246–276.
Baker, Frank B. 2001. *The Basics of Item Response Theory*. Washington, DC: ERIC.
Bansak, Kirk, Jens Hainmueller, Daniel J. Hopkins, and Teppei Yamamoto. 2018. "The Number of Choice Tasks and Survey Satisficing in Conjoint Experiments." *Political Analysis* 26, no. 1: 112–119.
Bansak, Kirk, Jens Hainmueller, Daniel J. Hopkins, and Teppei Yamamoto. 2021. "Beyond the Breaking Point? Survey Satisficing in Conjoint Experiments." *Political Science Research and Methods* 9, no. 1: 53–71.
Barnett, Carolyn, Amaney A. Jamal, and Steve L. Monroe. 2021. "Earned Income and Women's Segmented Empowerment: Experimental Evidence from Jordan." *American Journal of Political Science* 65, no. 4: 954–970.
Baviskar, Siddhartha, and Mary Fran T. Malone. 2004. "What Democracy Means to Citizens—And Why It Matters." *Revista Europea de Estudios Latinoamericanos y del Caribe/European Review of Latin American and Caribbean Studies*, 3–23.
Bayat, Asef. 2010. *Life as Politics: How Ordinary People Change the Middle East.* Stanford, CA: Stanford University Press.
Bayat, Asef. 2017. *Revolution Without Revolutionaries*. Palo Alto, CA: Stanford University Press.
Bechtel, Michael M., and Kenneth F. Scheve. 2013. "Mass Support for Global Climate Agreements Depends on Institutional Design." *Proceedings of the National Academy of Sciences* 110, no. 34: 13763–13768.
Behr, D., M. Braun, L. Kaczmirek, and W. Bandilla. 2014. "Item Comparability in Cross-National Surveys: Results from Asking Probing Questions in Cross-National Web Surveys About Attitudes Towards Civil Disobedience." *Quality & Quantity* 48, no. 1: 127–148.
Beinin, Joel. 2015. *Workers and Thieves: Labor Movements and Popular Uprisings in Tunisia and Egypt*. Palo Alto, CA: Stanford University Press.
Bellin, Eva. 2018. "The Puzzle of Democratic Divergence in the Arab World: Theory Confronts Experience in Egypt and Tunisia." *Political Science Quarterly* 133, no. 3: 435–475.
Benstead, Lindsay J. 2014. "Does Interviewer Religious Dress Affect Survey Responses? Evidence from Morocco." *Politics and Religion* 7, no. 4: 734–760.
Benstead, Lindsay J. 2015. "Why Do Some Arab Citizens See Democracy as Unsuitable for Their Country?" *Democratization* 22, no. 7: 1183–1208.
Benstead, Lindsay J. 2018. "Survey Research in the Arab World: Challenges and Opportunities." *PS: Political Science & Politics* 51, no. 3: 535–542.

Berman, Chantal E. 2021. "Policing the Organizational Threat in Morocco: Protest and Public Violence in Liberal Autocracies." *American Journal of Political Science* 65, no. 3: 733–754.

Bermeo, Nancy. 2016. "On Democratic Backsliding." *Journal of Democracy* 27, no. 1: 5–19.

Bishara, Dina. 2021a. "The Generative Power of Protest: Time and Space in Contentious Politics." *Comparative Political Studies* 54, no. 10: 1722–1756.

Bishara, Dina. 2021b. "Precarious Collective Action: Unemployed Graduates Associations in the Middle East and North Africa." *Comparative Politics* 53, no. 3 (April): 453–476.

Black, Antony. 2011. *History of Islamic Political Thought: From the Prophet to the Present*. Edinburgh: Edinburgh University Press.

Blackman, Alexandra Domike, and Marlette Jackson. 2019. "Gender Stereotypes, Political Leadership, and Voting Behavior in Tunisia." *Political Behavior* 43: 1037–1066.

Blaydes, Lisa, Justin Gengler, and Noora Ahmed Lari. 2021. "Understanding Cultural Constraints to Female Labor Force Participation: How Family Dynamics Influence Women's Employment in Qatar and the Arab Gulf States." Semantic Scholar. Corpus ID: 239849660.

Blaydes, Lisa, and Rachel M. Gillum. 2013. "Religiosity-of-Interviewer Effects: Assessing the Impact of Veiled Enumerators on Survey Response in Egypt." *Politics and Religion* 6, no. 3: 459–482.

Boix, Carles, Michael Miller, and Sebastian Rosato. 2013. "A Complete Data Set of Political Regimes, 1800–2007." *Comparative Political Studies* 46, no. 12: 1523–1554.

Bratton, Michael. 2003. "Briefing: Islam, Democracy and Public Opinion in Africa." *African Affairs* 102, no. 408: 493–501.

Bratton, Michael. 2009. "Democratic Attitudes and Political Participation: An Exploratory Comparison Across World Regions." Paper presented at the Congress of the International Political Science Association, Santiago, Chile, July.

Breznau, Nate, Valerie A. Lykes, Jonathan Kelley, and Mariah Debra R. Evans. 2011. "A Clash of Civilizations? Preferences for Religious Political Leaders in 86 Nations." *Journal for the Scientific Study of Religion* 50, no. 4: 671–691.

Cammett, Melani, Dominika Kruszewska-Eduardo, Christiana Parreira, and Sami Atallah. 2021. "Coethnicity Beyond Clientelism: Insights from an Experimental Study of Political Behavior in Lebanon." *Politics and Religion* 15, no. 2: 417–438.

Cammett, Melani, Christiana Parreira, Dominika Kruszewska-Eduardo, and Sami Atallah. 2022. "Commitment to the 'National' in Post-Conflict Countries: Public and Private Security Provision in Lebanon." *Journal of Conflict Resolution* 66, no. 7–8: 1235–1262.

Campante, Filipe R., and Davin Chor. 2012. "Why Was the Arab World Poised for Revolution? Schooling, Economic Opportunities, and the Arab Spring." *Journal of Economic Perspectives* 26, no. 2: 167–188.

Canache, Damarys. 2012. "Citizens' Conceptualizations of Democracy: Structural Complexity, Substantive Content, and Political Significance." *Comparative Political Studies* 45, no. 9: 1132–1158.

Carnes, Nicholas, and Noam Lupu. 2016. "Do Voters Dislike Working-Class Candidates? Voter Biases and the Descriptive Underrepresentation of the Working Class." *American Political Science Review* 110, no. 4: 832–844.

Carrión, Julio F. 2008. "Illiberal Democracy and Normative Democracy: How Is Democracy Defined in the Americas." In *Challenges to Democracy in Latin*

248 Works Cited

America and the Caribbean: Evidence from the Americas Barometer, edited by Mitchell A. Seligson, 21–46. Nashville: LAPOP.

Chaney, Eric, George A. Akerlof, and Lisa Blaydes. 2012. "Democratic Change in the Arab World, Past and Present." In *Brookings Papers on Economic Activity: Spring 2012*, edited by David H. Romer: and Justin Wolfers, 363–414. Washington, DC: Brookings Institution Press.

Cheibub, José Antonio, Jennifer Gandhi, and James Raymond Vreeland. 2010. "Democracy and Dictatorship Revisited." *Public Choice* 143, no. 1: 67–101.

Cho, Youngho. 2015. "How Well Are Global Citizenries Informed About Democracy? Ascertaining the Breadth and Distribution of Their Democratic Enlightenment and Its Sources." *Political Studies* 63, no. 1: 240–258.

Ciftci, Sabri. 2010. "Modernization, Islam, or Social Capital: What Explains Attitudes Toward Democracy in the Muslim World?" *Comparative Political Studies* 43, no. 11: 1442–1470.

Ciftci, Sabri. 2013. "Secular-Islamist Cleavage, Values, and Support for Democracy and Shari'a in the Arab World." *Political Research Quarterly* 66, no. 4: 781–793.

Ciftci, Sabri. 2022. *Islam, Justice, and Democracy*. Philadelphia: Temple University Press.

Claassen, Christopher. 2020. "In the Mood for Democracy? Democratic Support as Thermostatic Opinion." *American Political Science Review* 114, no. 1: 36–53.

Clark, Andrew, Yannis Georgellis, and Peter Sanfey. 2001. "Scarring: The Psychological Impact of Past Unemployment." *Economica* 68, no. 270: 221–241.

Cohu, Medhi, Christelle Maisonneuve, and Benoit Testé. 2021. "One Conception of Secularism for All? A Comparison of Conceptions of Laïcité Among Nonbelievers, Catholics, and Muslims in France." *Journal for the Scientific Study of Religion* 60, no. 1: 103–112.

Collier, David, and Robert Adcock. 1999. "Democracy and Dichotomies: A Pragmatic Approach to Choices About Concepts." *Annual Review of Political Science* 2, no. 1: 537–565.

Collier, David, and Steven Levitsky. 1997. "Democracy with Adjectives: Conceptual Innovation in Comparative Research." *World Politics* 49, no. 3: 430–451.

Coppedge, Michael, John Gerring, Carl Henrik Knutsen, Staffan I. Lindberg, Jan Teorell, David Altman, Michael Bernhard, et al. 2020. "V-Dem Codebook v10." Varieties of Democracy (V-Dem) Project.

Corstange, Daniel. 2014. "Foreign-Sponsorship Effects in Developing-World Surveys: Evidence from a Field Experiment in Lebanon." *Public Opinion Quarterly* 78, no. 2: 474–484.

Cronbach, Lee J., and Paul E. Meehl. 1955. "Construct Validity in Psychological Tests." *Psychological Bulletin* 52, no. 4: 281.

Dahl, Robert A. 2008 [1971]. *Polyarchy: Participation and Opposition*. New Haven, CT: Yale University Press.

Dalmasso, Emanuela. 2012. "Surfing the Democratic Tsunami in Morocco: Apolitical Society and the Reconfiguration of a Sustainable Authoritarian Regime." *Mediterranean Politics* 17, no. 2: 217–232.

Dalton, Russell J., Doh C. Shin, and Willy Jou. 2007. "Understanding Democracy: Data from Unlikely Places." *Journal of Democracy* 18, no. 4: 142–156.

Davis, Nicholas T., Kirby Goidel, and Yikai Zhao. 2021. "The meanings of Democracy among Mass Publics." *Social Indicators Research* 153: 849–921.

De Regt, Sabrina. 2013. "Arabs Want Democracy, but What Kind?" *Advances in Applied Sociology* 3, no. 1: 37.

Desilver, Drew. 2020. "In Past Elections, U.S. Trailed Most Developed Countries in Voter Turnout." Pew Research Center. November 3.

Diamond, Larry, and Leonardo Morlino. 2004. "The Quality of Democracy: An Overview." *Journal of Democracy* 15, no. 4: 20–31.

Doherty, David, Conor M. Dowling, and Michael G. Miller. 2019. "Do Local Party Chairs Think Women and Minority Candidates Can Win? Evidence from a Conjoint Experiment." *Journal of Politics* 81, no. 4: 1282–1297.

Doherty, David, and Jessica Mecellem. 2013. "Conceptions of Democracy in the Arab World." University of Chicago.

Doorenspleet, Renske. 2015. "Where Are the People? A Call for People-Centred Concepts and Measurements of Democracy." *Government and Opposition* 50, no. 3: 469–494.

Dunne, Michele Durocher. 2006. *Evaluating Egyptian Reform*, vol. 66. Carnegie Endowment for International Peace.

El Badawi, Ibrahim, and Samir Makdisi. 2007. "Explaining the Democracy Deficit in the Arab World." *Quarterly Review of Economics and Finance* 46, no. 5: 813–831.

El Fadl, Khaled Abou. 2015. *Islam and the Challenge of Democracy*. Princeton, NJ: Princeton University Press.

El Safty, Sarah. 2023. "Egypt to Sell Discounted Bread to Fight Inflation." Reuters. January 16.

El-Ghobashy, Mona. 2021. *Bread and Freedom: Egypt's Revolutionary Situation*. Palo Alto, CA: Stanford University Press.

"El-Sisi Wins Egypt's Presidential Race with 96.91%." 2014. *Ahram*. June 3.

Esposito, John L. 1998. *Islam and Politics*. Syracuse, NY: Syracuse University Press.

Fatas-Villafranca, Francisco, Dulce Saura, and Francisco J. Vázquez. 2011. "A Dynamic Model of Public Opinion Formation." *Journal of Public Economic Theory* 13, no. 3: 417–441.

Feldman, Noah. 2020. *The Arab Winter*. Princeton, NJ: Princeton University Press.

Ferrín, Mónica, and Hanspeter Kriesi, eds. 2016. *How Europeans View and Evaluate Democracy*. Oxford: Oxford University Press.

Ferwerda, Jeremy, and Justin Gest. 2021. "Pull Factors and Migration Preferences: Evidence from the Middle East and North Africa." *International Migration Review* 55, no. 2: 431–459.

Fetterolf, Janell. 2018. "Negative Views of Democracy More Widespread in Countries with Low Political Affiliation." Pew Research Center. March 8.

Fish, M. Steven. 2002. "Islam and Authoritarianism." *World Politics* 55, no. 1: 4–37.

Fox, Jonathan. 2007. "Do Democracies Have Separation of Religion and State?" *Canadian Journal of Political Science / Revue canadienne de science politique* 40, no. 1: 1–25.

Franchino, Fabio, and Francesco Zucchini. 2015. "Voting in a Multi-Dimensional Space: A Conjoint Analysis Employing Valence and Ideology Attributes of Candidates." *Political Science Research and Methods* 3, no. 2: 221–241.

Freedom House. 2021. *"Freedom in the World 2021* Methodology."

Fuchs, Dieter, and Edeltraud Roller. 2006. "Learned Democracy? Support of Democracy in Central and Eastern Europe." *International Journal of Sociology* 36, no. 3: 70–96.

Fukuyama, Francis. 2006. *The End of History and the Last Man*. New York: Simon & Schuster.

García-Peñalosa, Cecilia, and Maty Konte. 2014. "Why Are Women Less Democratic Than Men? Evidence from Sub-Saharan African Countries." *World Development* 59: 104–119.

Gengler, Justin J., Mark Tessler, Russell Lucas, and Jonathan Forney. 2019. "'Why Do You Ask?' The Nature and Impacts of Attitudes Towards Public Opinion Surveys in the Arab World." *British Journal of Political Science* 51, no. 1: 115–136.

250 Works Cited

Gouda, Moamen, and Shimaa Hanafy. 2020. "Islamic Constitutions and Democracy." *Political Research Quarterly* 75, no. 4: 994–1005.

Graham, Matthew H., and Milan W. Svolik. 2020. "Democracy in America? Partisanship, Polarization, and the Robustness of Support for Democracy in the United States." *American Political Science Review* 114, no. 2: 392–409.

Groh, Matthew, and Casey Rothschild. 2012. "Oil, Islam, Women, and Geography: A Comment on Ross 2008." *Quarterly Journal of Political Science* 7, no. 1: 69–87.

Haerpfer, C., R. Inglehart, A. Moreno, C. Welzel, K. Kizilova, J. Diez-Medrano, M. Lagos, et al., eds. 2020. World Values Survey: Round Seven—Country-Pooled Datafile. Madrid, Spain, and Vienna, Austria: JD Systems Institute & WVSA Secretariat. doi.org/10.14281/18241.1.

Hainmueller, Jens, Dominik Hangartner, and Teppei Yamamoto. 2014. "Do Survey Experiments Capture Real-World Behavior? External Validation of Conjoint and Vignette Analyses with a Natural Experiment." *Proceedings of the National Academy of Sciences* 112, no. 8: 2395–2400.

Hainmueller, Jens, Daniel J. Hopkins, and Teppei Yamamoto. 2014. "Causal Inference in Conjoint Analysis: Understanding Multidimensional Choices via Stated Preference Experiments." *Political Analysis* 22, no. 1: 1–30.

Harkness, Janet, Beth-Ellen Pennell, and Alisú Schoua-Glusberg. 2004. "Survey Questionnaire Translation and Assessment." In *Methods for Testing and Evaluating Survey Questionnaires*, edited by Stanley Presser, Jennifer M. Rothgeb, Mick P. Couper, Judith T. Lessler, Elizabeth Martin, Jean Martin, and Eleanor Singer, 453–473. New York: Wiley.

Hassan, Mazen, Elisabeth Kendall, and Stephen Whitefield. 2018. "Between Scylla and Charybdis: Religion, the Military and Support for Democracy Among Egyptians, 2011–2014." *Democratization* 25, no. 2: 273–292.

Hatim, Yahia. 2020. "Morocco's 2021 General Elections to Take Place in September." *Morocco World News*. November 9.

Hegasy, Sonja. 2007. "Young Authority: Quantitative and Qualitative Insights into Youth, Youth Culture, and State Power in Contemporary Morocco." *Journal of North African Studies* 12, no. 1: 19–36.

Hibou, Béatrice. 2011. "Le mouvement du 20 février, le Makhzen et l'antipolitique. L'impensé des réformes au Maroc." Sciences Po.

Hobolt, Sara B., James Tilley, and Thomas J. Leeper. 2020. "Policy Preferences and Policy Legitimacy After Referendums: Evidence from the Brexit Negotiations." *Political Behavior* 44: 839–858.

Hoerger, Michael. 2010. "Participant Dropout as a Function of Survey Length in Internet-Mediated University Studies: Implications for Study Design and Voluntary Participation in Psychological Research." *Cyberpsychology, Behavior, and Social Networking* 13, no. 6: 697–700.

Hoffman, Michael. 2020. "Religion, Sectarianism, and Democracy: Theory and Evidence from Lebanon." *Political Behavior* 42: 1169–1200.

Hoffman, Michael, and Amaney Jamal. 2012. "The Youth and the Arab Spring: Cohort Differences and Similarities." *Middle East Law and Governance* 4, no. 1: 168–188.

Hoffman, Michael, and Amaney Jamal. 2014. "Religion in the Arab Spring: Between Two Competing Narratives." *Journal of Politics* 76, no. 3: 593–606.

Hong, Wai Mun. 2019. "Demographic Pressure, Social Demands, and Instability in the Maghreb." In *The Lure of Authoritarianism: The Maghreb After the Arab Spring*, edited by Stephen J. King and Abdeslam M. Maghraoui, 68–93. Bloomington: Indiana University Press.

Horiuchi, Yusaku, Daniel M. Smith, and Teppei Yamamoto. 2018. "Measuring Voters' Multidimensional Policy Preferences with Conjoint Analysis: Application to Japan's 2014 Election." *Political Analysis* 26, no. 2: 190–209.

Huber, John D., and Piero Stanig. 2011. "Church-State Separation and Redistribution." *Journal of Public Economics* 95, no. 7–8: 828–836.

Huntington, Samuel P. 1991. "Democracy's Third Wave." *Journal of Democracy* 2, no. 2: 12–34.

Huntington, Samuel P. 2000. "The Clash of Civilizations?" In *Culture and Politics*, edited by Lane Crothers and Charles Lockhart, 99–118. New York: Palgrave Macmillan.

Iannaccone, Laurence R. 1992. "Sacrifice and Stigma: Reducing Free-Riding in Cults, Communes, and Other Collectives." *Journal of Political Economy* 100, no. 2: 271–291.

Inglehart, Ronald. 2003. "How Solid Is Mass Support for Democracy: And How Can We Measure It?" *PS: Political Science & Politics* 36, no. 1: 51–57.

Inglehart, Ronald, and Pippa Norris. 2003. "The True Clash of Civilizations." *Foreign Policy* 135 (March–April): 63–70.

"International Reactions to Morsi's Removal." 2013. *Al-Jazeera*. July 4.

Isani, Mujtaba, and Bernd Schlipphak. 2020. "The Role of Societal Cues in Explaining Attitudes Toward International Organizations: The Least Likely Case of Authoritarian Contexts." *Political Research Exchange* 2, no. 1: 1771189.

Ismail, Amina, and Ali Abdelaty. 2018. "Ex-Military Chief of Staff to Run in Egyptian Presidential Election." Reuters. January 19.

Jacobsen, Jannes, and Lukas Marian Fuchs. 2020. "Can We Compare Conceptions of Democracy in Cross-Linguistic and Cross-National Research? Evidence from a Random Sample of Refugees in Germany." *Social Indicators Research* 151: 669–690.

Jamal, Amaney. 2007. *Barriers to Democracy*. Princeton, NJ: Princeton University Press.

Jamal, Amaney A. 2006. "Reassessing Support for Islam and Democracy in the Arab World? Evidence from Egypt and Jordan." *World Affairs* 169: 51.

Jamal, Amaney, and Irfan Nooruddin. 2010. "The Democratic Utility of Trust: A Cross-National Analysis." *Journal of Politics* 72, no. 1: 45–59.

Kalmoe, Nathan P., and Lilliana Mason. 2022. *Radical American Partisanship: Mapping Extreme Hostility, Its Causes, and the Consequences for Democracy*. Chicago: University of Chicago Press.

Kaufmann, Karen M. 2004. "The Partisan Paradox: Religious Commitment and the Gender Gap in Party Identification." *Public Opinion Quarterly* 68, no. 4: 491–511.

Khanani, Ahmed. 2021. *All Politics Are God's Politics: Moroccan Islamism and the Sacralization of Democracy*. Rutgers University Press.

Kiewiet de Jonge, Chad P. 2016. "Should Researchers Abandon Questions About 'Democracy'? Evidence from Latin America." *Public Opinion Quarterly* 80, no. 3: 694–716.

King, Stephen J. 2019. "Elections Before and After the Arab Spring in North Africa." In *The Lure of Authoritarianism: The Maghreb After the Arab Spring*, edited by Stephen J. King and Abdeslam M. Maghraoui, 191–209. Bloomington: Indiana University Press.

King, Stephen Juan. 2011. "The Constitutional Monarchy Option in Morocco and Bahrain." Middle East Institute. May 1.

Kirshner, Alexander S. 2010. "Proceduralism and Popular Threats to Democracy." *Journal of Political Philosophy* 18, no. 4: 405–424.

252 Works Cited

Kuran, Timur. 1991. "Now Out of Never: The Element of Surprise in the East European Revolution of 1989." *World Politics* 44, no. 1: 7–48.

Kuran, Timur. 1997. *Private Truths, Public Lies*. Cambridge, MA: Harvard University Press.

Kuran, Timur. 2012. *The Long Divergence*. Princeton, NJ: Princeton University Press.

Kurd, Dana El. 2022. "Gateway to Dissent: The Role of Pro-Palestine Activism in Opposition to Authoritarianism." *Democratization* 29, no. 7: 1230–1248.

Labott, Elise, and Aida Alami. 2011. "Morocco Approves Constitutional Reforms." CNN. July 1.

Lagos, Marta. 2008. "The Democracy Barometers (Part II): Latin America's Diversity of Views." *Journal of Democracy* 19, no. 1: 111–125.

Laessing, Ulf. 2018. "Miners' Protest Raises Political Temperature in Morocco." Reuters. February 2.

Lawson, Marian L., and Susan B. Epstein. 2019. "Democracy Promotion: An Objective of U.S. Foreign Assistance." Congressional Research Service. January 4.

Leeper, Thomas J., Sara B. Hobolt, and James Tilley. 2020. "Measuring subgroup preferences in conjoint experiments." *Political Analysis* 28, no. 2: 207–221.

Leeper, Thomas J., and Rune Slothuus. 2014. "Political Parties, Motivated Reasoning, and Public Opinion Formation." *Political Psychology* 35: 129–156.

"Legislative Elections: RNI Leads Ahead of PAM and Istiqlal Party (Provisional Results)." 2021. Kingdom of Morocco. September 9.

Lerner, Daniel. 1958. *The Passing of Traditional Society: Modernizing the Middle East*. New York: The Free Press.

Lewis, Bernard. 2002. *What Went Wrong? Western Impact and Middle Eastern Response*. Oxford: Oxford University Press.

Lindberg, Staffan. 2009. "A Theory of Elections as a Mode of Transition." In *Democratization by Elections: A New Mode of Transition*, edited by Staffan Lindberg, 314–341. Baltimore: Johns Hopkins University Press.

Linz, Juan J., and Alfred Stepan. 1996. *Problems of Democratic Transition and Consolidation: Southern Europe, South America, and Post-Communist Europe*. Baltimore: Johns Hopkins University Press.

Lupia, Arthur, and Mathew D. McCubbins. 1998. *The Democratic Dilemma: Can Citizens Learn What They Need to Know?* Cambridge: Cambridge University Press.

Lupu, Noam, and Kristin Michelitch. 2018. "Advances in Survey Methods for the Developing World." *Annual Review of Political Science* 21: 195–214.

Lust, Ellen. 2009. "Democratization by Elections? Competitive Clientelism in the Middle East." *Journal of Democracy* 20, no. 3: 122–135.

Lyberg, Lars, Beth-Ellen Pennel, Kristen Cibelli Hibben, Julie de Jong, Dorothée Behr, Jamie Burnett, Rory Fitzgerald, et al. 2021. *AAPOR/WAPOR Task Force Report on Quality in Comparative Surveys*. April. https://wapor.org/wp-content/uploads/AAPOR-WAPOR-Task-Force-Report-on-Quality-in-Comparative-Surveys_Full-Report.pdf

Maghraoui, Abdeslam E. M. 2015. "The Stabilising Effect of Turbulence in Authoritarian Regimes: How the Moroccan Monarchy Ducked the Arab Spring." *Orient* 56, no. 2: 30–41.

Maghraoui, Abdeslam M. 2002. "Democratization in the Arab World? Depoliticization in Morocco." *Journal of Democracy* 13, no. 4: 24–32.

Maghraoui, Abdeslam M. 2019. "From Authoritarian Pluralism to Centralized Autocracy in Morocco." In *The Lure of Authoritarianism: The Maghreb After the Arab Spring*, edited by Stephen J. King and Abdeslam M. Maghraoui, 264–282. Bloomington: Indiana University Press.

Magone, José M. 2014. "Introduction: The 'Great Transformation' of European Politics: A Holistic View." In *Routledge Handbook of European Politics*, edited by José Magone, 45–82. London: Routledge.

Malik, Adeel, and Bassem Awadallah. 2013. "The Economics of the Arab Spring." *World Development* 45: 296–313.

Marcus, Richard R., Kenneth Mease, and Dan Ottemoeller. 2001. "Popular Definitions of Democracy from Uganda, Madagascar, and Florida, USA." In *A Decade of Democracy in Africa*, pp. 113–132. Brill.

Marshall, Monty G., and Ted Robert Gurr. 2020. "Polity 5: Political Regime Characteristics and Transitions, 1800–2018." Center for Systemic Peace.

Maseland, Robbert, and André Van Hoorn. 2011. "Why Muslims Like Democracy Yet Have So Little of It." *Public Choice* 147, no. 3–4: 481–496.

Mattes, Robert, and Michael Bratton. 2007. "Learning About Democracy in Africa: Awareness, Performance, and Experience." *American Journal of Political Science* 51, no. 1: 192–217.

Mernissi, Fatima. 1992. *Islam et démocratie*. Paris: Alban Michel.

Meyerrose, Anna M. 2021. "International Sources of Democratic Backsliding." In *Routledge Handbook of Illiberalism*, edited by András Sajó, Renáta Uitz, and Stephen Holmes, 888–906. London: Routledge.

Minkenberg, Michael. 2007. "Democracy and Religion: Theoretical and Empirical Observations on the Relationship Between Christianity, Islam and Liberal Democracy." *Journal of Ethnic and Migration Studies* 33, no. 6: 887–909.

Miller, Michael K. 2021. *Shock to the System*. Princeton, NJ: Princeton University Press.

Mohamad-Klotzbach, Christoph, and Oliver Schlenkrich. 2016. "Determinanten input-und outputorientierter Demokratievorstellungen in der arabischen Welt: Eine Mehrebenenanalyse." In *"Demokratie" jenseits des Westens*, edited by Sophia Schubert and Alexander Weiss, 404–436. Baden-Baden: Nomos Verlagsgesellschaft mbH & Co. KG.

Munck, Gerardo L., and Jay Verkuilen. 2002. "Conceptualizing and Measuring Democracy: Evaluating Alternative Indices." *Comparative Political Studies* 35, no. 1: 5–34.

Neustadt, Ilja. 2011. "Do Religious Beliefs Explain Preferences for Income Redistribution? Experimental Evidence." *CESifo Economic Studies* 57, no. 4: 623–652.

Nugent, Elizabeth R. 2020. *After Repression*. Princeton, NJ: Princeton University Press.

Nyhan, Brendan, and Thomas Zeitzoff. 2018. "Conspiracy and Misperception Belief in the Middle East and North Africa." *Journal of Politics* 80, no. 4: 1400–1404.

Obama, Barack. 2011. "Remarks by the President on the Middle East and Africa." May 19. https://obamawhitehouse.archives.gov/the-press-office/2011/05/19/remarks-president-middle-east-and-north-africa.

"Opposition Claims Massive Fraud in Egypt Electoral Poll." 2005. *Forbes*. September 8.

Oser, Jennifer, and Marc Hooghe. 2018a. "Democratic Ideals and Levels of Political Participation: The Role of Political and Social Conceptualisations of Democracy." *British Journal of Politics and International Relations* 20, no. 3: 711–730.

Oser, Jennifer, and Marc Hooghe. 2018b. "Give Me Your Tired, Your Poor? Support for Social Citizenship Rights in the United States and Europe." *Sociological Perspectives* 61, no. 1: 14–38.

Ottaway, Marina. 2019. "Religious Conservatism, Religious Extremism, and Secular Civil Societies in North Africa." In *The Lure of Authoritarianism: The Maghreb After the Arab Spring*, edited by Stephen J. King and Abdeslam M. Maghraoui, 15–41. Bloomington: Indiana University Press.

254 Works Cited

Papacharissi, Zizi. 2021. *After Democracy*. New Haven, CT: Yale University Press.

Pérez, Efrén O. 2011. "The Origins and Implications of Language Effects in Multilingual Surveys: A MIMIC Approach with Application to Latino Political Attitudes." *Political Analysis* 19, no. 4: 434–454.

Peytchev, Andy. 2009. "Survey Breakoff." *Public Opinion Quarterly* 73, no. 1: 74–97.

Pfeiffer, Karen. 2019. "Shifting Courses: Economies of the Maghreb After 2011." In *The Lure of Authoritarianism: The Maghreb After the Arab Spring*, edited by Stephen J. King and Abdeslam M. Maghraoui, 94–136. Bloomington: Indiana University Press.

Plattner, Marc F. 2019. "Illiberal Democracy and the Struggle on the Right." *Journal of Democracy* 30, no. 1: 5–19.

Potrafke, Niklas. 2013. "Democracy and Countries with Muslim Majorities: A Reply and Update." *Public Choice* 154, no. 3: 323–332.

Przeworski, Adam. 1991. *Democracy and the Market: Political and Economic Reforms in Eastern Europe and Latin America*. Cambridge: Cambridge University Press.

Przeworski, Adam, R. Michael Alvarez, Michael E. Alvarez, Jose Antonio Cheibub, Fernando Limongi, and Fernando Papaterra Limongi Neto. 2000. *Democracy and Development: Political Institutions and Well-Being in the World, 1950–1990* Cambridge: Cambridge University Press.

Rachik, Abderrahmane. 2016. *La société contre l'Etat: mouvements sociaux et stratégie de la rue au Maroc*. Editions la Croisée des chemins.

Rafiqi, Arzoo. 2019. "A Clash of Civilizations? Muslims, Christians, and Preferences for Democracy." *Journal for the Scientific Study of Religion* 58, no. 3: 689–706.

Rawłuszko, Marta. 2021. "And if the Opponents of Gender Ideology Are Right? Gender Politics, Europeanization, and the Democratic Deficit." *Politics & Gender* 17, no. 2: 301–323.

Reuters. 2009. "Moroccan Magazines Seized over Royal Opinion Poll." Reuters. August 1.

Ridge, Hannah. 2019. "Effect of Religious Legislation on Religious Behavior: The Ramadan Fast." *Interdisciplinary Journal of Research on Religion* 15: 1–39.

Ridge, Hannah. 2021 "Conspiracy Belief and Attitudes Toward Democracy in the Middle East." Paper presented at the American Political Science Association Conference, Seattle, Washington, September.

Ridge, Hannah M. 2020. "State Regulation of Religion: The Effect of Religious Freedom on Muslims' Religiosity." *Religion, State & Society* 48, no. 4: 256–275.

Ridge, Hannah M. 2022a. "Dismantling New Democracies: The Case of Tunisia." *Democratization* 29, no. 8: 1539–1556.

Ridge, Hannah M. 2022b. "Illiberal Democrats in Egypt." *Journal of the Middle East and Africa* 13, no. 4: 363–384.

Rizzo, Helen, Abdel-Hamid Abdel-Latif, and Katherine Meyer. 2007. "The Relationship Between Gender Equality and Democracy: A Comparison of Arab Versus Non-Arab Muslim Societies." *Sociology* 41, no. 6: 1151–1170.

Rollinde, Marguerite, and Didier le Saout. 1999. *Emeutes et mouvements sociaux au Maghreb*. Paris: Karthala.

Rose, Richard. 2002. "How Muslims View Democracy: Evidence from Central Asia." *Journal of Democracy* 13, no. 4: 102–111.

Ross, Michael L. 2008. "Oil, Islam, and Women." *American Political Science Review* 102, no. 1: 107–123.

Ross, Michael L. 2001. "Does Oil Hinder Democracy?" *World Politics* 53, no. 3: 325–361.

Works Cited   255

Rowley, Charles K., and Nathanael Smith. 2009. "Islam's Democracy Paradox: Muslims Claim to Like Democracy, So Why Do They Have So Little?" *Public Choice* 139, no. 3–4: 273–299.

Salevurakis, John William, and Sahar Mohamed Abdel-Haleim. 2008. "Bread Subsidies in Egypt: Choosing Social Stability or Fiscal Responsibility." *Review of Radical Political Economics* 40, no. 1: 35–49.

Sarkissian, Ani. 2012. "Religious Regulation and the Muslim Democracy Gap." *Politics and Religion* 5, no. 3: 501–527.

Sartori, Giovanni. 1987. *The Theory of Democracy Revisited*. Vol. 2. Chatham, UK: Chatham House Publishing.

Sayer, Andrew. 2009. "Contributive Justice and Meaningful Work." *Res Publica* 15, no. 1: 1–16.

Schaffer, Frederic Charles. 2000. *Democracy in Translation: Understanding Politics in an Unfamiliar Culture*. Ithaca, NY: Cornell University Press.

Schaffer, Frederic Charles. 2014. "Thin Descriptions: The Limits of Survey Research on the Meaning of Democracy." *Polity* 46, no. 3: 303–330.

Schmitter, Philippe C., and Terry Lynn Karl. 1991. "What Democracy Is . . . and Is Not." *Journal of Democracy* 2, no. 3: 75–88.

Schumpeter, Joseph A. 2008. *Capitalism, Socialism and Democracy*. 3rd ed. New York: Harper Collins.

Sen, Maya. 2017. "How Political Signals Affect Public Support for Judicial Nominations: Evidence from a Conjoint Experiment." *Political Research Quarterly* 70, no. 2: 374–393.

Shafiq, M. Najeeb. 2010. "Do Education and Income Affect Support for Democracy in Muslim Countries? Evidence from the Pew Global Attitudes Project." *Economics of Education Review* 29, no. 3: 461–469.

Shamir, Michal, and Jacob Shamir. 1995. "Competing Values in Public Opinion: A Conjoint Analysis." *Political Behavior* 17, no. 1: 107–133.

Shockley, Bethany, and Justin J. Gengler. 2020. "Social Identity and Coethnic Voting in the Middle East: Experimental Evidence from Qatar." *Electoral Studies* 67: 102213.

Şiviloğlu, Murat R. 2018. *The Emergence of Public Opinion: State and Society in the Late Ottoman Empire*. Cambridge: Cambridge University Press.

Sklar, Richard L. 1983. "Democracy in Africa." *African Studies Review* 26, no. 3–4: 11–24.

Snider, Erin A. 2022. *Marketing Democracy: The Political Economy of Democracy Aid in the Middle East*. Cambridge Middle East Studies 64. Cambridge: Cambridge University Press.

Stacher, Joshua. 2020. *Watermelon Democracy: Egypt's Turbulent Transition*. Syracuse, NY: Syracuse University Press.

Stasavage, David. 2020. *The Decline and Rise of Democracy*. Princeton, NJ: Princeton University Press.

Stegmueller, Daniel, Peer Scheepers, Sigrid Roßteutscher, and Eelke De Jong. 2012. "Support for Redistribution in Western Europe: Assessing the Role of Religion." *European Sociological Review* 28, no. 4: 482–497.

Stepan, Alfred, ed. 2018. *Democratic Transition in the Muslim World: A Global Perspective*. New York: Columbia University Press.

Stepan, Alfred, and Juan J. Linz. 2013. "Democratization Theory and the 'Arab Spring.'" *Journal of Democracy* 24, no. 2: 15–30.

Stepan, Alfred C., and Graeme B. Robertson. 2003. "An 'Arab' More Than a 'Muslim' Democracy Gap." *Journal of Democracy* 14, no. 3: 30–44.

256 *Works Cited*

Stepan, Alfred C. 2000. "Religion, Democracy, and the 'Twin Tolerations.'" *Journal of Democracy* 11, no. 4: 37–57.

Tessler, Mark. 2002. "Do Islamic Orientations Influence Attitudes Toward Democracy in the Arab World? Evidence from Egypt, Jordan, Morocco, and Algeria." *International Journal of Comparative Sociology* 43, no. 3–5: 229–249.

Tessler, Mark A., and Eleanor Gao. 2005. "Gauging Arab Support for Democracy." *Journal of Democracy* 16, no. 3: 83–97.

Thompson, Gene, and Karen Dooley. 2019. "Ensuring Translation Fidelity in Multilingual Research." In *The Routledge Handbook of Research Methods in Applied Linguistics*, edited by Jim McKinley and Heath Rose, 63–75. London: Routledge.

Treier, Shawn, and Simon Jackman. 2008. "Democracy as a Latent Variable." *American Journal of Political Science* 52, no. 1: 201–217.

Truex, Rory, and Daniel L. Tavana. 2019. "Implicit Attitudes Toward an Authoritarian Regime." *Journal of Politics* 81, no. 3: 1014–1027.

Ulbricht, Tom. 2018. "Perceptions and Conceptions of Democracy: Applying Thick Concepts of Democracy to Reassess Desires for Democracy." *Comparative Political Studies* 51, no. 11: 1387–1440.

Verme, Paolo, Khalid El-Massnaoui, and Abdelkrim Araar. 2014. "Reforming Subsidies in Morocco." *Economic Premise* 134 (February).

Vicente, Paula, and Elizabeth Reis. 2010. "Using Questionnaire Design to Fight Nonresponse Bias in Web Surveys." *Social Science Computer Review* 28, no. 2: 251–267.

Wedeen, Lisa. 2007. "The Politics of Deliberation: Qāt Chews as Public Spheres in Yemen." *Public Culture* 19, no. 1: 59–84.

Welzel, Christian. 2021a. "Democratic Horizons: What Value Change Reveals About the Future of Democracy." *Democratization* 28, no. 5: 992–1016.

Welzel, Christian. 2021b. "Why the Future Is Democratic." *Journal of Democracy* 32, no. 2: 133.

Westwood, Sean J., Justin Grimmer, Matthew Tyler, and Clayton Nall. 2022. "Current Research Overstates American Support for Political Violence." *Proceedings of the National Academy of Sciences* 119, no. 12: e2116870119.

Wike, Richard, Katie Simmons, Bruce Stokes, and Janell Fetterolf. 2017. "Globally, Broad Support for Representative and Direct Democracy." Pew Research Center. October 16.

Williams, Daniel, and Robin Wright. 2005. "Controversy Swirls over Egypt Vote." *Washington Post*. September 8.

Williamson, Vanessa. 2019. "Public Ignorance or Elitist Jargon? Reconsidering Americans' Overestimates of Government Waste and Foreign Aid." *American Politics Research* 47, no. 1: 152–173.

Woodberry, Robert D. 2012. "The Missionary Roots of Liberal Democracy." *American Political Science Review* 106, no. 2: 244–274.

World Factbook. 2019. "Egypt."

World Factbook. 2020. "Morocco."

"World Leaders Put Egypt on Notice over Democracy." 2013. *CBC*. July 5.

Wuttke, Alexander, Konstantin Gavras, and Harald Schoen. 2020. "Have Europeans Grown Tired of Democracy? New Evidence from Eighteen Consolidated Democracies, 1981–2018." *British Journal of Political Science* 52, no. 1: 416–428.

Yildirim, A. Kadir, and Meredith McCain. 2019. *The Aftermath of the Arab Spring Protests: What a Public Opinion Survey Tells Us*. Policy Brief no. 03.21.19. Rice University's Baker Institute for Public Policy, Houston, Texas.

Index

Adalet (justice), 24, 88, 189
al-Adl wal-Ihsan Party, 135
Africa, 33, 48*n*7, 69, 81*n*8, 189
Afrobarometer (survey), 9–10, 92
Agadir, Morocco, 76*tab*, 148*tab*, 150*tab*
Age, 42–43*tab*, 49*n*15, 74*tab*, 100*tab*, 102*tab*, 117, 143; Arab Spring and, 110; political behavior and, 91*tab*
Alaouite dynasty, Morocco, 134
AlAzzawi, Shireen, 17, 57
Albrecht, Holger, 114, 144, 146
Alexandria, Egypt, 76*tab*, 123*tab*
Algeria, 2, 37, 37*tab*, 40, 72, 74, 85
AMCE. *See* Average marginal component effect
Amir al-mu'minin (commander of the faithful), Moroccan, 38, 135, 153–154
Anocracies, 39
Antidemocracy, 153, 161; Islam treated as, 7, 118, 128; parliamentary monarchies and, 179
Antigovernment sentiment, 8, 154
Antimonarchical sentiment, 139–140, 152–154
Arab Barometer, 9–10, 88–89, 92, 105*n*1, 128, 141, 163, 181; on Arab Spring, 86, 186–187; *dimuqratiyya* level rated, 19–20, 36–41, 37*tab*, 40*tab*, 42–44*tab*, 45–46, 116, 177–179; *dimuqratiyya* predictors from, 68–69, 70*tab*, 71*tab*, 72–74, 74*tab*, 75–76*tab*, 76–78; V, 37*tab*, 74*tab*, 86; on political participation, 21, 82,

88–90, 89*tab*, 104–105, 128, 141, 167; on political parties, 86; VI, 60, 129–130, 188; on voter turnout, 85; III, 110, 183–184; Wave 1, 39, 40*tab*, 42–44*tab*, 93–94, 93tab, 96, 100–101*tab*; Wave 2, 39, 40*tab*, 42–44*tab*, 59, 93–94, 96, 96*tab*, 101*tab*, 103*tab*; Wave 3, 39, 40*tab*, 42–44*tab*, 49*n*18, 93, 96, 101, 102–103*tab*, 103; Wave 4, 9, 39, 40*tab*, 42–44*tab*; Wave 5, 39, 40*tab*, 42–44*tab*, 49*n*18, 73–74, 74*tab*, 88–89
"Arab exceptionalism," 8–9, 174
Arab Spring, 2, 81*n*12, 105, 130, 158, 177, 183–185; Arab Barometer on, 86, 186–187; constitutional referendums following, 162; Egypt and, 21, 108, 110–112; Morocco and, 133–136, 140; NDP after, 163; public suicides starting, 138; Tunisia and, 59–60, 97, 113
Arab uprisings, 24, 102–103, 105, 183, 186
Arab Winter, 2, 183
Arab World. *See specific topics*
Arabic (language), 19, 24–25, 25*n*6, 117, 143, 166, 190
Aristotle, 35–36
Arrests, 131*n*1, 137, 139
Athenian democracy, 27–28
Austerity programs, 138
Authenticity and Modernity Party, Moroccan, 135

257

258 Index

Authoritarian democracy, 17, 66
Authoritarianism, 5, 45, 130, 132n6,
175–176, 188; democracy and, 16,
32, 73, 111; Egyptians on, 126, 128;
in Morocco, 137; persistence, 24,
187; protest against, 1, 182–185, 187
Autocracy, 5, 32, 108, 129, 182
Average marginal component effect
(AMCE), conjoint analysis, 165–168,
172

Backsliding, democratic, 127, 190
Bahrain, 44tab, 101tab, 103tab
Barriers/restrictions to political
participation, 158–159, 163, 166–167,
169, 171; electoral democracy vs.,
172–173
Basic necessities, state provision of,
53fig, 55fig, 60–62, 164, 166–167,
169, 171–172; Egyptians on, 62–
63tab, 68tab; Moroccans on,
64–65tab, 69tab
Behavior, political, 26n16, 87–89, 89tab,
90, 91–92, 106n1; Arabic speakers
and, 3; dimuqratiyya and, 90–91tab;
religion and, 6
Ben Ali, Zine El Abidine, 1, 38
Bias, translation, 11–13, 22, 24–25,
25n8
Boycotts, 85, 113, 136
Bread Intifada (1977), 164

Canada, 119, 130
Candidate preferences, 161–163
Casablanca, Morocco, 146, 161
Chants/slogans, protests, 1, 9, 60, 107–
108, 183–185, 191; Arab Spring, 21,
112, 130
Characteristics of dimuqratiyya, 58–62,
66–67, 72–74, 80n5; in Egypt, 62–
63tab, 68tab, 70tab; in Morocco,
64–65tab, 69tab, 71tab
China, 25, 189
Christianity, 43tab, 75tab, 90tab, 100tab,
102tab; Egyptians, 113, 123tab, 127;
Moroccan, 147tab, 149tab; Muslims
compared to, 92; PCD and, 78;
secularism and, 121
Circle of Justice, 36, 48n12
Civil liberties, 12, 32, 177–178; protests
for, 184
Civil rights, 14–15, 17, 93–97, 99

Civil society, 9, 43tab, 99, 100tab,
102tab, 130; Egyptian, 113–114;
Islam and, 4; Moroccan, 136–137;
PCD and, 77
Civil War: Libya, 105; Yemeni, 87
Clientelism, 119, 130, 137, 161
Climate-regulation, 161
College education, 43tab, 100tab,
102tab, 123tab, 147tab, 150tab; in
Morocco, 77; poitical behavior and,
91–92, 91tab
Colonialism, 4, 43tab, 91tab, 100tab,
103tab; French, 35, 41, 76
Commander of the faithful (amir al-
mu'minin), Moroccan, 38, 135,
153–154
Competitive elections, 11, 20, 27, 29, 46,
51, 162
Conjoint experiment/analysis (Egypt and
Morocco), 52, 161–168, 172–176,
176nn7–9; committed democrats in,
169–170; conception of dimuqratiyya
in, 170–171
Consolidation, democratic, 114, 121,
132n5, 144, 146
Constitutional referendums, 113, 136, 162
Constitutions, state, 2, 109, 131n1;
Islamic law and, 67, 168; Moroccan,
134–137
Construct validity, 10
consultation (shūrā), 35, 155n1
Consultative National Assembly,
Moroccan, 134
Corruption, 38, 42tab, 61, 119, 168, 178;
in Egypt, 54fig, 62–63tab, 68tab,
110–112; in Morocco, 56fig, 64–
65tab, 69tab, 136–137; protests on,
184–185
Cosectarianism, 161–162
Coup d'état, 131n1, 131n4, 140, 148;
Egyptian military, 2, 21–22, 38, 105,
108–109, 113, 126, 128, 131n2; self-
coup as, 2, 185; Tunisian, 59, 185
Covariates, 91–92, 99, 119 121, 144, 146
Criticism, government, 53fig, 55fig, 59,
62–63tab, 64–65tab, 68tab, 69tab
Culture, democratic, 5–6, 33, 129, 144,
187–188

DAP. See Democracy-autocracy
preference battery
Deaths, 1, 86, 137–138

Index 259

Delta, Egypt, 76*tab*, 123*tab*
Democracia, 72, 88, 98, 189
Democracy. *See specific topics*
Democracy deficit, 3–10, 20, 84, 181–182. *See also* Paradox, democracy
"Democracy promotion," US, 128, 186
Democracy-autocracy preference (DAP) battery, 93–94, 99, 102–103*tab*, 106*n*3
Democracy-*dimuqratiyya* gap, 22, 47, 159, 174, 179; in Egypt, 107–108, 127, 133; in Morocco, 133–134, 141, 151
Democratic culture theory, 5, 33, 144
Democratic transition, 6, 131*n*1
Democratization, 2–3, 27, 131*n*1, 170, 176, 181; African, 33–34; development and, 80; Egypt and, 107–112, 116, 128; free elections and, 46; Huntington on, 48*n*8; Islam and, 4–7, 159; Morocco and, 133, 135, 141–142; PCD and, 157; Polity2 scores rating, 39; polyarchy as measure of, 30; religious minorities and, 128; social movements and, 183, 187–188; urban areas and, 118; women and, 6
Democrats, committed/Democratic commitment, 26*n*10, 95, 159, 169–170, 173–174; construct validity and, 10; *dimuqratiyya* and, 22, 92–93; in Egypt, 108, 114–117, 121, 169; in Morocco, 140–144, 145*tab*, 147–148*tab*, 151–152, 169; PCD citizens as, 122, 124, 127
Democrats, singular, 93, 114; in Egypt, 114–116, 121, 123*tab*, 126; in Morocco, 142, 144, 145*tab*, 148*tab*, 151
Demos, 28, 35, 178
"Depoliticization," 22, 138, 152
Development, 3, 4, 6; democratization and, 80; economic, 7, 34, 69, 72, 118–119, 136, 192*n*2; in Morocco, 135–136, 155
Dictatorships, 21, 29, 32, 48*n*7, 157
Dignity, 39, 57, 173, 184
Dimuqratiyya, 83, 96–99, 96*tab*, 99*tab*, 100–101*tab*, 119, 155*n*1; ambiguous meaning of, 19, 105, 180–182, 189–191; Arab Barometer rating, 19–20, 36–41, 37*tab*, 40*tab*, 42–44*tab*, 45–46, 116, 177–179; Arab Spring and,

185; characteristics of, 58–62, 62–63*tab*, 64–65*tab*, 66–67, 68*tab*, 69*tab*, 70*tab*, 71*tab*, 72–74, 80*n*5; DAP battery and, 93–94, 102–103*tab*; democratic commitment and, 22, 92–93; as distinct from democracy, 27, 35–42, 40*tab*, 92–93, 114–115, 134, 177–180, 182, 187–188; economic dimensions of, 158–159; Egyptian conception of, 38, 75–77*tab*, 107–109, 116–117, 120*tab*, 121–122, 124, 126–131; Moroccan conception of, 39, 75–77*tab*, 133, 138–141, 143–144, 145*tab*, 146, 151–155; Moroccan Islamists on, 155*n*1, 160–161; political participation and, 84–87; predictors of, 68–69, 70*tab*, 71*tab*, 72–74, 74*tab*, 75–76*tab*, 76–78; religious dimensions of, 158–159; slogans, 184–185; State-structures and, 170–171, 174; welfare systems in, 164. *See also* PCD (political conception of *dimuqratiyya*); SECD (socioeconomic conception of *dimuqratiyya*)
dimuqratization, 24, 80, 188, 192

Economy/economic, 30, 42*tab*, 45, 100*tab*, 102*tab*, 153, 158; in conjoint analysis, 166, 170–173; development, 7, 34, 69, 72, 118–119, 136, 152, 192*n*2; *dimuqratiyya* and, 61, 66, 80*n*5; Egyptian, 109–111, 130, 131*n*4; equality, 127, 161, 182, 188; protests about, 22, 110–111, 137–138, 184–187. *See also* SECD (socioeconomic conception of *dimuqratiyya*)
Education, 4, 31, 143, 155, 162; college, 43*tab*, 77, 90*tab*, 91–92, 100*tab*, 102*tab*, 123*tab*, 147*tab*, 150*tab*; foreign aid and, 188; high school, 161; income and, 118; in Morocco, 136; women pursuing, 183
Effectivity, government (regime efficacy), 32, 46, 51; in Egypt, 122*tab*, 124*tab*; in Morocco, 147*tab*, 149*tab*, 152–153
Egalitarianism, gender, 7, 121, 129, 153
Egypt, 37*tab*, 44*tab*, 91*tab*, 101*tab*, 103*tab*, 131*n*1, 172; Arab Spring and, 21, 108, 110–112; authoritarianism

and, 126, 128; Bread Intifada in, 164; Cairene Muslims in, 8, 126, 162, 168; characteristics of *dimuqratiyya* in, 53–54*fig*, 62–63*tab*, 68*tab*; Christianity in, 113, 127; committed democrats in, 108, 114–117, 121, 169; conception of *Dimuqratiyya* in, 38, 75–77*tab*, 107–109, 116–117, 120*tab*, 121–122, 124, 126–131; corruption in, 54*fig*, 62–63*tab*, 68*tab*, 110–112; democracy-*dimuqratiyya* gap in, 107–108, 127, 133; democratic preferences in, 107–108; democratization and, 107–112, 116, 128; economy, 109–111, 130, 131*n*4; electoral democracy and, 115–116, 120*tab*, 124–126; electoral institutions, 53*fig*, 62–63*tab*, 68*tab*, 108–109, 112–113, 120*tab*, 121, 122*tab*, 126–127; gender traditionalism in, 75*tab*, 122*tab*, 148; government efficacy in, 122*tab*, 124*tab*; government law and order in, 54*fig*, 62–63*tab*, 68*tab*, 70*tab*, 81*n*6, 81*n*6; income in, 53*fig*, 75*tab*, 123*tab*; Islam in, 119, 121, 154; Islamists in, 112–113, 126–127; military coup in, 2, 21–22, 38, 105, 108–109, 126, 128, 131*n*2; Mixed PCD in, 61, 100*tab*, 117–118, 120*tab*, 122*tab*, 124*tab*, 126; Mixed SECD in, 61, 100*tab*, 102*tab*, 117*n*3, 120*tab*, 122*tab*, 124*tab*; multiparty elections and, 1 21, 116, 127; Muslim Brotherhood and, 38, 67, 109–113, 126, 131*n*2; NDP, 109, 113, 163; Parliament, 109, 113, 126, 163; PCD, 108, 117–119, 120*tab*, 121–122, 122*tab*, 124, 124*tab*, *126–127*; prayer in, 74–75*tab*, 121, 122*tab*, 124*tab*; religion in, 54*tab*, 62–63*tab*, 117, 123*tab*; SECD, 108, 117–119, 120*tab*, 121–122, 122*tab*, 124, 124*tab*, *126–128*, 159, 171; secularism, 75*tab*, 121, 122*tab*, 126, 129; singular democrats in, 114–116, 121, 123*tab*, 126; state-structures in, 111, 121–122, 122–123*tab*, 124, 124–125*tab*, 126–131, 131*n*4; unemployment in, 75*tab*, 123*tab*. *See also* Conjoint experiment/analysis (Egypt and Morocco); *specific cities*

Ekklesia (Athenian assembly), 28
electoral democracy, 32, 34, 66, 158–160, 166–170, 174; barriers to political participation *vs.*, 172–173; Egyptians on, 115–116, 120*tab*, 124–126; liberal values and, 95; modernization theory and, 118; Moroccans on, 69*tab*, 140–142, 145*tab*, 146, 152–155; unelected governments and, 22
Electoral institutions/structures, 29–30, 47*n*5, 85–86, 114–115, 187; abolition of, 124–125*tab*, 146, 149–150*tab*; competition in, 11, 20, 27, 29, 46, 51, 162; in *dimuqratiyya*, 58–59; Egyptian, 53*fig*, 62–63*tab*, 68*tab*, 108–109, 112–113, 120*tab*, 121, 122*tab*, 126–127; free, 14–15, 40–41, 42*tab*, 45, 96; MENA, 177–178; Moroccan, 55*fig*, 64–65*tab*, 134–136, 145*tab*, 146, 149–150*tab*, 155; single-party, 166, 179. *See also* Multiparty elections
Emigration, 162, 181, 185
Employment, 23, 26*n*14, 59, 162
English (language), 35, 117, 155*n*2, 176*n*9
Ennahda party, 109
Environmentalism, 118
Equality, 14, 28, 31; economic, 127, 161, 182, 188
Europe/European, 12, 17, 86–88, 119, 130, 176*n*1; colonialism, 4; protectorate powers, 134

al-Farabi (philosopher), 35
February 20 Movement, 22, 135–137, 140
Fès, Morocco, 76*tab*, 148*tab*, 150*tab*
First Intifada, 162
Food insecurity, 130, 175
Foreign aid, 80, 131*n*4, 132*n*9, 181, 191; US, 110, 129–130, 135, 188, 192*n*2
Foreign intervention, 130, 154–155
France, 43*tab*, 76, 91*tab*, 101*tab*, 103*tab*, 139, 173; colonialism by, 35, 41, 76
Free elections, 14–15, 40, 42*tab*, 45, 96
Free will, 88
Freedom House (nonprofit), 48*n*6, 183
Freedoms, 6, 11, 28–30, 33; political, 110–111, 184
French (language), 48*n*10, 52, 57, 96

Gaddafi, Muammar, 38

Index   261

Gap, income, 31, 59, 61; Egyptians on, 53*fig*, 62–63*tab*, 68*tab*; Moroccans on, 55*fig*, 64–65*tab*, 69*tab*
GDP. *See* Gross domestic product
Gender, 25*n*6, 117, 143; egalitarianism, 7, 121, 129, 153
Gender traditionalism, 77–78, 92, 99, 100*tab*, 102*tab*, 129, 177; in Egypt, 75*tab*, 122*tab*, 148; in Morocco, 75*tab*, 147*tab*, 148, 149*tab*, 153; political behavior and, 90*tab*
Global democracies, 168, 188–190
Global South, 164
Goals, of social movements, 183–184, 187, 192*n*1
Greek (language), 11, 35
Gross domestic product (GDP), 34, 41, 43*tab*, 91*tab*, 101*tab*, 103*tab*, 110
Group rights, 26*n*15, 191
Gulf wars, 5

Hassan II (King), 134–135, 140
health care, 31, 60, 136
High school, 161
Hirak Rif protests, 105, 137
Hogra movement, 105
Human rights, 4, 6, 24, 30, 33–34, 137, 186, 191; in Egypt, 110; in Morocco, 135, 137; social rights and, 60; in Tunisia, 1
Hungary, 86

Ibn Rushd (philosopher), 35
Illiberal democracy, 6, 19, 26*n*15, 95, 188
Ilsāmiyūn, Moroccan, 57, 160, 190
Income, 59, 61, 72, 90*tab*, 118, 178; in Egypt, 53*fig*, 75*tab*, 123*tab*; gaps, 31, 53*fig*, 55*fig*, 59, 61, 62–63*tab*, 64–65*tab*, 68*tab*, 69*tab*; in Morocco, 55*fig*, 75*tab*, 147*tab*, 149*tab*
Individual rights, 26*n*15, 191
Inflation, 130, 137
infrastructure, 132*n*9, 135, 153, 188
"Input-oriented" democracy, 72–73
interest, political, 72, 74*tab*, 79, 100*tab*, 102*tab*, 109, 121; in Egypt, 75*tab*, 129; PCD and, 77; political behavior and, 90*tab*
International Monetary Fund, 130
Iran, 59, 86, 189, 191
Iraq, 5, 37*tab*, 44*tab*, 91*tab*, 101*tab*, 103*tab*

Islam et démocratie (Mernissi), 1, 35
Islamic law (shari'a), 4, 67, 94, 119, 126, 168; elections and, 116, 121, 122*tab*, 142, 147*tab*, 149*tab*, 154; Moroccans on, 146, 147*tab*, 149–150*tab*, 151
Islamists/Islamist parties, 26*n*15, 67, 109, 129, 158, 160, 174, 191; democratization and, 6, 159; Egyptian, 112–113, 126–127; Moroccan, 142, 147, 155*n*1, 160–161; social movements by, 183–184
Islam/Muslims, 3, 17, 67, 78, 91; democratization and, 4–7, 159; Egyptian, 119, 121, 154; majority countries, 6, 16–17, 173; Moroccan, 8, 151, 154, 161. *See also* Men, Muslim
Israel, 4, 5, 162
Italy, 41, 43*tab*, 76, 91*tab*, 101*tab*, 103*tab*

Janissary Corp, 8, 112
Jordan, 37, 37*tab*, 44*tab*, 72, 91*tab*, 101*tab*, 103*tab*; elections in, 85–86
Justice (*adalet*), 24, 88, 189
Justice and Development Party (PJD), Moroccan, 135–136, 138, 146, 147, 154

Kenitra, Morocco, 76*tab*, 148*tab*, 150*tab*, 162
"Khobzists," 117, 158, 187
Kratos, 39, 178
Kuwait, 37, 37*tab*, 44*tab*, 101*tab*, 103*tab*

Laïcité, 191
Language/s, 13, 48*n*10, 92, 114–115, 188–191; Arabic, 19, 24–25, 25*n*6, 117, 143, 166, 190; English, 35, 117, 155*n*2, 176*n*9; French, 48*n*10, 52, 57, 96. *See also* Translation
Latin America, 12, 88
Law and order, government provision of, 38, 58–61, 88–89; Egyptians on, 54*fig*, 62–63*tab*, 68*tab*, 70*tab*, 81*n*6, 81*n*6; Moroccans on, 56*fig*, 64–65*tab*, 69*tab*, 71*tab*
Lebanon, 37*tab*, 44*tab*, 72, 91*tab*, 101*tab*, 103*tab*; foreign aid and, 188; religion in, 164; security policies in, 161
Liberal democracy, 12, 33–34, 81*n*9, 99, 104, 154, 162; as distinct from other

262 Index

democracies, 19; Obama on, 2;
  Ulbricht on, 16
Liberal values, 3, 19–20, 33–34, 81*n*9,
  94–95, 118, 188; Dahl on, 30;
  dimuqratiyya as distinct from, 182; of
  Moroccan women, 153; Schumpeter
  on, 47*n*1
Liberalization, 110, 135
Liberty, 26*n*11, 72, 88, 189
Libya, 2, 37*tab*, 41, 49*n*18, 105, 111
Logistic regression models, 73–74, 90,
  99, 121, 144

Majoritarianism, 29, 33, 127
Makhzen (Moroccan governing
  institution), 137, 139, 154, 155*n*1
Marginal mean in conjoint analysis, 165–
  167, 172
Marginal value hypothesis, 7
Marrakech, Morocco, 38, 76*tab*, 141,
  148*tab*, 150*tab*
Maximalist views of democracy, 20, 29–
  30, 106*n*4, 190
Membership, Party, 89, 132*n*6, 163, 167
Men, 43*tab*, 77, 90*tab*, 91–92, 100*tab*,
  102*tab*; Egyptian, 75*tab*, 123*tab*;
  Moroccan, 75*tab*, 147*tab*, 149*tab*;
  Muslim, 8, 126, 168, 196; on
  elections, 141–142, 162–163
MENA. *See* Middle East/North Africa
Middle East. *See specific topics*
Middle East/North Africa (MENA), 2,
  26*n*14, 27–28, 51, 85, 107, 127;
  electoral institutions in, 177–178;
  emigration, 162; foreign aid and, 188;
  non-Arab, 189; PCD *vs.* SECD in, 84,
  88, 134; religion in, 163–164;
  secularists, 151; social movements,
  182–183; US foreign aid and, 129–
  130; YouGov, 49*tab*, 117
Military interventions, 15, 116–117, 126,
  131*n*1, 146, 179
Military rule/governments, 21–23, 93,
  108–117, 126, 142, 149–150*tab*, 151,
  178; *dimuqratiyya* and, 38
Miller, Michael, 32
Minimalist views of democracy, 27, 29–
  32, 37, 46–47, 114–115
Ministries of Sovereignty, Moroccan, 22,
  135
Mixed PCD, 98*tab*, 99; in Egypt, 61,
  100*tab*, 117–118, 120*tab*, 122*tab*,

124*tab*, 126; in Morocco, 143,
  145*tab*, 147tab, 149*tab*
Mixed SECD, 98*tab*, 99; in Egypt, 61,
  100*tab*, 102*tab*, 117*n*3, 120*tab*,
  122*tab*, 124*tab*; in Morocco, 143–
  144, 145*tab*, 146, 147–148*tab*, 148,
  149–150*tab*, 151–155
Modern democracy, 28–29, 47
Modernization theory, 73, 118, 128, 144
Mohammed VI (King), 135
Monarchies, 5, 36
Monarchy, parliamentary, 22, 133–140,
  142–143, 146, 152–153, 179;
  abolition of, 149–150*tab*, 151
Morocco, 39, 44*tab*, 91*tab*, 101*tab*,
  103*tab*, 172; *Amir al-mu'minin*, 38,
  135, 153–154; Arab Spring and, 133–
  136, 140; characteristics of
  dimuqratiyya in, 55–56*fig*, 61–62,
  64–65*tab*; committed democrats in,
  140–144, 145*tab*, 147–148*tab*, 151–
  152, 169; conception of *Dimuqratiyya*
  in, 39, 75–77*tab*, 133, 138–141, 143–
  144, 145*tab*, 146, 151–155;
  corruption in, 56*fig*, 64–65*tab*, 69*tab*,
  136–137; democratization and, 133,
  135, 141–142; development in, 135–
  136, 155; electoral democracy and,
  69*tab*, 140–142, 145*tab*, 146, 152–
  155; electoral institutions in, 55*fig*,
  64–65*tab*, 134–136, 145*tab*, 146,
  149–150*tab*, 155; gender
  traditionalism in, 75*tab*, 147*tab*, 148,
  149*tab*, 153; government effectivity
  in, 147*tab*, 149*tab*, 152–153;
  government provision of law and
  order, 56*fig*, 64–65*tab*, 69*tab*, 71*tab*;
  income in, 55*fig*, 75*tab*, 147*tab*,
  149*tab*; Islamic law in, 146, 147*tab*,
  149–150*tab*, 151; Islamists, 142, 147,
  155*n*1, 160–161; men, 75*tab*, 147*tab*,
  149*tab*; Mixed PCD, 143, 145*tab*,
  147tab, 149*tab*; mixed SECD in, 143,
  145*tab*, 147*tab*, 149*tab*; multiparty
  elections and, 142–143, 149–150*tab*,
  151; Muslims, 142, 147, 155*n*1, 160–
  161; nondemocratic regimes and, 143,
  146, 151–154; PCD in, 117, 133–134,
  143–144, 145*tab*, 146, 147–148*tab*,
  148, 149–150*tab*, 151–155, 174; PJD,
  135–136, 138, 146, 154; prayer in,
  147*tab*, 149*tab*; protests, 134–139,

155n2; reforms, 22, 135–139; religion in, 56*fig*, 64–65*tab*, 135, 147*tab*, 149*tab*, 154; SECD in, 133–134, 159; secularism in, 75*tab*, 147*tab*, 149*tab*, 151, 154; singular democrats in, 142, 144, 145*tab*, 148*tab*, 151; state-structures in, 22, 146, 149–150*tab*; unemployment in, 75*tab*, 137, 147*tab*, 149*tab*; urban, 75*tab*, 78, 147*tab*, 150*tab*; women, 8, 20, 153–154. *See also* Conjoint experiment/analysis (Egypt and Morocco); Parliamentary monarchy; *specific cities*

Moulay 'Abdal-'Aziz (Sultan), 139

Movements, social, 84, 90, 111, 138, 182, 185–186; democratization and, 183, 187–188; goals of, 183–184, 187, 192n1. *See also* Protests; *specific movements*

Mubarak, Hosni, 38, 109–113, 128, 163, 184

Muhammad (Prophet), 134

Multiparty democracy, 121, 124, 126, 142, 144, 146, 153, 169

Multiparty elections, 59, 81n6, 95, 124–125*tab*, 126, 151, 160, 179; in conjoint analysis, 166, 169, 171; Egyptians on, 116, 121, 127; Moroccans on, 142–143, 149–150*tab*, 151

Muslim Brotherhood, 38, 67, 109–113, 126, 131n2

al-Nahyan, Sheikh Abdullah bin Zayed, 108–109

Nasser, Gamal Abdel, 109–110

National Democratic Party (NDP), Egyptian, 109–110, 113, 163

Nationalism, 4, 24

NDP. *See* National Democratic Party

New Democratic Party, Egypt, 117

News consumption, 75*tab*, 100*tab*, 102*tab*; Egyptian, 122*tab*, 124*tab*; Moroccan, 147*tab*, 149*tab*

NGOs. *See* nongovernmental organizations

Nichomachian Ethics (Aristotle), 35

Nida Touns (party), 109

Nondemocracy/nondemocratic regimes, 2, 32, 49n13, 106n3, 119, 126, 188; African, 33, 48n7; coups and, 109;

democratic commitment and, 128; *dimuqratiyya* and, 38, 46; *dimuqratiyya* ratings and, 77; Egyptians on, 112, 121; Moroccans on, 143, 146, 151–154; oil as source of, 5; PCD on, 134

Nongovernmental organizations (NGOs), 79, 183

Noninstitutional political participation, 83, 85–87, 92, 163, 175, 178; Arab Barometer on, 88–89. *See also* Protests

"Nonmovements," 182–183

Normative values, 57–58, 79

North Africa, 164

Obama, Barack, 2, 131n1, 188

Official/state religion, 142, 154, 159, 172–173, 176n9, 179–180; Islam as, 67, 162–164, 168; SECD and, 170–171

Oil, 5, 7–8, 185

One-party systems, 116–117, 126, 132n6, 142, 149–150*tab*, 151, 163

Orientalism (Said), 51

Ottoman Empire, 4, 9, 36, 112

Palestine, 37*tab*, 41, 44*tab*, 72, 86, 91*tab*, 101*tab*, 103*tab*; foreign aid and, 188

Paradox, democracy, 2–3, 7, 18, 24, 84, 181–182

Parliamentary monarchy, 22, 133–140, 142–143, 146, 152–154, 179; abolition of, 149–150*tab*, 151

Parliaments, 94, 99, 101, 104; Egyptian, 109, 113, 126, 163

Participatory democracy, 132n6, 155n1

Participatory governments, 113, 128, 152, 159

Party systems/parties, 86, 89*tab*, 90–91*tab*, 163; membership, 89, 132n6, 163, 167; Moroccan, 134–136; One-party, 116, 132n6, 142, 151; "Right-wing," 94, 96*tab*

PCD (political conception of *dimuqratiyya*), 18–20, 97–99, 98*tab*, 100*tab*, 102*tab*, 104; as committed democrats, 122, 124, 127; *dimuqratiyya* predictors and, 72, 77–78; Egyptian, 108, 117–119, 120*tab*, 121–122, 122*tab*, 124, 124*tab*, *126–127*;

264 Index

electoral democracy supported by, 160; on essential characteristics of *dimuqratiyya*, 61; Moroccan, 117, 133–134, 143–144, 145*tab*, 146, 147–148*tab*, 148, 149–150*tab*, 151–155, 174; political interest and, 77; protests and, 188; SECD *vs.*, 51–52, 84–87, 157, 159, 170–171, 175–176, 178–180; state structures and, 170–171, 174. *See also* Mixed PCD
"people-centered" democracy, 106*n*2
Persianate empire, 36, 48*n*12
Persistence, authoritarian, 24, 187
Petitions, 84–86, 87–90, 89*tab*, 90–91*tab*, 167
Philosophy, 35–36
PJD. *See* Justice and Development Party
Plato, 35–36
Pluralism, 4, 17, 48*n*6, 126–127, 185
"Pluralization" of power, 22, 135
Police, 86, 136–138
Political: preferences, 9, 80, 85, 103–104, 107, 180; rights, 30, 48*n*6, 59–60, 62–64*tab*, 68*tab*, 69*tab*, 94–95, 97, 127, 170
Political freedom, 110–111, 184
Political participation, institutional, 80, 83, 178; Arab Barometer on, 21, 82, 88–90, 89*tab*, 104–105, 128, 141; committed democrats on, 159–160; PCD and, 2, 84–87, 157. *See also* Barriers/restrictions to political participation; Noninstitutional political participation
Political science, 20, 23–24, 27–34, 47*n*4
Politically motivated violence, 21, 84, 87, 104, 178
Polity (score system), 32, 39, 49*n*18, 51, 59; Polity2, 39, 41, 44*tab*, 49
Polyarchy, 30–32, 48*n*6, 51
Populism, 21–22, 72, 81*n*9, 130, 131*n*2
Poverty, 6, 39, 110, 137, 161
Prayer, 78, 90*tab*, 91, 100*tab*, 102*tab*; in Egypt, 74–75*tab*, 121, 122*tab*, 124*tab*; in Morocco, 147*tab*, 149*tab*
Predictors, *dimuqratiyya*, 68–69, 70*tab*, 71*tab*, 72–74, 74*tab*, 75–76*tab*, 76–78
Preference concealment, 158
Preference falsification, 7–8, 193
Presidents, 94; Egyptian, 21, 109, 113
Prime minister, Moroccan, 135–136

Privatization, 110
Pro-democracy, 7, 15, 24, 108, 134, 140, 184–185
Protectorates, 41, 134, 138–139
Protests, 24, 86, 89, 89*tab*, 90–91*tab*, 105; against autocratic regimes, 182; in conjoint analysis, 167–168; economic, 22, 110–111, 137–138, 184–187; Egyptian, 110, 184; Iranian, 191; Moroccan, 134–139, 155*n*2; PCD and, 175; slogans/chants, 1, 9, 21, 60, 107–108, 112, 130, 183–185, 191; Tunisian, 1, 110

Qatar, 108–109, 161–162
Quietism, political, 88

Rabat, Moroccan, 76*tab*, 136, 148*tab*, 150*tab*
Recessions, 34, 185
Redistribution, 72, 161, 176*n*1
Referendums, 15, 85, 109; constitutional, 113, 136, 162
Reforms, 28; Egyptian, 110–112; Moroccan, 22, 135–139
Regression analyses, 52, 119, 144
Religion/s, 28, 43*tab*, 60, 67, 100*tab*, 102*tab*, 118, 168–169; in Egypt, 54*tab*, 62–63*tab*, 117, 123*tab*; governments and, 160–161; in MENA countries, 163–164; minorities, 92, 99, 128, 154; in Morocco, 56*fig*, 64–65*tab*, 135, 147*tab*, 149*tab*, 154; SECD and, 78, 160, 170; secularism and, 112, 176*n*1; separation of government and, 60–61, 67, 68*tab*, 70*tab*, 71*tab*. *See also* Official/state religion
Religious leaders in government, 23, 38, 121, 164, 168, 172–173
Representation, 5, 10, 31, 41, 109, 139, 143, 175, 187
"Representative democracy," 117
Repression, 122
Rights, 28–29, 54*fig*, 56*fig*, 68*tab*, 69*tab*, 109, 118; civil, 14–15, 17, 93–97, 99; to criticize government, 53*fig*, 55*fig*, 59, 62–63*tab*, 64–65*tab*, 68*tab*, 69*tab*; group, 26*n*15, 191; political, 30, 48*n*6, 59–60, 62–64*tab*, 68*tab*, 69*tab*, 94–95, 97, 127, 170; social, 12–13, 31, 60, 72, 87–88; of women,

6, 16–17, 129–130, 132*n*9, 136–137, 153–154, 188, 191. *See* Human rights
"Right-wing" parties, 94, 96*tab*
Rule of law, 12, 15, 19, 26*n*11, 49*n*6, 94, 192*n*2; in minimalist/maximalist democracy frameworks, 30–32; US supporting, 186
Russia, 189

Sadat, Anwar, 163
Salé, Morocco, 76*tab*, 148*tab*, 150*tab*
Sasanian empire, 48*n*12
Satisfaction, government/regime, 40, 46, 119, 130; in Morocco, 140, 144, 146, 152
Saudi Arabia, 101*tab*, 103*tab*, 109, 132 163–164
Scripture reading: in Egypt, 121, 122*tab*, 124*tab*; in Morocco, 147*tab*, 149*tab*
SECD (socioeconomic conception of *dimuqratiyya*), 19–20, 94, 97–99, 98*tab*, 100*tab*, 102*tab*, 104; *dimuqratiyya* predictors and, 72–74, 77–78; Egyptian, 108, 117–119, 120*tab*, 121–122, 122*tab*, 124, 124*tab*, *126–128*, 159, 171; on essential characteristics of *dimuqratiyya*, 61; MENA, 107; Moroccan, 143–144, 145*tab*, 146, 147–148*tab*, 148, 149–150*tab*, 151–155; PCD *vs.*, 84–87 51–52, 157, 159, 170–171, 175–176, 178–180; protests and, 188; religion and, 160–161; state structures and, 170–171. *See also* Mixed SECD
Secularism/secular, 90*tab*, 99, 100*tab*, 102*tab*, 132*n*7, 160–161, 173, 191; civil society, 136–137; democracy and, 58; democratization and, 118; *dimuqratiyya* and, 67, 77–78; in Egypt, 75*tab*, 121, 122*tab*, 126, 129; Europe promoting, 4; framed as democratic, 128; in Morocco, 75*tab*, 147*tab*, 149*tab*, 151, 154; religion and, 112–113; violence and, 91
Self-coup, 2, 59, 185
Self-determination, 2–3, 17, 29, 188
Self-immolation, 1, 138
Senegal, 26*n*16, 52–53, 87–88, 180
Separation of religion and government, 60–61, 67, 68*tab*, 70*tab*, 71*tab*
Shari'a. *See* Islamic law

Shūrā (consultation), 155*n*1
Single-party elections/systems, 109, 151, 166, 179. *See also* One-party systems
Slavery, 4–5, 28
Slogans/chants, protests, 1, 9, 60, 107–108, 183–185, 191; Arab Spring, 21, 112, 130
Social capital theory, 144
Social justice, 78, 98, 111, 136, 160
Social movements. *See* Movements, social
Social rights, 12–13, 31, 60, 72, 87–88
"Soft capitalism," 47*n*3
South America, 17, 76, 86
Sovereignty, 33, 57
Soviet Union (USSR), 1–2
State-structures/regime type, 2, 23, 80*n*1, 158–161, 163–164, 173–176, 176*n*1; in conjoint analysis, 166, 168–170, 179; Egyptian, 111, 121–122, 122–123*tab*, 124, 124–125*tab*, 126–131, 131*n*4; Moroccan, 22, 146, 149–150*tab*; understanding of *dimuqratiyya* and, 170–171, 174
Strongman governance, 93, 101, 116–117, 126, 142, 146, 151
Sudan, 37*tab*, 44*tab*, 59, 87, 101*tab*, 103*tab*
Suffrage, universal, 20, 29, 48*n*2
Supreme Council of the Armed Forces, Egyptian, 91*tab*, 113
System satisfaction, 130, 144

Tahrir Square, 21, 108
Tangier, Morocco, 76*tab*, 148*tab*, 150*tab*
taxes, 14–15, 17, 160
Tolerance, 5, 38, 118, 187
Transition, democratic, 6, 131*n*1
Translation, 10, 25*n*7, 35, 48*n*10, 155*n*2, 191; bias, 11–13, 22, 24–25, 25*n*8
Trust, 42*tab*, 90*tab*, 100*tab*, 102*tab*, 122*tab*, 147*tab*, 149*tab*, 153
Tunisia, 44*tab*, 101*tab*, 103*tab*, 109–110, 117, 154, 158; Arab Spring and, 59–60, 97, 113; democracy rating for, 37, 37*tab*; political violence in, 87; self-coup, 2, 59, 185; social movements in, 1–2, 183–184
Turkey, 9, 109, 189

Umayyad caliphate, 48*n*12
Unelected governments, 114, 116, 141, 175

266 Index

Unelected offices/officers, 39, 142, 152
Unemployment, 6, 17, 158–161, 164, 170, 173, 179–180; in conjoint analysis, 166 170–172; Egyptian, 75*tab*, 123*tab*; Moroccan, 75*tab*, 137, 147*tab*, 149*tab*; political behavior and, 90*tab*; protests against, 110, 185
United Arab Emirates, 108–109
United Kingdom, 173
United States (US), 2, 12, 85, 87, 119, 130, 173; "democracy promotion," 128, 186; foreign aid, 110, 129–130, 135, 188, 192*n*2
Universal suffrage, 20, 29, 48*n*2
Upper Egypt, 75*tab*, 123*tab*
Urban: Egypt, 75*tab*, 78, 123*tab*; Morocco, 75*tab*, 78, 147*tab*, 150*tab*
US. *See* United States
USSR. *See* Soviet Union

Varieties of Democracy Project (V-Dem), 32, 48
Violence, 112, 132*ni4*, 182, 191; politically motivated, 21, 84, 87, 89–90, 89*tab*, 90–91*tab*, 104, 178
Voter turnout, 85, 105*n*1, 110, 136

Welfare state/system, 26*n*11, 80*n*1, 164, 178–179, 186; committed democrats and, 160; Egyptians on, 127; PCD on, 174; unemployment and, 173. *See also* Personal necessities, state provision of
Welzel, Christian, 17–18, 33, 72, 81*n*9
West, time spent in the, 42*tab*, 100*tab*, 102*tab*, 130; by Egyptians, 75*tab*, 121, 123*tab*; by Moroccans, 75*tab*, 148*tab* 150*tab*
Western Europe, 86, 179
Wolof (language), 48*n*10, 52–53, 180
Women, 77, 162, 183; Moroccan, 8, 20, 153–154; Muslim, 8, 143; rights of, 6, 129–130, 132*n*9, 136–137, 153–154, 188, 191
World Values Survey, 9–10, 12, 14–17, 52, 60, 66, 92–93

Yemen, 2, 37*tab*, 44*tab*, 59, 86–87, 101*tab*, 103*tab*
YouGov MENA, 49*tab*, 77, 117
Youth, 105, 110, 164

About the Book

The Middle East and North Africa comprise by all measures one of the least democratic regions in the world. At the same time, decades of research show robust support for democracy among MENA residents. A paradox . . . or is it?

Hannah Ridge explores the "democracy paradox" by parsing the meanings that citizens assign to the Arab word *dimuqratiyya*. Drawing on Arab Barometer data from across the region, as well as original surveys in Egypt and Morocco, she shows that democracy and *dimuqratiyya* are typically not the same thing—and how conflating the two has led to misconceptions about public support for democratic governance.

Hannah M. Ridge is assistant professor of political science at Chapman University.